Barcode →

VIOLENCE & GENDER

REEXAMINED

The LAW AND PUBLIC POLICY: PSYCHOLOGY AND THE SOCIAL
SCIENCES series includes books in three domains:

> *Legal Studies*—writings by legal scholars about issues of relevance to
> psychology and the other social sciences, or that employ social science
> information to advance the legal analysis;

> *Social Science Studies*—writings by scientists from psychology and the other
> social sciences about issues of relevance to law and public policy; and

> *Forensic Studies*—writings by psychologists and other mental health scientists
> and professionals about issues relevant to forensic mental health science and
> practice.

The series is guided by its editor, Bruce D. Sales, PhD, JD, ScD(*hc*), University of
Arizona; and coeditors, Bruce J. Winick, JD, University of Miami; Norman J.
Finkel, PhD, Georgetown University; and Stephen J. Ceci, PhD, Cornell
University.

* * *

The Right to Refuse Mental Health Treatment
    Bruce J. Winick
Violent Offenders: Appraising and Managing Risk
    Vernon L. Quinsey, Grant T. Harris, Marnie E. Rice, and Catherine A. Cormier
Recollection, Testimony, and Lying in Early Childhood
    Clara Stern and William Stern; James T. Lamiell (translator)
Genetics and Criminality: The Potential Misuse of Scientific Information in Court
    Jeffrey R. Botkin, William M. McMahon, and Leslie Pickering Francis
The Hidden Prejudice: Mental Disability on Trial
    Michael L. Perlin
Adolescents, Sex, and the Law: Preparing Adolescents for Responsible Citizenship
    Roger J. R. Levesque
Legal Blame: How Jurors Think and Talk About Accidents
    Neal Feigenson
*Justice and the Prosecution of Old Crimes: Balancing Legal, Psychological, and
    Moral Concerns*
    Daniel W. Shuman and Alexander McCall Smith
*Unequal Rights: Discrimination Against People With Mental Disabilities and the
    Americans With Disabilities Act*
    Susan Stefan
Treating Adult and Juvenile Offenders With Special Needs
    Edited by José B. Ashford, Bruce D. Sales, and William H. Reid
Culture and Family Violence: Fostering Change Through Human Rights Law
    Roger J. R. Levesque
*The Legal Construction of Identity: The Judicial and Social Legacy of American
Colonialism in Puerto Rico*
    Efrén Rivera Ramos
Family Mediation: Facts, Myths, and Future Prospects
    Connie J. A. Beck and Bruce D. Sales

Not Fair! The Typology of Commonsense Unfairness
   Norman J. Finkel
Competence, Condemnation, and Commitment: An Integrated Theory of Mental Health Law
   Robert F. Schopp
The Evolution of Mental Health Law
   Edited by Lynda E. Frost and Richard J. Bonnie
Hollow Promises: Employment Discrimination Against People With Mental Disabilities
   Susan Stefan
Violence and Gender Reexamined
   Richard B. Felson

VIOLENCE
& GENDER
REEXAMINED

RICHARD B. FELSON

AMERICAN PSYCHOLOGICAL ASSOCIATION

WASHINGTON, DC

Published by
American Psychological Association
750 First Street, NE
Washington, DC 20002
www.apa.org

To order
APA Order Department
P.O. Box 92984
Washington, DC 20090-2984
Tel: (800) 374-2721, Direct: (202) 336-5510
Fax: (202) 336-5502, TDD/TTY: (202) 336-6123
Online: www.apa.org/books/
Email: order@apa.org

In the U.K., Europe, Africa, and the Middle East, copies may be ordered from
American Psychological Association
3 Henrietta Street
Covent Garden, London
WC2E 8LU England

Typeset in Goudy by AlphaWebTech, Mechanicsville, MD

Printer: Port City press, Baltimore, MD
Cover designer: Anne Masters, Washington, DC
Technical/Production Editor: Jennifer Powers

The opinions and statements published are the responsibility of the authors, and such opinions and statements do not necessarily represent the policies of the American Psychological Association.

Library of Congress Cataloging-in-Publication Data
Felson, Richard B.
    Violence and gender reexamined / Richard B. Felson
        p. cm.—(Law and public policy)
    Includes bibliographical references and index.
    ISBN 1-55798-895-1 (hardcover : alk. paper)
        1. Women—Violence against—United States. 2. Violence in men—United States.
    3. Violence—United States—Psychological aspects. 4. Sexism—United States.
    I. American Psychological Association. II. Title. III. Series.

    HV6250.4.W65 F45 2002
    305.3 21   2002001966

British Library Cataloguing-in-Publication Data
A CIP record is available from the British Library.

Printed in the United States of America
First Edition

CONTENTS

Preface ix

Acknowledgments xi

I. Introduction 1

    Chapter 1.   Introduction 3

    Chapter 2.   A Theory of Instrumental Aggression 11

II. Violence Inside and Outside the Family 29

    Chapter 3.   Comparing Frequencies 31

    Chapter 4.   Gender Differences in Power and Status 51

    Chapter 5.   Chivalry 67

    Chapter 6.   Privacy and Police Intervention 83

    Chapter 7.   Controlling Women 95

    Chapter 8.   Love Triangles 107

III. Rape and Sexual Coercion 119

    Chapter 9.   Coercive versus Consensual Sex 121

    Chapter 10. Sexual Motivation 143

Chapter 11.   Sexism and Sexual Coercion 163

Chapter 12.   Sexual Coercion and the Law 183

IV. Conclusion 201

Chapter 13.   Conclusion 203

References 225

Author Index 255

Subject Index 263

About the Author 273

PREFACE

What is different about violence involving women? Does it have special motives, or is its motivation similar to violence between men? Are we more tolerant of violence against women than of violence against men? Is it more frequent? Are we more likely to blame the victim when it occurs?

Asking comparative questions is controversial because they raise the possibility that many common assertions about violence involving women are wrong. For example, it is commonly held that sexism motivates men to attack women. Attention to the broader study of violence might reveal that violence against women is like any violence and not an expression of sexism. However, when activists discuss the victimization of women they want a sympathetic ear, not statistical comparisons. This is understandable: Comparative statements dilute moral outrage.

In making comparisons between violence against the genders, my intention is not to minimize the effects of violence against either women or men. There is no question that violence is traumatic for female victims and that they deserve our sympathy and assistance. I do not oppose special measures to reduce violence against women, even when they ignore violence against men. However, I do believe that the study of violence against women within the larger context of violence will reveal important information about its causes. Without understanding causes and without the open discussion of these issues, prevention is impossible.

My approach developed out of my training in quantitative sociology at Indiana University in the 1970s. In graduate school, my interest in social psychology led me to take a course in interpersonal aggression in the psychology department. I wrote a paper applying the symbolic interactionist perspective to aggression, the most prominent theory in sociological social psychology at the time. The paper emphasized the social interaction leading to violence and the victim's role in the event (Felson, 1978). My focus was on violence between men and was not then controversial. In fact, I was a typical left-wing graduate student in sociology, tolerant of those considered criminals and deviants. The left's prevailing worldview at that time allowed room for an examination of the causal role of victims because it was sympathetic with offenders who were often poor and Black.

Much later, an interactionist approach became controversial because it appeared to assign blame to female victims of male violence. If cause is confused with blame, then assigning a causal role to a victim is offensive, especially if the victim is a member of a protected group. Blaming the victim is a "mortal sin," not only in academia but in society in general.

Because of this rather unpopular approach, throughout the years I have been subject to a fair amount of criticism. The negative reaction to my work reached its zenith when a colleague and I published a paper reporting evidence for sexual motivation in rape (Felson & Krohn, 1990). I responded to the angry reaction to this piece with a paper criticizing the impact of political correctness on sociology (Felson, 1991).

Several years later I wrote a paper on chivalry (Felson, 2000) that was controversial because it implied that women get more favorable treatment than men, a sensitive topic in certain feminist circles. I then coauthored some papers (Felson & Ackerman, 2001; Felson & Messner, 2000; see also Felson, Messner, & Hoskin, 1999a) examining the issue of whether violence against women is different from violence against men. To publish these papers in major journals, we disguised the negative implications they had for the commonly accepted, feminist approach to violence. I decided to write this book so that I could be more explicit about my perspective.

ACKNOWLEDGMENTS

I appreciate the editors at APA Books for their willingness to take on a project that one reviewer said would undermine the publisher's reputation. I wish to thank Jeff Ackerman, Hannah Gaw, Sharon and George Gmelch, Michael Johnson, Marv Krohn, Ed Meidenbauer, Lisa Miller, Luna Munoz, and Glenna Spitze for comments on earlier drafts of the manuscript. I also wish to thank various members of the Felson clan for their comments: my siblings, Steve, Nancy, Marcus, and Ed; my niece, Sabrina; my wife, Sharon; and my son, Jacob. Discussions of these matters produced lively, and sometimes heated, discussions at family reunions, because we are a liberal family sympathetic with women's rights and because some of the women in my family are feminist activists. Fortunately, blood is thicker than ideology.

I

INTRODUCTION

1

INTRODUCTION

Suppose a patriarchal state placed millions of women into prison camps. The male guards in these camps shaved the women's heads, stripped them of their clothes, and murdered most of them. Those women who were not murdered were starved, beaten, raped, and subjected to the most inhumane and humiliating treatment. Wouldn't this be an appalling and clear case of sexism?

Not necessarily. This scenario occurred in Nazi Germany, but the Nazis imprisoned and killed millions of men as well. The Nazis were mostly men, but they chose their victims on the basis of ethnicity and politics, not gender. Yet, by focusing on the male perpetrators and female victims and ignoring the male victims, the scenario appears to be an example of sexism.

This same selective focus characterizes current scholarly and popular discussions of violence against women. Those discussions are dominated by a feminist approach that attributes violence against women to sexism(see, e.g., Belknap, 2001; Bograd, 1988; Brownmiller, 1975; DeKeseredy & MacLeod, 1997; R. E. Dobash & R. P. Dobash, 1979; Eigenberg, 2001; Harway & O'Neil, 1999; Jackson, 1978; Koss et al., 1994; Kurz, 1989; Mahoney, Williams, and West, 2001; Merlo & Pollock, 1995; Pence & Paymar, 1993; Ptacek, 1988; Stanko, 1985; Weis & Borges, 1973).

Feminist scholars tell us that, because of sexism, violence against women is at epidemic levels. For example, Koss and colleagues (1994) argued that

3

"wife abuse is not a rare and deviant phenomenon that results from the break-down of family functioning, but a predictable and common dimension of normal family life as it is currently structured in our society" (p. 14). These scholars fail to mention that the high rates of violence against women in this country are consistent with the overall high violent crime rate. Why should women be immune from the high rate of criminal violence? If offenders attacked people randomly, wouldn't half their victims be women? In fact, women are much less likely to be victims of violence than men (see further discussion in chapter 3). If we are interested in gender differences in victimization, we need to explain men's greater victimization, not women's. Man's inhumanity to man is the modal category.

Tunnel vision is also common in the study of motives for violence toward women. According to the feminist perspective, rapists and wife beaters are sexists who are motivated by the desire for power and control (e.g., Belknap, 2001; Brownmiller, 1975; R. E. Dobash & R. P. Dobash, 1979; Koss et al. 1994; Pence & Paymar, 1993). The perspective fails to recognize that the control motive plays a role in other types of violence as well. It fails to recognize that men assault women for a variety of reasons, often for the same reasons they attack men. Social relationships produce conflict regardless of gender, and that conflict sometimes results in violence. One should not assume that a special explanation is required when men hit women. The study of violence against women belongs under the study of violence, not gender.

Many of the students in my course on interpersonal violence disregard everything they have learned about violence when we get to the section on violence against women. They do not apply what they have learned about conflict, grievances, face-saving, or frustration. They behave as if they are studying a completely different behavior when the victim is a woman—they compartmentalize. Student views reflect what they have heard from their professors and from media sources: violence against women is special.

There *are* special characteristics of male violence against women, but I argue in this book that they have little or nothing to do with the oppression of women. First, violence against women is much more likely to occur within the family than violence against men, largely because women are much less likely to be victimized by strangers. Thus, the study of women and violence overlaps with the study of domestic violence. Second, sexual coercion typically involves male offenders and female victims. For this one crime, women are much more likely than men to be victims. Third, gender differences in size, strength, and the tendency to use violence shape the nature of violent encounters between men and women (Felson, 1996a). Physical advantage encourages men to use violence against women and discourages women from using violence against men. Finally, violence against women is perceived as less acceptable than violence against men because of the societal norm to protect women from harm (see chapter 5). Chivalry is alive and well in modern societies.

The central theme of this book is that violence against women should be understood as violence, not sexism. Violence is violence, regardless of the target. To understand it we should rely on theories of violence and aggression, not feminism. It makes no sense to consider the motives for violence against women without considering the motives for violence generally. Tests of feminist theory require comparisons between violence against women and violence against men to see if there are differences in motive.

I argue that hatred toward women (or misogyny) plays at most a trivial role in violence toward women—attacks on women are rarely "hate crimes." Typically, men who assault their wives are versatile offenders, not misogynists who specialize in violence toward women (see chapters 7 and 11). Men who assault women have similar attitudes toward women as do men who assault men. Men who commit rape or assault their wives commit other crimes as well. Low self-control and a lack of moral inhibitions allow these men to victimize both men and women. The versatility evidence suggests that misogyny and sexism play, at most, a minor role in producing violence against women.

I go even further, arguing that sexism—that is, traditional attitudes toward women—inhibits violence against women. Chivalry leads men to protect women, not harm them. Society views hitting a woman as worse than hitting a man. Beliefs in male dominance may play some role in spousal violence, but that role is trivial, at least in Western countries. Although the control motive may play a greater role in assaults on wives than it does in other forms of violence, I suggest that the desire for control is unrelated to attitudes toward women. In addition, evidence suggests that women are more likely than men to attempt to control their spouses, although men use violence more often for this purpose (see chapter 7).

Later in the book I examine whether sexism plays a role in the motivation for rape and sexual coercion or in the legal response to these crimes. I challenge the idea that rape is a method of controlling women or that it is perceived as legitimate behavior. Evidence on offender tactics, target choice, sexual aspirations, and gender differences in sexuality suggest that rape is usually sexually motivated.

To support my arguments, I review a wide range of evidence from a variety of disciplines. I discuss, for example, experimental studies of shock delivery, survey research on violent crime, and ethnographies of violence in tribal societies. I look at statistical distributions, primarily in the United States, to discern patterns of violent crime and determine whether they imply special motives or distinctive reactions to violence against wives or women. I compare incidents involving male violence against their female partners to incidents involving men, incidents involving women, and incidents involving nonintimate men and women to determine whether male violence against female partners is distinctive. Uniqueness should be demonstrated, not assumed, and differences in degree should not be treated as differences in kind.

At present, the study of causes of violence against women is theory laden and data deprived. My purpose in this book is to reorient the field. I challenge the conventional wisdom that there is an epidemic of violence against women in this country that is hidden from public view. I challenge the widely held notions that these acts are committed by sexist offenders and tolerated by a sexist society. I propose a reintegration of the study of violence against women into the general study of violence.

Some feminist writers have proposed a more eclectic approach that includes other perspectives. For example, Harway and O'Neil (1999) took a feminist approach but added some hypotheses about the effects of biological and psychological variables on violence against women. However, they still studied violence against women separately and viewed sexism as the key to its explanation. It is that perspective which I challenge in this book.

In describing feminist thought, I have attempted to avoid setting up a "straw feminist" by focusing on the most radical ideas. Although there is great variation in feminist thought, there is some consensus that sexism is a key factor promoting violence against women, that offenders are motivated by power and control, and that violence against women is frequent because society tolerates it. This book is concerned with the validity of these basic ideas, not of feminism itself. It is possible to be a feminist but not accept the feminist interpretation of violence involving women. It is possible to think sexism is bad and violence against women is bad but not link the two ideas. My brother, a well-known criminologist, calls the tendency to view social evils as going together the "pestilence fallacy" (M. Felson, 1998).

I discuss violence against women in the neutral tone of science, the same tone I use in the analysis of violence against men. Although I confess that on an emotional level I find violence against women more offensive and upsetting than violence against men, I do not think that sentimentality (or chivalry) should be included in the scientific treatment of the subject. The suffering produced by violence goes without saying.

Perhaps women suffer more from violence than men. Men are more likely than women to be the victims of violence and to be injured or killed (see chapter 3), but violence against women may have special characteristics that make it worse. For example, women are more likely to be injured by their partners than men (e.g., Archer, 2000), perhaps violence inflicted by a family member is more traumatic. In addition, women are much more likely to be victims of rape, and rape is usually more traumatic than robbery and assault, crimes that more typically target men. Finally, women have a greater fear of violent crime than men and are more likely to curb their activities to avoid it (e.g., Riger & Gordon, 1981). It is difficult to weigh these factors and determine which gender suffers more from violence. I think it is best to view violence as a human problem.

ORGANIZATION OF THE BOOK

In chapter 2, I describe an eclectic, gender-neutral approach to violence that borrows from the fields of social psychology, criminology, and sociology (see Tedeschi & Felson, 1994, for a more extended treatment of the topic). Like feminist scholars, I interpret violence as instrumental behavior. People sometimes use violence to punish someone who has wronged them—violence can be an act of justice or retribution carried out in righteous anger. Sometimes they use violence to influence or control another person's behavior. Sometimes they use violence to promote or defend their self-image. Whatever the actor's goal, the target's suffering is a means to an end, not an end in itself.

To a large extent, men and women have similar motives when they use violence. Both have grievances and a desire to punish the "guilty" party. Both have an interest in controlling the behavior of others for their own purposes. Both are likely to retaliate when attacked in order to avoid losing face, although men are more strongly motivated to protect their self-image in these contests. The major difference between men and women is in their use of physical violence. Testosterone and superior size and strength, as well as socialization and gender roles, contribute to male violence.

To understand violence, one must understand inhibitions as well as goals. People often avoid violence if they think it is too costly or morally wrong. These inhibitions prevent attacks on both men and women. However, violent encounters typically involve quick decisions, strong emotions, and alcohol and other drugs. People who are angry, hurried, and intoxicated often fail to consider costs, morals, or alternative approaches. Ill-considered decisions, rather than inner compulsions, result in irrational violence.

Chapters 3 through 8 focus on nonsexual assaults, particularly male violence against partners. Chapter 3 examines the frequency of violence against women relative to violence against men both inside and outside the family. I consider a variety of comparisons, including whether violence against women is more frequent in the United States than elsewhere and whether partner violence is frequent relative to the level of conflict between partners. I also examine whether gender differences in frequency reflect the tendency for men to precipitate their victimization with their own violence. The evidence shows that women are more likely than men to kill in self-defense or in response to a physical attack and that male victims are more likely to physically provoke their assailants than are female victims. However, gender effects are no different for couples than for people in other relationships: women who kill their husbands, for example, are no more likely to kill in self-defense than women who kill in other circumstances. This pattern is inconsistent with the notion of a "battered wife syndrome."

Chapter 4 focuses on gender differences in power and status. I challenge the feminist assertion that American men have more power in their personal relations with women, and more status and prestige, in addition to having more power in the public sphere. I also argue that the notion of women as property is a metaphor, not a description of real social relations now or even in the past. Men do have more coercive power because of their greater size and strength, and this is the key to women's vulnerability. Size and strength give men a tremendous advantage in a physical altercation with a woman, as do men's greater willingness to use violence and superior fighting skills. Why, therefore, isn't male violence against women more frequent?

In chapter 5, I address this question by showing how the chivalry norm discourages violence against women. I present evidence that men are more frequently victimized than women and that men who harm women are punished more severely than men who harm men. I discuss some of the history of society's treatment of violence against women, emphasizing the role of the competing value of privacy. I argue that the privacy of family life, not belief in male dominance, explains why violence against female partners has sometimes been tolerated. The reluctance of the state to intervene in domestic violence situations generally, not just violence against female partners, suggests that privacy concerns were not merely a justification for male dominance. Historical evidence suggests that attitudes toward violence against wives were similar in the past to current attitudes, but that privacy concerns were sometimes greater. Women are more vulnerable to violence by their male partners (and children are more vulnerable to parental violence) when privacy concerns are strong.

The offsetting effects of gender and privacy are apparent in the discussion of the role of the police in chapter 6. I present evidence on how gender and the victim's relationship to the offender affect whether violent incidents are reported to the police, whether the victim signs a complaint, and whether the police make an arrest. The evidence shows that women are not particularly reluctant to call the police or sign a complaint when the offender is their spouse or male partner, at least when they think a crime has been committed. Fear of future attack is more likely to encourage victims to call the police on their spouses and others they know than fear of reprisal is likely to discourage them. Third parties, on the other hand, do show reluctance to intervene on behalf of victims in any kind of partner violence. Gender sometimes has effects in these analyses, but it generally leads to more protection of women, not less.

Chapter 7 examines the idea that assaults by men against their female partners are more likely than other assaults to have a control motive. I show that there is some evidence for this hypothesis, but I argue that such violence is due to men's superior strength, not their sexist attitudes or their desire to control women. Some research suggests that women are more likely to attempt to control men than the reverse—they just use verbal means.

Chapter 8 examines the control motive as a factor in violence stemming from love triangles. I present evidence that love triangles are a more important motivator when women kill than when men kill. In addition, women usually kill their cheating partner, whereas men usually kill their rival—both tend to target men. The evidence does not support the idea that men who kill their partners in love triangles are more likely to have a control motive.

Chapters 9 through 12 are concerned with rape and sexual coercion. Chapter 9 examines the interaction leading to sexual coercion between people who know each other, pointing to the ambiguity of many "date rapes." In chapter 10, I provide evidence that most sexual coercion is sexually motivated rather than power motivated, as some feminists have claimed. Gender differences in sexuality provide the context for sexual coercion. Men are much more likely to be indiscriminate and casual in their attitudes toward sexual relations, whereas women are more likely to interpret sexual activity as romance. Differences in sexuality lead to a gender conflict in which men attempt to influence women to have sex using a variety of techniques. A man without moral qualms or fear of consequences can use force to have sex with anyone he wants.

In chapter 11, I discuss whether sexism plays a role in sexual coercion. I examine the feminist hypotheses that offenders are attempting either to control women or to show their power. I examine whether sexual coercion is different among heterosexuals than among homosexuals and compare the attitudes of men who engage in sexual coercion to the attitudes of other offenders. Chapter 12 examines whether the legal system treats rape and sexual coercion leniently because of prejudice or an interest in controlling women who violate gender roles. Studies that compare the legal system's response to rape and its response to other crimes do not reveal bias. I argue that concerns for due process rather than sexism explain the difficulties in prosecuting sexual assault cases.

In chapter 13, I summarize the main ideas presented in the book. I also discuss the implications of my approach for policy and for organizing and conducting future research on violence. I argue that it is important to study violence against women within the context of the general study of violence using a comparative approach. We must provide evidence showing that it is special before we specialize. An a priori focus on violence against women distorts the larger picture. However, greater attention to violence against women may be justifiable—in spite of its relative infrequency—because it offends us more than violence against men. Chivalry, not misleading claims about an epidemic, provides the rationale for our special concerns about violence against women.

2

A THEORY OF
INSTRUMENTAL AGGRESSION

In this chapter, I present the general approach to aggression and violence that guides this book (for a more complete treatment of the theoretical foundation, see Tedeschi & Felson, 1994). The ideas apply to violence against women as well as men. I begin by considering definitional issues, because without clear definitions of aggression and violence, meaningful dialogue is impossible. Then I criticize frustration–aggression theories, which interpret aggression as an innate response to frustration or aversive stimuli. It is important to consider these theories, because they are central to the study of violence and because the theory used in this book is a response to them.

Finally, I present a social psychological approach that views all aggression as instrumental—that is, as a means to an end rather than an end in itself. I discuss what people hope to accomplish when they harm other people. My treatment of violence as instrumental behavior is actually consistent with the approach of feminist scholars, however, they never explain why they ignore frustration–aggression theories in accounting for violence against women.

DEFINING AGGRESSION

People use the terms "aggression," "violence," and "abuse" loosely in everyday life. In social science, we should be more careful. We recognize that

11

there are no true definitions—dictionary meanings are based on common usage, not scientific truths. We must settle for a definition that is useful.

A definition should classify together behaviors that have similar motives and exclude behaviors that have completely different motives. The behavior of the aggressive salesmen should not be classified with the behavior of the serial killer if their motivations are different. The behavior of the punishing parent and the homicide offender, however, should be classified together if their motivations are similar (even though, of course, there are many differences between them). For example, both may be attempting to satisfy a grievance or deter their victim.

Interpersonal aggression is usually defined as any behavior involving an intent to harm another person. The definition includes the components of harm and intention. Harm is relatively straightforward. If you produce an outcome for me that I would prefer to avoid, you have harmed me.

People harm each other in a variety of ways using a variety of methods. They can use verbal methods (e.g., insults and threats), physical methods (e.g., punches and kicks, bodily force), or indirect methods (e.g., gossip). The term "violence" usually refers to actions that involve the use or threatened use of physical methods. Violence and other forms of aggression can be used to harm the target physically, psychologically, or materially. The method used to harm does not necessarily correspond to the type of outcome. For example, a push or shove may produce little or no physical pain, but it may be humiliating. Rape is a type of violence that results in psychological harm, but often no serious physical harm (see chapter 10).

For an action to be identified as aggression, the person must have intended to produce harm. Whether the attack was successful or not does not matter. For example, the sniper who shoots and misses is engaged in an act of aggression even if he harms no one. If harm has been done, it must have been done on purpose for the act to be aggression; it cannot be accidental. For example, the drunk driver who kills someone is engaged in an act of recklessness, not aggression, because he did not have the intent to harm.

The intent to harm does not necessarily imply that the aggressor preferred the victim to suffer or placed a positive value on the victim's suffering. For example, robbers may be indifferent about harming the victim. The typical robber desires the victim's compliance, which will bring him a profit, not harm. He makes a contingent threat to force the victim to give him money. The robber is willing to harm the victim, but it has no intrinsic value for him. The rapist may also be indifferent to the victim's suffering. He may use a contingent threat or bodily force to produce sexual compliance because he desires sex or power. In sum, a particular behavior can have a number of consequences, only some of which an aggressor desires. To understand the aggressor's behavior, we must examine his or her definition of the situation, not the victim's. The victim's point of view is only relevant to an understanding of the response to violence.

Not all behaviors that deliberately produce harm involve aggression. In competitive activities winners gain (deliberately) at the expense of losers, but we do not want to consider competitive behavior an act of aggression. For example, if two people are competing for a job and only one is hired, then a purposeful behavior has resulted in harm. However, the motives for seeking jobs are different from the motives for harming people, so these behaviors should not be classified together.

How, then, is the competitor different from the typical robber or rapist? Both are willing to harm someone, but neither typically attaches a positive value to that harm. One difference is that robbers and rapists use coercion, but the competitor does not. Robbers and rapists impose harm on unwilling victims, whereas competitors are engaged in a consensual activity. Another difference is that harm is a means to an end for robbers and rapists but an incidental outcome for the competitor.

These considerations lead to an amendment of the standard definition of aggression. I define *aggression* as coercive behavior in which an actor deliberately harms another person. People who use aggression expect that the target will be harmed (whether they value it or not), and they force harm on the target. In our work, we often prefer the term "coercion" over aggression (e.g., Tedeschi & Felson, 1994). Coercion involves verbal impositions (e.g., insults) as well as physical impositions. It does not imply that the motive is necessarily to influence the target's behavior; one may use coercion to promote a self-image or restore justice, for example.

An insult is an act of aggression because it is an imposition; it attempts to impose a negative identity or image on its target. The use of contingent threats or bodily force to force sexual activity, or engaging in sexual activity with an unconscious person, are acts of aggression because they involve coercion and harm. On the other hand, verbal persuasion and pressure for sexual activity are not acts of aggression, because the target can refuse to comply without suffering any harm. Robbery is aggression, but nonconfrontational theft is not because the former relies on coercion and the latter relies on stealth. The use of deception (e.g., pretending romantic interest) to encourage sexual activity involves trickery, not coercion.

We should not confuse anger with aggression (Berkowitz, 1993). When people are upset, they may curse or pound their fist, but that is not aggression because they have no intent to harm. Sometimes it is not even clear that the person is angry: Anger is difficult to distinguish from other forms of emotional upset. *Anger* is the emotional reaction people have to other people when they believe they have been treated unfairly—when they have a grievance. Sometimes anger leads to aggression, but more often it does not (Averill, 1983). In addition, people are not necessarily angry when they engage in aggression. However, a display of anger is an act of aggression if a person uses it to threaten others.

It is important not to allow value judgments to influence definitions. Thus, aggression should not be defined as harm-doing that is "antisocial" or "wrong" (Berkowitz, 1993). A moral approach leads to endless debate over whether a particular act of harm-doing was justified or not; perpetrators often view their behavior as just, whereas victims do not. It is better to say that people harm other people for good reasons and bad or, more precisely, that society approves of some acts of aggression and disapproves of others. We may approve of violence used in self-defense, for example, but it is still useful to describe it as an act of aggression because it involves coercion and an intent to do harm. In addition, it is important not to label some behavior aggression just because we disapprove of it (e.g., lying, drinking and driving)—not all antisocial behavior or harm-producing behavior is aggression.

Punishment is aggression given a positive face. When teachers, judges, and parents punish, they intentionally harm an offender to deter unwanted behavior and to encourage future compliance. Calling the aggression "punishment" legitimizes it because it implies that the target deserved to be harmed. However, there is still an intent to do harm, at least in the short term. (Over the long term a harm may help, by rehabilitating the target, for example.) If the target does not experience the punishment as a harm—that is, if it is not something they would have preferred to avoid—it is not effective punishment. Some criminal violence involves an attempt by an offender to punish someone for an alleged wrong.

The word "aggressive" is sometimes used as an adjective to describe intense effort or activity. However, the aggressive salesman who annoys us on the telephone is not engaged in aggression because he has no intent to harm and is not using coercion. Pete Rose was an aggressive base runner, but his intent was to reach the next base, not to injure the opposing player. If he did attempt to injure an opponent in a particular instance, as some have claimed, then in that instance he was engaged in an act of aggression.

FRUSTRATION AGGRESSION VERSUS INSTRUMENTAL AGGRESSION

One popular conception of aggression is that it is an irrational outburst. In the scientific literature, this point of view is expressed in the frustration–aggression hypothesis and its revisions (Berkowitz, 1989, 1993; Dollard, Doob, Miller, Mowrer, & Sears, 1939). The basic idea is simple: People become aggressive when their goals are blocked or when they experience aversive stimuli. Psychological stress, depression, anxiety, failure, physical pain, sadness, embarrassment, and guilt would all lead to aggression. People who experience these aversive stimuli sometimes just "snap."

According to this perspective, aggression satisfies an innate desire to harm other people when one is feeling bad or frustrated. People prefer to attack the source of their suffering, but if that is too costly, they displace their aggression onto a safer target. For example, a man mistreated by his boss might "take it out on" his wife. If women are safer targets, one might expect that violence against women is more likely to be displaced aggression than violence against men. Yet displacement and aversive stimuli are generally not used to explain men's violence against women. To say that a man assaulted a woman because of his own suffering might, to some extent, excuse his behavior, and that would be ideologically unacceptable.

Violence produced by aversive stimuli is called "emotional" or "reactive" aggression (Berkowitz, 1993). According to Berkowitz, aversive stimuli produce negative affect, which in turn produces aggressive behavior. A major problem with this approach is that people who feel bad generally do not engage in aggression. For example, the death of a loved one is one of the most negative of human experiences, yet aggression rarely occurs at funerals or other situations involving mourning. In addition, we feel worse when we blame ourselves for a problem, but it is blaming others, not self-blame, that leads to aggression. For example, in a study of love triangles to be described in chapter 8, blaming of partner and rival, not self-blame, was associated with anger or aggression. Finally, negative affect leads to risk-taking behavior generally, not just aggression (Baumeister, Heatherton, & Tice, 1994). Thus, Leith and Baumeister (1996) found that participants who experienced anger or embarrassment accompanied by arousal were more likely to pick long shots in a lottery because they were less likely to carefully analyze outcomes.

People respond to negative events in other ways. They become upset, they get drunk or stoned, they engage in problem solving, or they give up and try something else. Why would aversive stimuli have an innate link to aggression from an evolutionary standpoint? If such a link exists, it must have contributed to the survival of the species at some point in human history. It is difficult to imagine how striking out when negative experiences occur would have contributed to human survival.

From the perspective of instrumental aggression, the type of negative situation that leads to aggression is more specific. People tend to become aggressive when they believe that someone has attacked or wronged them in some way. In the laboratory, the best way to get research participants to be aggressive is to attack them, not frustrate them. An insult has much more impact than losing a contest, for example (Tedeschi & Felson, 1994). Some studies do show small effects of aversive stimuli, if the participant is also attacked, but aversive stimuli have no effect on propensity to use aggression by themselves. (In an alternative explanation, Berkowitz, 1993, argued that aversive stimuli do instigate the participants in laboratory studies to aggression, but that the attack is necessary to overcome their inhibitions.)

Aversive stimuli perceived as unjustifiably inflicted are more likely to lead to aggression, according to laboratory evidence. (Berkowitz, 1989, countered this argument by claiming that unjustifiable frustrations are more aversive than justifiable frustrations.) In other words, the attribution of blame is critical in determining whether a negative experience leads to aggression. In laboratory studies participants retaliated for intended shocks even when they did not actually receive the shock (Epstein & Taylor, 1967). "Bad intentions," not bad experiences, lead to aggression, because they imply blame. Other laboratory studies have shown that participants are more likely to retaliate when a person shocks them than when a machine shocks them (Sermat, 1967). The pain is the same, but the meaning differs. When someone zaps them, and participants think that the person has mistreated or humiliated them, they want to retaliate.

From the perspective described in this book, all aggression is instrumental. People use aggression to get what they want. They may want justice, they may want to save face, or they may want to influence someone's behavior. Whatever their goal, the victim's suffering has no intrinsic value for them—it is a means to some other end.

Aggression is similar to other human behavior in that it is oriented toward rewards and costs, not compelled by a mysterious biological inner force. The instrumental approach is preferable on grounds of parsimony: A special mechanism to account for aggression is unnecessary. I do not mean to deny the influence of biological factors, but I think that their effects are indirect. D. M. Buss (1989b) argued that temperament types, which have heritability components, can indirectly affect aggression. For example, a tendency to be impulsive increases the likelihood of aggressive behavior, whereas a tendency to be fearful inhibits it. In addition, evidence shows that testosterone plays a role in violence and other criminal behavior and helps explain sex differences (see Mazur & Booth, 1998, for a review). Perhaps testosterone produces dominance behavior or risk taking behavior—the causal mechanism is unknown.

DECISIONS, IMPULSIVE AND OTHERWISE

People use aggression when they think it will achieve something they value. They are likely to avoid using aggression if they think it will be too costly, such as if their antagonist is physically stronger or a third party is likely to inflict punishment. Potential aggressors are also likely to be inhibited by moral considerations, including their beliefs about the legitimacy of violence and violence against women. However, violent encounters often involve quick decisions, strong emotions, and alcohol and other drugs (e.g., Baumeister, Heatherton, & Tice, 1994; Gottfredson & Hirschi, 1990). People who are angry, hurried, and intoxicated often fail to consider costs, morals, or alternative approaches. Ill-considered decisions, rather than inner compulsions, result in "irrational" violence.

Aggression can also be like a bad habit. People may strike out habitually in certain circumstances, based on past rewards rather than the anticipation of future ones. For example, people may habitually scream at their spouses or children. Like people who smoke or overeat, aggressors may feel compelled or out of control, but they can break the habit if they want to badly enough. Some scholars have described these habitual responses as "scripted behavior" (e.g., Huesmann, 1988).

People often inhibit habitual aggression when they think the costs are too high. For example, spouses may refrain from attacking each other in public and wait until they are alone. On the other hand, if they are impulsive, they may lash out in front of others without giving it much thought. Low self-control (or self-regulation) is an important personality factor in explaining aggressive behavior (Baumeister, Heatherton, & Tice, 1994). It helps explain why people engage in behaviors that they think are wrong and why people who commit violent acts also commit other antisocial behavior, are accident prone, and do poorly in school (Gottfredson & Hirschi, 1990).

All acts of aggression, no matter how impulsive or spontaneous they appear, involves a string of decisions. Consider the baseball batter who charges the pitcher after being hit with a pitch. He is clearly angry, and to some he may appear completely out of control. But he remembers, on the way to the mound, to drop his bat, because he knows that going after the pitcher with a bat would mean the end of his career. As he approaches the pitcher, he has more decisions to make: Should he throw a punch? Should he grab or push the pitcher? Should he make verbal threats from a distance? When players, coaches, and umpires intercede, he allows himself to be contained, screaming all the while.

Even when people use violence in a rage, they are still engaged in decision making. They must decide whether to attack or bide their time, how to attack, and how to respond to their adversary's counterattack. Although they may behave impulsively in the sense that they fail to consider long-range consequences, they are still making decisions. The fact that decisions are sometimes impulsive does not mean that decisions are not being made. Of course, there is variation in the amount of thought given to decisions about whether to use aggression; sometimes people are calculating, and sometimes they are not. Frustrations or aversive stimuli (and the resulting emotion) can facilitate aggression if they interfere with the ability to make careful decisions, but they are not instigators of aggression. Their role in this theory is much more limited than their role in frustration–aggression theories.

What about violent offenders who kill someone when they know they will be caught and sent to prison? Perhaps they are so angry at the victim and so intent on punishment that they are willing to pay the price. More likely, they do not even consider the cost. They are acting in the heat of the moment, overwhelmed by their desire for revenge, or fooling themselves about the likely consequences. Perhaps frustration or emotional arousal interferes with careful thought (Leith & Baumeister, 1996). Perhaps things happen too quickly for much reflection. Perhaps they are lost in a cloud of drunkenness; alcohol interferes with the ability to make thoughtful decisions (e.g., Hull, 1981). However, they still have a purpose in mind.

Some readers may still find some violent behavior incomprehensible, devoid of any rationality, and want to attribute it to an inner compulsion. Perhaps that is because their moral inhibitions prevent them from understanding why someone would choose to commit heinous acts of violence. Maybe these readers have difficulty understanding this behavior because they have high self-control—they give more thought to their behavior than people who commit these acts. Someone who has enough self-control to read this book may find it difficult to gain a full understanding of impulsive violent offenders. If aggression is not due to an inner compulsion, then what is its motivation? Why do we sometimes impose harms on others? One needs to manage individuals with strong motives for using violence and relatively weak inhibitions.

MOTIVES FOR AGGRESSION

People engage in aggression primarily for three reasons: (1) to control the behavior of the target, (2) to gain retribution or justice, and (3) to promote or defend their self-image. (One could add a fourth motive: the desire for excitement [Katz, 1988]. The use of violence for entertainment has not received much attention in the literature.) A summary of our theory of motivation for violence is presented in Table 2.1 (Felson, 1993). The table distinguishes between dispute-related and predatory violence. *Dispute-related violence* refers to instances in which actors engage in violence in response to what they believe is a provocation; whether they have actually been provoked is irrelevant. *Predatory violence* refers to instances in which actors do not perceive any provocation, but attempt to use the target for their own purposes. Unlike most antagonists in disputes, the predatory actor is not usually angry.

The table lists the three general concerns of actors in violent incidents. In the case of dispute-related violence, violent actors may attempt to deter the target from some behavior they find objectionable. They may believe that justice dictates that they gain retribution by punishing the target for a wrongful act. Finally, they may retaliate to save face. In predatory violence, the actor uses coercion to compel the target to engage in some desired behavior. Robbery and rape are usually predatory crimes, although in some instances they stem from grievances and the desire to punish (see chapter 10). A second form of predatory violence involves redistributive justice or equity restoration. When people think that someone has received an unfair share of some reward, they may attempt to restore equity by harming the person, even

TABLE 2.1
Motives in Predatory and Dispute-Related Violence

Actor's concern	Type of violence	
	Predatory	Dispute-related
Compliance	"Compellence"	Deterrence
Justice	Redistribution	Retribution
Social identities	Assertive self-presentation	Defensive self-presentation

when they do not think that person has treated them unfairly. Some violence against rivals in love triangles and other attacks motivated by jealousy are examples. Finally, predatory violence may involve an attempt to establish or assert some self-image: the schoolyard bully is an example. (The distinction between assertive and defensive self-presentation is borrowed from Arkin, 1981).

Compliance and Control

It is in an individual's interest to attempt to influence or control the behavior of others. Parents want their children to behave, adults want to change their spouse's behavior when they find it offensive, robbers and rapists want their victims to comply, and judges want to deter criminals. Aggression is a social influence tactic, sometimes used as a last resort, sometimes as a first resort. It is used to compel a target to do something the target would otherwise not do or to deter a target from what he or she is doing.

For example, parents sometimes use persuasion at first to influence a resistant child to go to bed. However, children often disobey, responding with counterarguments and negotiation. Parents could promise a reward, but that requires time and resources and may interfere with ongoing activity. Instead, parents rely on threats. They become stern or angry to convey their threat, and if the child continues to resist, they make the threat explicit. The child understands this contingent threat and complies. Aggression is quick, easy, and often effective as an influence technique. (It can be costly and less effective in the long run, however; evidence suggests that reasoning with a child is important, e.g., Marion, 1983).

The contingent threat—communicated verbally or nonverbally—is a common method for controlling others through force. The robber displays a weapon, threatening to use it unless the victim complies. The stranger rapist uses the threat of harm to force a woman to engage in sexual relations. The blackmailer threatens to reveal incriminating information to the police unless the victim makes a payoff.

Agents of social control sometimes use violence as a method of influence, and their charges sometimes respond in kind. This helps explain violence involving parents and children, police and suspects, prison guards and inmates, debt collectors and debtors, and bartenders and patrons. Some commentators suggest that violent husbands and rapists act as agents of social control, attempting to force women to conform to gender roles (e.g., Brownmiller, 1975; R. E. Dobash & R. P. Dobash, 1979). I discuss this possibility in chapters 11 and 12.

Divergent interests—interpersonal conflict—is a ubiquitous aspect of social life and an important source of aggression and violence. When people want something that others have, or want others to do things they do not want to do, violence is one method of getting their way. If they want other people's money, or if they want to engage in sexual activity when others do not, some will use force. The more interpersonal conflict in a social group, the greater the incidence of aggression and violence. The more interpersonal conflict a person experiences, the more likely he or she is to be aggressive and violent.

Routine activities that lead to conflict or that result in contact between potential adversaries are therefore likely to result in violence (M. Felson, 1998). For example, violence is more likely at bars frequented by young men (Felson, Baccaglini, & Gmelch, 1986), at competitive sports contests, and during consensual sexual activity when partners disagree about how far to go (see chapter 10). The dependence of family members on each other and the necessity for joint decisions create opportunities for conflict. Thus, siblings fight over ownership and the use of tangible goods in the home and over the division of labor; the frequency is not affected by gender (Felson, 1983). When siblings get older and their interdependence and contact decrease, the frequency of violence dramatically decreases. Husbands and wives argue over sex and money (D. M. Buss, 1989a). Violence may also result from extramarital affairs, divorce settlements, and conflicts over child custody. Finally, the likelihood of violence is increased in the absence of capable guardians. For example, domestic violence occurs more frequently if the nuclear family is isolated from the extended family, because guardianship is reduced (Parke & Collmer, 1975).

Retribution

We punish those who offend us to achieve retributive justice (as well as to deter an injustice). When people do wrong—particularly when they wrong us—we believe they deserve to be punished. We believe the punishment should fit the crime—that is, the more serious the offense is, the more severe the punishment should be. The question is, Who should carry out the punishment?

Sometimes people rely on the criminal justice system to handle their grievances; sometimes they take the law into their own hands. Much criminal violence is similar to vigilantism or self-help, where someone with a grievance seeks retribution (Black, 1983). Self-help violence is more likely when the criminal justice system is unavailable or ineffective in addressing a grievance. For example, violence may occur in conflicts over illicit drug sales, because the police are not available to handle grievances (Goldstein, 1990). E. S. L. Peterson (1999) suggested that women use violence against their husbands as a form of self-help because the criminal justice system is ineffective in deterring their husbands' violence.

It is ironic that people who use violence often feel self-righteous. From their point of view, they are doing a good deed, and their behavior is an act of justice. From their perspective, nonaggression is immoral when someone deserves to be punished. To fail to punish the misdeeds of others would be wrong. Pacifists view violence as a clear moral evil, but for most people, moral values regarding the use of violence are ambiguous and context dependent.

If justice restoration is important in dispute-related aggression and violence, then the attribution of blame is critical. We punish people when we blame them for negative outcomes. We assign blame when we think that they have misbehaved intentionally or recklessly. We wish to harm people when we think they have done wrong to us, not when they have harmed us through no fault of their own. Thus, Tonizzo, Howells, Day, Reidpath, & Froyland (2000) found that men who were violent toward their partners were more likely than nonviolent men to interpret the negative behavior of their partners as intentional, selfish, and blameworthy.

People are not necessarily careful in their attributions of blame—sometimes they can be described as "blame-mongerers." That is, they tend to assign blame even when it is undeserved. They may ignore exonerating circumstances—committing the fundamental attribution error (Ross, Greene, & House, 1977)—or they may fail to understand the perspective of the person they accuse of wrong. Sometimes they blame others to avoid self-blame. For example, students can avoid their own responsibility for a failing grade by blaming their teacher. Sometimes blaming others can help explain traumatic events that are otherwise difficult to understand. For example, people may assign blame for a terrible accident even when it was unavoidable. The question of whether the amount of blame assigned to rape victims is higher than the amount of blame assigned to other crime victims is discussed in chapter 12.

Grievances are common in social life because people frequently break rules and offend each other. When people are dependent on each other and living together, conflict is inevitable, and there are many opportunities for grievances to develop. These conflicts can lead to domestic violence (e.g., Straus, 1980). Discussions of violence between husbands and wives must recognize the important role of conflict and grievances.

People often do not express their grievances to the offending party (Averill, 1983; Goffman, 1959). They do not confront the person because they want to avoid either an embarrassing scene or damage to their relationship. Politeness helps regulate interpersonal relations by preventing aggression, although sometimes it prevents conflicts from being resolved. (Some people have learned to be so polite that they then feel the need to express their grievances more often and purchase books and attend assertiveness training seminars that exhort them to do so.)

People under stress are more likely to generate grievances. Stress interferes with competent performance and people under stress may offend others because they are less likely to be polite and friendly. Support for this idea comes from a study that found that people who experienced stressful life events were more likely to be targets of aggression rather than be aggressive themselves (Felson, 1992). The relationship between stress and the frequency of their own aggression disappeared when the victimization measure was controlled. This finding suggests that the relationship between stress and violence generally reported in the literature may be due to the fact that people under stress are more likely to provoke others, get into conflicts, and then engage in aggression themselves. In addition, the negative effects of stress on decision making may also affect the likelihood of involvement in violence.

Some people are more likely than others to generate grievances because they engage in offensive behavior. Obnoxious people are more likely to become involved in violent interactions because they get people angry with them. Politeness is expected in social life, and the failure to follow ritualized forms of respect is sure to offend others.

Men probably generate more grievances than women because they engage in more deviant behavior. For example, alcohol abuse, more common in men, may lead them to offend their partners and others and make them more likely to become embroiled in conflicts. This deviance may play a role in men's higher levels of aggression and violence.

Women are more likely than men to experience anger and to express anger in a nonaggressive way when they have a grievance (see Brody, 1999, for a review). Women also express more intense anger than men, and their anger lasts longer. Similar gender differences are reported in the literature on making complaints. A meta-analysis revealed that women are more likely than men to complain when they have a grievance (Kowalski, 1996). Male reticence about complaining or displaying anger may reflect gender roles that encourage men to be stoic. Finally, women are more likely to talk over the incident with third parties (Brody, 1999). The literature on indirect aggression also suggests that women are more likely than men to gossip or say negative things about others behind their backs (e.g., Bjorkqvist, Lagerspetz, & Kaukiainen, 1992; Richardson & Green, 1999).

In domestic disputes, wives are more likely than husbands to express grievances (Stets & Burke, 1996). The content of husbands' and wives' grievances are different to some extent. A study of couples showed that men were more likely to be upset about their wives' moodiness, whereas women were more likely to complain about their husbands' condescension, neglect, and inconsiderateness (D. M. Buss, 1989a). Among dating couples, the study found that women were more likely than men to be angry about demands for sexual intimacy and touching their bodies without permission. Of course, these are only statistical tendencies: Men and women, to some extent, have similar complaints about their partners.

Levinson (1989) examined sources of grievances in spousal violence based on the ethnography of 90 tribal societies. Allegations of adultery were a common source of grievances leading to violence against wives in these societies (see also M. Daly & Wilson, 1988). A husband was also likely to hit his wife when she failed to perform her duties or when she failed to treat him with the degree of respect that he expected, suggesting that his belief in male dominance led him to use violence. However, the data did not address whether the women also became aggressive when their husbands failed to perform their duties or mistreated them (see chapter 5).

The aggrieved party is likely to have a different perspective than the target of the grievance. For example, Mikula and Heimgartner (1992) asked husbands and wives to report instances of unfair behavior by their spouses. Each was also asked to respond to a series of questions about the events the other partner thought were unfair. Those who engaged in the unfair behaviors rated the events as less serious and unjust, thought their causal contribution to the event was smaller, and considered their actions as more justified than did their partners (see also Mummendey, Linneweber, & Loschper, 1984).

The tendency for grievances to be concealed may also lead to a difference in perspective. An aggrieved party may have accumulated a set of grievances that he or she never expressed to the target. The unaware target may then perceive the anger expressed over the latest event as an unjustified overreaction (Baumeister, Stillwell, & Wotman, 1990). As a result of these differences in perspectives, disputes may escalate, leading to physical violence.

Self-Image

People use aggression to enhance or protect their self-images. For example, by using violence, a young man demonstrates that he is powerful, tough, and courageous. By showing skill with his fists, he can increase his status among his friends. If winning is impossible, standing up to the antagonist maintains some level of honor and provides a measure of satisfaction.

When someone insults another, the other may believe that he or she has been put down, or made to appear weak. By putting the adversary down in turn, the insulted party can nullify that image and make himself or herself appear powerful. Retaliation is a form of defensive self-presentation, a way of "saving face" or maintaining one's honor when one has been attacked. However, the counterattack is a put-down for the other person, who may then retaliate, creating a "conflict spiral." Adversaries try to win this face-saving contest rather than limit their punishments to fit the offense. In this way small disputes sometimes escalate into physical violence.

Escalation is particularly likely to occur when an audience is watching, because the threat to image is greater. Sometimes the audience eggs the adversaries on, making it difficult for them to back down without losing face. Sometimes the audience pulls the antagonists apart: third-party mediation allows both sides to back down without losing face (Felson, 1978). The response of third parties is thus a key factor in the escalation of aggressive interactions.

School-age bullies, who are usually boys, are typically attempting to promote a self-image—that is, they are engaged in assertive self-presentation (Besag, 1989; Olweus, 1978). These boys prey on vulnerable targets, usually in the presence of third parties, to show how tough they are. For the bully, dominating the victim is an accomplishment, a way of demonstrating power to himself and others. The bully targets other boys, presumably because dominating girls will not make him look strong and may even have the opposite effect. Some commentators have asserted that rape is also motivated by a concern for self-image—the rapist wants to show his power (e.g., Groth, Burgess, & Holmstrom, 1977). The question of whether rape is a form of bullying designed to display power is discussed in chapter 11.

Gender differences in aggression and violence are at least partly due to differences in gender role identities (i.e., self-images associated with gender). The identities of men and boys place more importance on power, courage, risk-taking, and skill in fighting. Research has also found that men take more risks than women (J. Block, 1983; Ginsburg & Miller, 1982). Presumably, these identities are valued because of the requirement that men serve as bodyguards and soldiers (Harris, 1997). Societies have relied on men, particularly young men, to protect their members, and thus the characteristics in men that help them in this endeavor are valued.

Evidence suggests that gender role identities help explain gender differences in violence among adolescents (Felson & Liska, 1984). We asked respondents to rate themselves on adjective pairs, such as sensitive–unfeeling, cowardly–brave, and rough–smooth, and to indicate which of their peers fought the most. Regression analyses indicated that the strong gender differences in frequency of fighting were greatly reduced when self-ratings of gender-relevant identities were controlled. The pattern suggests that gender role identities to some extent mediate or explain gender differences in violence.

When men confront other men, their actions are particularly likely to precipitate identity contests with other men, who are also motivated to protect their masculine identities. Verbal conflicts between men are more likely to escalate to physical violence than intergender conflicts, particularly if an audience is present (Felson, 1982). The presence of an audience makes the issue of social identities more salient. However, the presence of an audience inhibits escalation in conflicts between men and women, suggesting that physical violence during these conflicts does not enhance identities. The antagonist's behavior is also likely to depend on the perceived values of the audience (e.g., Borden, 1975). Because men are more favorable toward violence, violence is more likely to occur when men are watching than when women are watching.

Men and women respond differently to different types of identity attacks. Laboratory studies have shown that men are more likely than women to respond with aggression to attacks on their competence (Bettencourt & Miller, 1996). College men report that they would be more apt to retaliate for implications of homosexuality, whereas women reported that they would react most strongly to insults that indicated sexual promiscuity (Jay, 1980). These same gender differences were observed in a study of the content of insults directed to men and women (Preston & Preston, 1987). People apparently know what insults hurt, and they use them. Also, different slurs are used in attacks on men and women: A woman is called a "bitch," and a man is called an "asshole." The latter was the most frequently used slur in verbal conflicts coded in the Albany data (described in chapter 3) probably reflecting the higher rates of aggression targeting men than targeting women.

Alcohol use is also associated with the male identity for some men. Men drink and get drunk twice as often as women, and they are three to four times more likely to be alcoholics (Cahalan, 1978; Hartford & Gerstel, 1981; Malin, Wilson, Williams, & Aitken, 1986). Moreover, men drink more often in public places than women (Hartford, 1978; Leland, 1982), creating opportunities for violence with other men. These gender differences in routine activities help explain gender differences in violence.

Multiple Motives

A particular violent incident may involve all of these motives. For example, people often retaliate when they believe they have been attacked. First, retaliation deters the aggressor and others from engaging in future attacks. Second, targets are likely to perceive an attack as wrongdoing and therefore deserving of punishment. Finally, by retaliating, targets save face by making adversaries look weak.

In some instances retributive justice provides a justification for behavior and is not its motivation. The person retaliates to save face and is able to legitimate the counterattack by claiming that the target deserved it. One might describe this as a case of "justice in the service of revenge." In general, we must be skeptical of offenders' explanations of their motives for committing violence. This will become an issue in the consideration of rapists' reports about their motives (see chapter 10).

Concerns for justice and self-image do not always have the same effects. For example, aggrieved individuals are interested in seeing that the wrongdoer receives a punishment that is proportional to the offense, whereas individuals concerned with face-saving want to dominate the antagonist, if necessary, by delivering greater harm than they received. Those who are aggrieved are not concerned about who carries out the punishment, but those who are more concerned with face-saving want to punish the wrongdoer themselves.

Most violent disputes begin with criticism and other attempts at social control. The offended party's desire for redress of grievances and deterrence is central in the initial stage of the encounter (Felson, 1984). Those who have been accused often see things differently. They interpret the criticism as an attack, and they retaliate in response. Verbal attacks are reciprocated as the incident escalates into a battle to save face. One of the adversaries may then engage in a physical attack, perhaps under the impression that he or she is losing the verbal battle. Whether women's superior verbal skills sometimes lead men to retaliate with violence in verbal conflicts with them has never been examined.

Nor has research examined whether the gender of the antagonists or their relationship to each other affects the sequence of events leading to violence. We do not know, for example, if men's violence against women or wives is more likely to begin with a social control sequence than is other violence. In addition, it may be difficult to attribute a single motive to an incident of couple violence, because the motive may change during the event.

EXPLAINING DISPLACEMENT

The motive for aggression almost always has something to do with the victim. Either the offender has had a dispute with the victim, or the victim has something the offender wants. This pattern enables the police to catch offenders and prosecutors to "establish motive" and get a conviction. Violence rarely involves displaced aggression, such as attacks on innocent third parties (Felson, 1984; Luckenbill, 1977).

Although serial killers and "random" attacks on victims receive much media attention, they are rare. Even serial killers may have some imagined grievance against the strangers they victimize (Hickey, 1991). People respond to their own definitions of the situation, and if their paranoia leads them to think they are under attack, they may think they are defending themselves. Violent actions based on delusional thinking are still purposive. Perhaps some offenders experience a compulsion to commit violence. However, if a theory of compulsive violence could be developed, it would not necessarily involve a response to aversive stimuli.

Laboratory studies indicate that displaced aggression does occur and therefore requires explanation (Marcus-Newhall, Pedersen, Carlson, & Miller, 2000). Why, after some provocation, does someone attack an innocent third party? Berkowitz (1989) attributed displaced aggression to the negative affect produced by aversive stimuli, which can lead to aggression against anyone. But how can a theory of instrumental aggression account for displacement?

First, the misperception of aggression leads to an exaggeration of the frequency of displacement. When people are in a bad mood, they tend to be irritable and impolite, with no intent to do harm. Because people are expected to be warm and friendly to each other, the failure to show proper etiquette may be misperceived as displaced aggression. For example, when a man is irritable with his wife after a tough day at work, she perceives it as aggression, becomes aggrieved, and admonishes him. He is offended by her behavior—he now has an intent to harm—and he retaliates.

Second, evidence suggests that displacement may reflect a concern for self-image after a failure or loss of face (e.g., Melburg & Tedeschi, 1989). A successful attack against a third party may help the person restore a favorable image as tough or competent. By putting another person down, people can bring themselves up in comparison. By changing competitors, the actor shifts to a contest that is winnable: "If you can't beat 'em, beat someone else." Wills (1981) described this process as "downward comparison," whereby actors lower the standing of the target on some dimension and thereby look good in comparison.

Third, displaced aggression may also be due to guilt by association when the offending party and the third party are members of the same group. The aggressor may assign collective guilt to all members of the group. Blood feuds and bias crimes are examples of aggression carried out against members of a group. Groth, Burgess, and Holmstrom (1977) interpreted some rapes as displaced aggression against women due to the rapist's conflict with his wife or mother.

Finally, some acts of displacement involve attempts to produce redistributive justice or equity restoration (see Donnerstein & Hatfield, 1982; Tedeschi & Norman, 1985). When a person believes that a distribution of rewards and costs is unfair, he or she may attempt to restore equity by harming the person perceived as privileged, even when that person is not held responsible for the injustice. By increasing the costs or reducing the rewards of the overbenefited party, they can produce equity or distributive justice. Such a process helps explain why jealousy might lead to violence against rivals in love triangles (see chapter 8).

This process has been demonstrated in an experiment in which participants had to wait for another participant who did not show up for a research appointment (Nacci & Tedeschi, 1977). After waiting, participants engaged in a learning task in which they were given the opportunity to deliver shocks to someone who was allegedly recruited to take the place of the missing partner. Participants who had to wait delivered more shocks to their partner, but not if the partner had experienced a similar delay. That partners delivered greater shocks only to partners who had not experienced the delay suggests that they were attempting to restore equity rather than address their negative affect (Tedeschi & Norman, 1985).

CONCLUSION

There are reasons to be skeptical of the assertion that aggression is an innate response to any type of aversive stimuli or a drive triggered by frustration. I have suggested that aversive stimuli and negative affect facilitate but do not instigate aggression. Whereas many social psychologists distinguish emotional from instrumental aggression, I have suggested that all aggression is instrumental, even aggression carried out with great emotion. In other words, harming others is a means to various ends, not an end in itself. Sometimes aggressive behavior reflects careful calculation of reward and costs, and sometimes it is impulsive or habitual. In either case, we do not need a special mechanism to explain it; it is readily understood using well-established social psychological principles.

Most feminist discussions of violence imply that their authors also believe that aggression is instrumental behavior (e.g., R. E. Dobash & R. P. Dobash, 1979; Eigenberg, 2001; Koss et al., 1994). The motives they attribute to violent men (control or power) suggest that they believe that aggression is a means to an end, although they do not say this explicitly. To my knowledge, they do not mention frustration–aggression theories. In the case of battered wife syndrome, the woman's violence is sometimes interpreted as noninstrumental; she kills her abusive husband because she is suffering from a form of posttraumatic stress syndrome (e.g., Browne, 1987; Walker, 1984). More often, it is argued that she killed him in self-defense—an instrumental motive—but the possibility that she killed her husband in retaliation—to promote justice or save face—is not considered (see chapter 3). Women do engage in retaliatory aggression. In fact, gender differences in retaliatory aggression are weaker than gender differences in unprovoked aggression according to experimental research (Bettencourt & Miller, 1996).

I suspect that the idea that violence is an instrumental act motivated by power and control appeals to feminist activists for ideological reasons. Men's power and their control of women are central features of feminist ideology. In addition, to say that a man's violence against a woman is an emotional, involuntary outburst in response to aversive stimuli makes the male perpetrator appear less blameworthy. To say that he might have had a grievance implies that she might be blameworthy. On the other hand, a calculating male offender seeking to dominate the victim looks worse. A woman who kills her husband in self-defense, or because she is suffering from battered wife syndrome, is less blameworthy, and her victim is more so. As a result of these concerns about blame (not the social psychological evidence), frustration–aggression theories are generally ignored in discussions of violence against women. Whether aversive experience is an important instigator of violence or merely an occasional facilitator (as I have argued), it is likely to have similar effects on violence against women and men.

II

VIOLENCE INSIDE AND OUTSIDE THE FAMILY

3

COMPARING FREQUENCIES

Every 15 seconds, in the United States . . . someone comes up with a bogus statistic.

The purpose of most statistical research on violence against women is to demonstrate its frequency. Activists use this research to argue that there is an epidemic of violence against women in the United States (e.g., Bograd, 1988; Koss et al., 1994). Epidemics draw public attention to violence against women as a social problem (see Best, 1995). If the public is convinced that violence against women is epidemic, then it will allow more of its tax money to be used for research and for battered women's shelters.

Activists are also trying to influence the criminal justice system. They want to increase the certainty and severity of punishment for men who use violence against women and provide more lenient treatment of battered women who commit violence against men (e.g., Belknap, 2001; Koss et al., 1994; Walker, 1979). Finally, belief in an epidemic of violence against women is useful in increasing support for other feminist causes, because it provides dramatic evidence for the oppression of women. It is an ideal political issue because almost everyone is sympathetic with the victims and angry at the offenders.

In this chapter, I examine gender differences in the frequency of violent offending and victimization. In answering questions about frequency, it is important to be clear about the comparison. This chapter focuses on the following questions:

- Are women more likely than men to be the victim of violence?
- Is the victimization of women relative to men particularly high in the United States?
- Are women more likely than men to be victimized by their partners?
- When a woman is the victim of violence, is the perpetrator typically a male partner?
- Is violence between husbands and wives frequent relative to the level of verbal conflict?
- Is the level of violence involving heterosexual couples frequent as compared to the level of violence involving homosexual couples?
- Are women's violent acts against their male partners more likely to involve victim precipitation than other types of violence?

The comparisons implied in these questions are important for an understanding of how frequent violence against women is in the United States or elsewhere. For example, violence against women may be more frequent in the United States than in other Western countries, but so may violence against men. Violence between husbands and wives may be more frequent than other types of violence but infrequent relative to the level of contact and verbal conflict produced by domestic relations. Women may be just as violent toward their partners as men, but only because they act in self defense.

GENDER DIFFERENCES IN VIOLENCE AND OTHER AGGRESSION

Before discussing gender differences in victimization, it is important to consider gender differences in offending. If men are more violent than women, then husbands should be more violent than wives, and wives should be victimized more than husbands. It is necessary to take into account gender differences in violent behavior when thinking about patterns of offending and victimization.

One of the best sources of information on violence is the U.S. Justice Department's National Crime Victimization Survey (NCVS). The NCVS involves a large, nationally representative survey of hundreds of thousands of households in the United States. Respondents are asked about victimizations in the previous six months, and if they report an incident to the interviewer, they are questioned about the circumstances of the crime.

The NCVS relies on extensive questioning to reveal whether the respondent was the victim of a violent crime. These probes are designed to address criticisms of the earlier National Crime Survey as undercounting incidents that involve sexual assault and family members and incidents that victims do not define as crimes. Respondents to the NCVS are asked if anyone attacked or threatened them at various locations. Later, after stating that "people often don't think of incidents committed by someone they know," the interviewer asks them whether they had been attacked or threatened by various people they might know. After describing these behaviors, respondents are asked to mention an incident even "if you are not certain it was a crime."

The NCVS has been criticized for both undercounting and overcounting incidents of violent crime, particularly family violence and violence against women. Respondents may have been reluctant to report incidents to interviewers out of fear or embarrassment. They may not have reported violence that they did not realize was criminal, even though the survey asked about specific behaviors rather than criminal behavior. On the other hand, the probes about specific behavior may have elicited reports of relatively minor incidents that were not criminal. These criticisms must be kept in mind in using statistics from the NCVS.

Table 3.1 presents data from the NCVS on gender differences in offending for various violent crimes committed by lone offenders (Bureau of Justice Statistics, 1997a). The statistics on arrest are based on data from the 1998 *Uniform Crime Reports*. The table shows that men were much more likely to commit all types of violence. The gender difference in rape is the most pronounced: Almost all of the rape offenders were male.

These gender differences reflect differences in intent to harm, methods used, exposure to provocation, and opportunity. Experimental studies that control for provocation and opportunity also have shown that men are more likely than women to engage in violence. According to a meta-analysis of these studies, gender differences are stronger for physical aggression than for verbal aggression and for unprovoked aggression than retaliatory aggression (Bettencourt & Miller, 1996).

Parental violence is an apparent exception to the generalization that men are more violent than women. Mothers are more likely than fathers to use physical punishment against their children (e.g., Straus, Gelles, & Steinmetz, 1980). This gender reversal can be attributed to the fact that mothers are usually the primary caretakers. The amount of time spent with children was presumably controlled in studies comparing the behavior of fathers and mothers in single-parent families. Estimates of the rate of severe violence for single fathers (189 per 1,000) is substantially greater than the rate for single mothers (130 per 1,000) (Gelles, 1987; see also Pagelow, 1984). Thus, when time spent caretaking is controlled, fathers are more violent than mothers.

Another apparent exception to greater male aggression is suggested by the literature on "indirect aggression." Studies based on both self-reports and peer nominations indicate that girls are more likely than boys to say negative

TABLE 3.1
Gender Distribution in Offending for Various Crimes

Crime	National Criminal Victimization Survey offenders		Uniform Crime Report offenders	
	Male (%)	Female (%)	Male (%)	Female (%)
Crimes of violence	82.7	16.8	—	—
Rape or sexual assault	99.4	0.6	98.8	1.2
Robbery	86.5	12.0	90.0	10.0
Aggravated assault	88.8	10.5	80.4	19.6
Simple assault	79.2	20.5	77.6	22.4
Homicide	—	—	88.8	11.2

Note. Dashes indicate the data were not gathered. The data are from Bureau of Justice Statistics (1997a) report based on NCVS data and Supplemental Homicide Reports (Fox, 2001). Numbers do not sum to 100% because of missing data.

things about others behind their backs (e.g., Bjorkqvist, Lagerspetz, & Kaukiainen, 1992). The evidence is more inconsistent concerning whether adult women engage in more indirect aggression than adult men (e.g., Richardson & Green, 1999). However, it is unclear whether these studies are actually measuring aggression, because gossip does not necessarily involve an intent to do harm. It may be that these studies reflect the gender difference in the tendency to complain (Kowalski, 1996).

GENDER DIFFERENCES IN VICTIMIZATION

Assertions about an epidemic of violence against women are misleading if they do not consider the frequency of violence against men as well. Rates of violence against women may appear high when examined in isolation but not when examined in the larger context of violence. To address this issue, Table 3.2 presents gender differences in victimization for various violent crimes based on data from the NCVS and the *Uniform Crime Reports*. With the exception of rape, the results show that men are more likely to be the victims of violence. Although women are much more likely to be the victims of rape and sexual assault, these crimes occur much less frequently than other violent crimes, so they play only a minor role in statistics on violent crime. Rape or sexual assault is involved in approximately 4% of violent crimes reported in the NCVS and 8.7% of the incidents involving violence against women.

The table also shows that the more serious the (nonsexual) assault, the less likely it is for the victim to be female. Nineteen percent of homicide victims are female, as are 34.7% of aggravated assault victims and 42.6% of victims of simple assault. Thus, the results suggest that not only are women assaulted less frequently than men, but their victimizations tend to be less

TABLE 3.2
Gender Differences in Victimization for Various Crimes (1994)

Crime	Male victims (%)	Female victims (%)
Simple assault	57.4	42.6
Aggravated assault	65.3	34.7
Homicide	81.0	19.0
Rape or sexual assault	7.1	92.9
Robbery	65.9	34.1

Note. The data are from Bureau of Justice Statistics (1997a) based on National Crime Victimization Survey data and Supplemental Homicide Reports.

severe. There are at least three explanations for this pattern. First, it may be that offenders are more punitive toward male victims because they anticipate or experience more violence from male victims (see chapter 4). Second, men may be inhibited by the norm of chivalry from harming women seriously (see chapter 5). Third, it may be that women are more likely to tell interviewers about minor incidents than men. Women are more likely to report incidents to the police and more likely to sign a complaint, particularly if the assailant is their husband (see chapter 6). More generally, as indicated earlier, when women have a grievance, they are more likely than men to complain to the offender and to third parties (Kowalski, 1996). Of course, this explanation cannot explain the results on homicide, because they are not based on self-report—dead men (and women) don't talk.

The International Crime Survey, a victimization survey, shows that men have higher victimization rates than women in other Western countries as well (van Dijk, Mayhew, & Killias, 1990). If violence against women reflects sexism, one might expect that women's victimization rates—relative to men's—would be lower in more egalitarian societies. However, there is no evidence that gender differences in victimization depend on the political or ideological climate of countries. For example, gender differences in assault victimization rates in the United States are similar to rates in Finland, Switzerland, Belgium, and Scotland.

Gender differences in homicide victimization for 1991–1992 for selected countries are presented in Table 3.3 (World Health Organization, 1995). These figures show that men are much more likely to die from homicide than women in every country. The table also shows that countries with high rates of violence against women have high rates of violence against men. If we compute the correlation between the victimization rates of men and women, we see that it is quite high ($r = .88$). Finally, the table shows that women's victimization rates relative to men's are lowest in countries with relatively high homicide rates such as Mexico, the United States, Italy, and Colombia. This suggests that there is less variation across countries in rates of violence against women than in rates of violence against men. When a country has a high rate of violence—what might be called an epidemic—it is primarily

TABLE 3.3
Gender Differences in Homicide Victimization Rates 1991–1992
(per 100,000 population)

Country	Male	Female	% Female
Argentina	7.3	1.4	16.1
Canada	2.9	1.4	32.6
China–urban	3.4	1.5	30.6
China–rural	2.8	1.0	26.3
Columbia	167.6	12.6	7.0
Germany	1.4	1.0	41.7
Israel	1.5	.7	31.8
Italy	5.2	.7	11.9
Japan	0.8	.5	38.5
Mexico	33.9	3.7	9.8
Russian Federation	37.6	9.9	20.8
Spain	1.3	.5	27.8
Sweden	1.8	1.0	35.7
United States	16.7	4.4	20.9

Note. World Health Statistics Annual, 1995 (World Health Organization).

because many men are being killed. The findings suggest that we do not have an epidemic of violence against women in this country and that we are unlikely to find epidemics of violence against women anywhere in the world.

Perhaps the rates of violence against women vary over time independently of the rates of violence against men, reflecting changing attitudes toward women. Marvell and Moody's (1999) examination of homicide victimization from 1930 to 1995 in the United States reveals similar trends for men and women. Their time series analyses revealed that similar factors were responsible for changes in rates of male and female victimization over time. The dramatic changes in female labor and divorce rates during this time period had little, if any, effect on homicide victimization rates for either men or women. Homicide victimization rates for both men and women decreased during World War II, increased during the crack cocaine epidemic, and were negatively associated with incarceration rates.

In sum, rates of violence against women correlate highly with rates of violence against men over time and geography. Violence against women is much less frequent than violence against men, and when it occurs, it tends to be less serious. The risk of victimization was lower for women in every country where statistics were available. In understanding gender patterns, the issue is not to understand why men victimize women, but to understand why men do not victimize women.

PARTNER VERSUS OTHER VIOLENCE

Discussions of violence against women often focus on violence by partners. It is well known that violence against women is more likely to involve

TABLE 3.4
Victim-Offender Relationships by Gender for Nonlethal Violence and Homicide

Relationship	Nonlethal violence (%)		Homicide (%)	
	Female	Male	Female	Male
Intimates	20.7	2.8	31.0	3.8
Other relatives	6.6	3.6	7.0	3.9
Friend or acquaintance	34.3	30.2	23.9	34.4
Stranger	38.4	63.4	7.9	15.0
Unknown	—	—	30.1	42.9
Totals	100	100	100	100

Note. Dashes indicate unknown: data was not included in computing percentages. Data are from the 1994 National Crime Victimization Survey (Bureau of Justice Statistics, 1997b) and Supplemental Homicide Reports.

partners and family members than violence against men (e.g., Browne & Williams, 1993; Kruttschnitt, 1994; A. J. Reiss & Roth, 1993). This relationship is revealed in Table 3.4 (Bureau of Justice Statistics, 1997b). The table shows that when women are victims of nonlethal violence, the perpetrator is much more likely to be a partner than when men are victimized (20.7% vs. 2.8%). The perpetrator is also slightly more likely to be some other person the victim knows when the victim is a woman. The proportion of violence committed by people the victim knows may be underestimated if respondents (of both genders) are reluctant to tell interviewers about these incidents. For homicide, where this methodological problem does not exist, the gender difference in partner involvement is stronger. When women (age 12 or older) are killed, 31.0% of the offenders are partners, compared to only 3.8% of males (Bureau of Justice Statistics, 1997b).

These gender differences contribute to an inaccurate stereotype about violence against women. When one thinks of violence against women, one typically thinks of violence committed by their male partners. However, the evidence presented in Table 3.4 suggests that only about one fifth of violent crimes against women and slightly less than one third of homicides are committed by their partners; most of their victimizations are committed by other people. Given the reporting biases and the rarity of homicide, a reasonable estimate is that partners commit about one quarter of incidents involving violence against women. Thus, women are less likely to be victimized by partners than they are by strangers, friends, and acquaintances. One must be careful in characterizing the typical act involving violence against women as involving partners.

Women typically have one partner at a particular time but are exposed to many strangers, friends, and acquaintances. A partner is likely to pose a greater risk than any other single person. On the other hand, people spend much more time with their partners, so there is a much greater opportunity for conflict. None of the statistical comparisons in Table 3.4 control for these opportunity factors.

VIOLENCE VERSUS VERBAL CONFLICT

According to a feminist approach, violence against female partners is frequent at least in part because the behavior is perceived as legitimate (e.g., R. E. Dobash & R. P. Dobash, 1979; Pagelow, 1984). From this perspective, a man should be more likely to use violence during a verbal conflict when the antagonist is his wife rather than someone else, because he is likely to perceive violence as more legitimate against wives than against other people. Straus and his colleagues (1980), on the other hand, emphasized the legitimation of spousal or domestic violence generally. For example, they described a marriage license as a "hitting license." From their perspective, both men and women should be more likely to engage in violence during verbal conflicts with spouses than with other people.

An alternative perspective is that the frequency of domestic violence reflects the relatively high level of contact and verbal conflict between family members. Family members typically live together in the same household. The more time people spend together, the more opportunities there are for disputes and the violence that can develop out of disputes. In addition, continual contact prevents people from avoiding each other once they have a conflict (Baumgartner, 1988). Perhaps more important than the extent of contact is the conflict produced by the interdependence of family members (Felson, 1983; Steinmetz & Straus, 1974). Family members have a critical interest in influencing each other's behavior because that behavior strongly affects their own outcomes. The interdependence of family life and the necessity for joint decisions create greater opportunity for conflicts of interest and reciprocal harm (Stafford & Gibbs, 1993). From this perspective, the frequency of physical violence should reflect the frequency of verbal conflict, which can be viewed as a measure of the total number of conflicts. The ratio of physical violence to verbal aggression should be no higher for couples than for antagonists in other relationships. (Violent disputes almost always begin with verbal aggression; Felson, 1984.)

We examined the relative frequency issue using data based on interviews of individuals in Albany County, NY, in 1980 (Kaplan & Felson, 1999). Two samples were used: (1) a representative sample from the general population ($N = 245$) and (2) a sample of exoffenders ($N = 141$). Respondents were asked how often they had engaged in verbal aggression, minor violence (i.e., pushing or slapping), and serious violence (i.e., hitting) in the preceding year against different targets. We then computed the ratios of violence to verbal aggression for different targets.

TABLE 3.5
Percentages of Respondents Reporting Violence in Previous Year and Ratios of Violence to Verbal Aggression

Measure	Type of relationship				
	Spouse	Child	Other family	Other known	Stranger
	Percentages				
Verbal aggression	87.0	66.7	52.8	57.5	30.3
Minor violence	19.5	38.0	8.0	18.2	13.7
Serious violence	6.8	5.4	4.0	16.1	12.4
	Ratios				
Minor violence to verbal aggression	.22	.57	.15	.32	.45
Serious violence to verbal aggression	.08	.08	.08	.28	.41

The top part of Table 3.5 presents the percentages of respondents who engaged in verbal aggression, minor violence, and serious violence during the year. The results show that a relatively high percentage of respondents engaged in minor violence (slapping or shoving) toward their children. Relatively few engaged in minor violence toward family members other than their spouses and children. Violence against spouses and other people the respondent knew occured at only a slightly higher rate than violence against strangers. Serious violence (hitting with a fist or object) was much less likely to be directed at family members than at people outside the family.

The bottom half of the table presents the ratios of violence to verbal aggression for each type of target. In general, the ratio of violence to verbal aggression was much lower for couples and other family members than for strangers. The ratio for other people the respondent knew was somewhere in between. The results show that people are much less likely to engage in violence against family members than against strangers relative to their level of verbal aggression.

There is one exception to this pattern. For parents, the ratio of minor violence to verbal aggression is higher than any other category. Parents are more likely to slap or shove their children than they are to slap or shove other people relative to the level of verbal aggression. These results suggest that legitimation does play a role in minor violence against children, which is not surprising given the high frequency of corporal punishment (e.g., Straus et al., 1980). (Some of the respondents' children were adults. If we eliminated respondents with adult children, this ratio would be even higher.)

The ex-offenders had higher rates of violence than the general population (not presented), but the ratios are similar. In contrast to a feminist argument, similar results were obtained when we analyzed male and female respondents separately. In more recent analyses of additional data, we have found that men are particularly reluctant to hit their female partners. The results suggest that relative to the level of verbal aggression, men and women are less (not more) likely to be violent toward spouses than toward strangers. In general, partner and family violence is infrequent relative to the level of verbal aggression. This pattern suggests that conflicts between adults are less likely to become violent within the family than outside it.

We also performed a situational analysis in an attempt to determine whether incidents involving domestic conflict were more likely than incidents involving strangers to escalate to violence. The respondents were asked to describe incidents involving physical violence and verbal aggression. We reconstructed the data set so that the incident was the unit of analysis and then examined whether gender and the relationship between the antagonists predicted whether the incident was physical or verbal. The results were consistent with the individual level of analyses. Incidents involving partners and other family members were much less likely to involve violence than incidents involving strangers.

We also found that verbal disputes were more likely to become violent when the antagonist was a man. In addition, the effects of gender and social relationships are additive: Both men and women were less likely to become violent with people they knew than with strangers. In contrast to a feminist approach, during a verbal dispute, men (as well as women) are less likely to become violent with a partner than a stranger.

In general, our findings suggest that the level of domestic violence is infrequent relative to the level of verbal conflict in the home. During a verbally aggressive dispute, both men and women are less likely to become violent when the antagonist is someone they know, particularly a family member. In other words, family disputes are less likely to become physically violent than disputes outside the family. The results suggest that people have special inhibitions about using violence against spouses and other family members (with the exception of children). They do not support the notion that a marriage license is a hitting license or that spousal violence or violence against wives is perceived as legitimate. Instead, they suggest that domestic violence stems from the level of contact and conflict in the family. Family life produces more conflict, more grievances, and more disputes than life outside the family. Some of these incidents escalate into physical violence, but a smaller percentage than for disputes outside the family.

GENDER DIFFERENCES IN PARTNER VIOLENCE

A feminist approach implies that because of their concern for dominance, men should be more likely than women to engage in violence against their heterosexual partners (see chapter 7). Hundreds of survey studies have examined gender differences in the frequency of partner violence (e.g, Arias & Johnson, 1989; Pan, Heidig, & O'Leary, 1994; Stets & Straus, 1990; Straus & Gelles, 1986; see Straus, 1993, for a review). A recent meta-analysis of those studies showed that women are slightly more likely than men to engage in physical violence against their spouses and lovers and that they engage in violence with greater frequency (Archer, 2000). The gender difference is greater for younger, dating couples than older, married couples. However, when reports of partners rather than self-reports are used, the gender difference disappears. The meta-analysis also suggests that violence is mutual in a large proportion of cases (see also Moffitt, Robins, & Caspi, 2001). However, men are more likely than women to injure their partners.

By contrast, analyses of police records, emergency room data, and the NCVS indicate that men are much more likely than women to engage in partner violence (e.g., R. P. Dobash et al., 1992; see Fagan & Browne, 1994, for a review). For example, analyses of the NCVS find that women are much more likely than men to report being assaulted by their spouse (Bureau of Justice Statistics, 1997b). In 1994, 84.4% of partner assaults reported to the NCVS involved men attacking women. Homicide data also indicate greater violence by men against their partners, but the differences are not as strong as they are for assault. In 1999, 74 % of persons murdered by an intimate partner were female (Bureau of Justice Statistics, 2001).

The discrepancy between the two types of studies just described is primarily due to the types of violence examined. Police records, emergency room data, and criminal victimization data tap more severe violence than do surveys of self-reported violence in the general population. The Conflict Tactics Scale (CTS) typically used in surveys assesses primarily slaps and pushes that do not produce injury. Men are much more likely than women to engage in injurious violence against their partners, but because injurious violence is relatively rare, the difference is not apparent in the survey data. When studies examine injury rather than acts of violence, the greater violence of men is revealed (e.g., Archer, 2000). Straus and Gelles (1986) still found sexual symmetry when they used a subscale restricted to more severe forms of violence on their CTS (see also Stets & Straus, 1990). However, the subscale includes such behaviors as kicking and punching, whose seriousness depends on the severity of the blow. More minor incidents are likely to dominate this measure as well. In addition, Straus and Gelles's measure included attacks using various weapons (e.g., objects thrown) that are favored by women.

Reporting biases may also help explain the discrepancy between results from self-report surveys and other research. Controlling for the seriousness of the violence, men are less likely to seek medical attention, less likely to call the police, and less likely to view violence against them by their partners as criminal (see chapter 6). Studies based on data that depend on these actions and perceptions are therefore likely to underestimate the level of violence against men. On the other hand, because there is a greater stigma attached to violence against women, both men and women may be less likely to tell interviewers that it occurs in their families.

The National Violence Against Women Survey relied on the CTS, but it found that men are more likely than women to use violence against their partners (Tjaden & Thoennes, 2000). The study is noteworthy because it is based on a large, nationally representative sample. The difference in results may be due to identification of the survey to respondents as a study of personal safety, which may elicit reports of more serious incidents (see Straus, 1999).

Gender differences in partner violence may be different in non-Western countries. Archer (2000) reviewed studies based on surveys of community samples showing that men have higher rates of violence against their partners than women in Nigeria, Korea, Japan, and India. Perhaps these non-Western countries have higher rates of male violence toward wives because they are less egalitarian than the United States. Research suggests that there is more tolerance of violence against wives in some non-Western countries (see chapter 5). However, Kumagai and Straus (1983) found that Japanese and Indian men were no more violent toward their wives than were American men. On the other hand, the women in these countries were less violent toward their husbands than American women, suggesting that it is primarily wives' violence that varies across countries, not husbands'.

HOMOSEXUAL COUPLES VERSUS HETEROSEXUAL COUPLES

Tjaden and Thoennes (2000) also compared heterosexual and homosexual couples. A comparison of homosexual and heterosexual couples allows one to sort out the effects of gender and social relationships. If homosexual men are just as violent toward their partners as heterosexual men, it suggests that male violence against partners is not based on the gender of the victim. Tjaden and Thoennes (2000) found that heterosexual men were no more violent toward their partners than homosexual men. The fact that the gender of the victim did not affect frequency suggests that male violence against female partners is not a function of male dominance or special attitudes toward women. Note that men were more likely than women to use violence against their partners, but this was true regardless of sexual orientation. Men are simply more violent than women. (However, Turrel [2000] found, using a small sample, that lesbians were more likely than gay men to be victimized by their partners.)

A report based on the NCVS provides additional evidence that heterosexual men are not more violent toward their partners than homosexual men (Bureau of Justice Statistics, 2001). According to data collected from 1993 to 1999, 10% of incidents of intimate violence against men involved male partners. This percentage is considerably higher than estimates of the percentage of couples who are homosexual. Laumann et al. (1994), for example, finds that less than 3% of men report having engaged in a homosexual activity in the last year. This evidence suggests that gay men are *more* likely to be violent toward their partners than are heterosexual men. In other words, women are less likely than men to be victims of violence from male partners.

American women are more likely than women in other countries to kill their husbands. Men are more likely than women to kill their spouses everywhere, but the ratio of husband-to-wife victimization is more symmetrical in the United States than in other countries (Wilson & Daly, 1992). The U.S. ratios are apparently affected by a special pattern in the African American community. For some reason, Black women are more likely than Black men to kill their spouses.

REPEATED VIOLENCE AGAINST PARTNERS

The literature on the social construction of social problems describes how social activists attempt to influence decision makers and the public to consider a particular issue a social problem (e.g., Best, 1995). In making claims about a particular social problem, the activists choose labels and present examples that they believe will be most likely to gain support. Their "typifications" of social problems are often dramatic and extreme and reflect political concerns rather than their concerns for scientific accuracy and representativeness.

The activists have had a strong influence on the language of research in domestic violence. Thus, researchers often use the term "wife beating" or "battering" to describe the general pattern of male violence toward their female partners. However, these terms imply repeated and severe violence within a single incident when the violence scales actually measure any kind of violence. Reports of the frequency of actual beatings are, of course, much lower than reports of serious violence. There is tremendous variation in the severity of violence, and we should avoid characterizing violence with a term that refers to its most extreme manifestations. Although male violence tends to be more severe than female violence, these terms exaggerate its severity.

Another example of exaggeration is when researchers use the phrase "continual abuse" as a general description of men's violence toward their partners. The term implies that men who commit violence against their partners typically repeat the behavior over and over. Research on the extent to which violence against female partners is repeated or continual is limited. Feld and Straus (1989) found that 19% of husbands who engaged in one or two severe assaults in the first year of the survey (and continued in the relationship) engaged in a severe assault in the following year. Forty-two percent engaged in some violent act in the second year. Quigley and Leonard (1996) found higher rates of repeat victimization in the second and third year of marriage. Presumably the higher rates reflected the longer time period examined and the youthfulness of the couples. These findings suggest that violence, particularly when it is serious, is often repeated, but it does not justify the use of the phrase "continual abuse." In addition, Archer's (2000) meta-analysis of studies using the CTS found that wives were actually more likely than husbands to engage in repeated violence.

Tjaden and Thoennes (2000) found higher levels of repeated violence using the CTS. Approximately two thirds of both men and women who had been the victim of violence by a partner were targeted again by that partner. Of those who were victimized multiple times, about a third were victimized more than once in a single year. In contrast to Archer's (2000) meta-analysis of the CTS, the average number of multiple victimizations during adulthood was higher for women than men (6.9 vs. 4.4), indicating that men who have used violence against their partners are likely to use it more frequently than women who have used violence against their partners. It must be kept in mind that the CTS focuses on minor forms of violence; the proportion of these cases that are appropriately described as "continual abuse" is unclear.

VICTIM PRECIPITATION

Another ambiguous and misused concept in the literature on couple violence is "victim precipitation" (see C. R. Block, 1993; Karmen, 1996; and Polk, 1997, for discussions). In its most expansive meaning, it refers to any behavior on the part of the victim that plays a causal role in initiating a violent encounter. Physical attacks by the victim can precipitate an offender's attack, but so can verbal attacks and other offensive behavior that does not involve aggression (e.g., infidelity). The offensive behavior may not seem offensive to the observer, and it may be trivial by any objective standard, but it is the offender's perspective that counts. The offender may then use violence in an attempt to gain retribution, save face, or prevent future attacks (Tedeschi & Felson, 1994). Most violent disputes involve victim precipitation if the concept is defined very broadly (Felson & Steadman, 1983; Luckenbill, 1977).

Victim precipitation can also refer to incidents in which a physical attack by the victim provokes the offender's counterattack (Wolfgang & Ferracuti, 1967). The specific motivation underlying the offender's counterattack could be retribution, face-saving, or an attempt to incapacitate or deter the adversary from continuing or repeating the attack. This latter motive is typically characterized as "self-defense."

From the perspective of the legal system, homicide is justifiable as an act of self-defense if the victim's behavior posed an imminent threat of death or serious bodily injury to the defendant. One cannot assume that an incident involves self-defense just because the victim attacked the defendant before, even if the attacks were "continual." Such incidents could just as easily be interpreted as retaliation, motivated by the desire for retribution or face-saving. Even a defensive attempt to incapacitate or deter would not necessarily be recognized by the legal system as self-defense if the defendant did not anticipate death or serious bodily injury.

Unfortunately, the term "victim precipitation" is sometimes used to refer to a claim about the relative blameworthiness of the actions of the offender or victim. In this kind of usage, a homicide is described as victim precipitated if the defendant's behavior is judged to be morally justifiable, given the provocation. In other words, the victim "deserved to die." Ideological concerns have produced a controversy over this concept of victim precipitation. Feminist activists blame male homicide victims for provoking the wives who kill them, but they denounce as "blaming the victim" those who cite the causal effects of the behavior of female victims of violence (e.g., Belknap, 2001; Eigenberg, 2001). The controversy is based on a confusion of cause and blame. Cause is a necessary, but not sufficient, condition for the assignment of blame (see chapter 12). Whether the victim's behavior played a causal role in a particular incident is a scientific question. Whether the behavior is blameworthy is a matter of moral judgment and a question for the courts and public opinion. For example, the behavior of a murdered husband played a causal role in the event regardless whether his wife was responding to his infidelity, his obnoxious behavior, or his plans to kill her. Although there are multiple causal factors, the incident would not have occurred without the provocation. The type of provocation should affect our moral and legal response, but it should not affect our causal analysis. The use of value judgments in the conceptualization of victim precipitation leads to confusion and polemics, and therefore I prefer to conceptualize victim precipitation using the causal language of social science (see Felson, 1991).

Gender and Victim Precipitation

Some commentators have argued that frequency counts of partner violence are misleading because the women's violence is used in self-defense (e.g., R. P. Dobash et al., 1992). Men choose to be violent toward their wives (for purposes of domination), whereas women have little choice—they are just defending themselves. If one took into account the context of violence, these commentators argue, the gender symmetry of partner violence found with the CTS would disappear.

Archer's (2000) meta-analysis does not support this argument: The studies in the analysis show that women are actually more likely to initiate violence, at least the minor violence measured by the CTS. In addition, a longitudinal analysis using this scale found evidence challenging the idea that violent wives are otherwise nonviolent people (Giordano et al., 1999). The relationship between adolescent delinquency and spousal violence 10 years later was just as high among women as among men. Also, the relationship between spousal violence and respondents' tendency to describe themselves as angry and aggressive was actually higher for women than for men.

Similarly, a study of couples in New Zealand found that "negative emotionality" was just as strongly associated with violence against partners for women as for men (Moffitt et al., 2001). In addition, negative emotionality predicted victimization by partners equally for men and women; highly emotional people apparently provoke their spouses, regardless of gender. The results point to the importance of interpersonal conflict not gender in couple violence.

Perhaps the pattern is different for more serious violence. It is frequently argued that when women kill their husbands, the incident is usually precipitated by the husband's violent behavior and motivated by self-defense (e.g., R. P. Dobash et al., 1992; Goetting, 1995; Saunders, 1986; Schwartz & DeKeseredy, 1993; Websdale, 1999; Yllö, 1988). When a woman kills her husband, according to this perspective, the apparent offender is really the victim, and the apparent victim, the offender. This point of view has been stated forcefully by R. P. Dobash et al. (1992):

> The evidence is overwhelming that a large proportion of the spouse-killings perpetrated by wives, but almost none of those perpetrated by husbands, are acts of self-defense. Unlike men, women kill male partners after years of suffering physical violence, after they have exhausted all available sources of assistance, when they feel trapped, and because they fear for their own lives. . . . (p. 81)

In contrast to this assertion, there is not much evidence regarding the motives of women who kill their husbands. This is not surprising, given the difficulty of establishing motive. It is particularly difficult to determine whether offenders killed in self-defense because they have a strong interest in justifying their behavior; a successful plea of self-defense enables the defendant to avoid punishment (see Mann, 1988). Self-defense is the most frequent account provided by homicide defendants generally (Felson, 1981).

Homicides and other violence committed by women against their male partners are sometimes attributed to a "battered wife syndrome" (e.g., Browne, 1987; Eber, 1981; Pagelow, 1984; Thar, 1981; Walker, 1984). This syndrome can be used to either excuse or justify the offender's behavior. The excuse involves a plea of a type of temporary insanity or posttraumatic stress syndrome resulting from a long history of abuse. The stress of prior abuse produces an irrational violent outburst that the defendant cannot control because of her diminished state. The syndrome excuses the offender's violent behavior because it denies or minimizes her personal causality and thus her responsibility for the incident. This excuse was used successfully in 1993 to convince a jury to acquit Lorena Bobbit of an assault on her husband's genitals.

Battered wife syndrome can also be used to justify the behavior of women who kill or injure their husbands. In the case of justification, the woman accepts personal causality for her behavior but claims that violence was legitimate, in this particular instance, because of the threat to her life. Battered wife syndrome extends the meaning of self-defense to instances where the victim is not in imminent danger: The woman kills her abusive husband because she believes that he will kill her later on. Perhaps she thinks that the police are incapable of defending her or that she is incapable of escaping him. Her justification implies that she was engaged in an instrumental act of aggression and that her behavior was quite rational (in contrast to the use of battered wife syndrome as an excuse). For example, in a famous case that was the subject of a movie (C. Schreder & Greenwald, 1984), a battered woman set a bed on fire while her husband was sleeping in it. She said that she believed he was going to kill her and that the police could not protect her.

The assertion that wives are likely to kill their husbands in self-defense is potentially misleading because it could refer to a range of possible contrasts. The statement that killings of husbands are typically in self-defense implies a comparison between the frequency of the self-defense motive and other motives. One could also hypothesize that when women kill their husbands, the incidents are more likely to involve self-defense than when husbands kill their wives, or when women kill other men, or when women kill women. Battered wife syndrome implies that self-defense is particularly likely to be involved when women kill their husbands, i.e., when the offender's gender is female, the victim's gender is male, and the relationship between the two adversaries is an intimate one.

A Study of Victim Precipitation in Homicide

We examined statistical interactions between gender and relationships in a study of victim precipitation in homicide (Felson & Messner, 1998). We used two different conceptualizations of victim precipitation in our analyses of homicide incidents. The first is the narrow view of victim precipitation as self-defense, based on prosecutors' judgments. Self-defense involved behaviors on the part of victims that prompted offenders to kill them to protect themselves from bodily harm. Second, we determined whether a physical attack by the victim provoked the offender's lethal attack, regardless of whether the offender's motive was self-defense. If the victim provoked the offender's attack by his or her own physical attack or by brandishing a weapon, or if the victim was suspected of having engaged in these actions, we coded the incident as victim precipitated.

We also examined the issue of victim precipitation indirectly by examining whether the victim had a violent history. We treated the victim's violent history as an indicator of a general propensity toward violence that may have precipitated the offender's lethal attack. We assumed that victims with prior histories of violence were more likely to have engaged in violent behavior that played a causal role in their death. In other words, we assumed that generally violent people were more likely to be violent in a particular incident. This assumption is supported by research showing that past violence is the best predictor of future violence (Farrington, 1989).

We also examined victim precipitation indirectly by determining the violent history of the offender. We assumed that an offender with a clean record was more likely than an offender with a prior arrest for violent crime to have committed the homicide in response to a significant provocation. It requires much more provocation to motivate a nonviolent person to kill than it does to motivate a violent person to kill. Those offenders who killed in response to a significant provocation should therefore be less likely to have a violent history than offenders who killed in response to minor or no provocation. In other words, similar to our approach to the victim's violent history, we treat the offender's violent history as an indicator of the offender's general propensity toward violence, which might lead an offender to kill even in the absence of provocation by the victim.

The bivariate results (see Table 3.6) show that only about 10% of women who killed their partners were acting in self-defense. If we believe prosecutions, it is unusual for female offenders to be motivated by self-defense. On the other hand, they were about 20 times more likely to be motivated by self-defense than the men who killed their partners (0.5%). We also observed a striking gender difference for physical attack by the victim. Almost half of the incidents in which women killed their partners were precipitated by a physical attack, whereas about one out of 10 homicides involving male offenders were precipitated in this way (see also Curtis, 1974; Felson, 1996a; Jurik & Winn, 1990; Langan & Dawson, 1995; Wilbanks, 1984; Wolfgang & Ferracuti, 1967). Finally, female offenders and victims are much less likely than male offenders and victims to have a history of violence.

Table 3.6 shows that men who kill their wives tend to be more violent than women who kill their husbands. However, men are more violent than women generally. The gender differences shown in the table were no greater than the gender differences in homicides not involving couples. In other words, there were no significant statistical interactions between gender and offender–victim relationship. Thus, the results indicate that that there is nothing special about incidents in which women kill their male partners. When women kill their male partners, it is not particularly likely to involve victim-precipitation. These women are just as likely to have a violent history as women who kill other people. The tendency for women to kill their partners in response to an immediate violent provocation reflects the fact that they are women, and their partners are men, and men are more violent than women. Their relationship to each other does not matter. This evidence runs counter to the notion of a battered wife syndrome, since such a syn-

TABLE 3.6
Gender Differences in Characteristics of Homicides Involving Heterosexual Couples

Characteristics of homicide	Offender's gender	
	Male	Female
Offender killed in self-defense	0.5	9.6
Victim physically attacked offender first	11.1	46.2
Victim had a violent record	1.6	10.7
Offender had a violent record	30.7	11.3
N	192	115

drome implies that women who kill their male partners are special (see also, Mann, 1988).

CONCLUSION

The evidence shows that women are less likely than men to be the victims of violence, and when they are victimized, the incident tends to be less serious. A comparative approach reveals that if there is an epidemic, it is an epidemic of violence, not violence against women. Trends over time in the rates of violence against women mirror trends in the rates of violence against men. The high rates of lethal violence against women and wives in this country reflect the high rate of lethal violence generally. In addition, the frequency of violence against women varies much less cross-culturally than the frequency of violence against men. This pattern suggests that epidemics of violence against women do not occur anywhere.

Women are just as likely as men to be the victims of violence from their partners, at least in Western countries. On the other hand, women are more likely than men to be the victims of serious violence by their partners. However, when women are the victims of serious violence, the perpetrators are not typically their partners.

Violence between husbands and wives appears to reflect the high level of conflict in this relationship. Violence involving homosexual couples is probably more frequent. In addition, a verbal conflict between spouses is actually less likely to become violent than a verbal conflict between strangers. A man is less likely to engage in violence during a verbal conflict with his wife than he is during a verbal conflict with some other antagonist. In addition, gender differences in partner violence should be considered in comparison to gender differences in other forms of violence. Although men are no more likely to use violence against their partners than are women, they are much more likely to be violent toward strangers. Given men's greater tendency toward violence, the question we should be asking is, Why don't men hit their wives more often?

Much violence between husbands and wives is reciprocal. Wives are slightly more likely to be the first to engage in minor violence. On the other hand, in homicides, men are much more likely than women to have provoked the offender with violence, and women are more likely to kill in self-defense. Because this pattern is not restricted to couples, it casts doubt on the battered wife syndrome as an explanation for why women kill their male partners. Perhaps the battered wife syndrome is better understood as a reflection of the community's attitude toward violence against wives and women. We are so angry at these violent men that we are sometimes willing to excuse and justify vigilante death sentences carried out by their victims.

The analyses presented in this chapter underscore the dangers of specialization in the study of violence. Research that examines only incidents involving intimates will be unable to demonstrate the distinctive effects of gender and intimacy. Violence against women is special in some respects, but in other respects it resembles other forms of violence. If social scientists study it in isolation, we are likely to fail to detect these commonalities. Studying specific forms of violence in a larger context using a comparative approach permits an examination of when special theories are required and when more general, parsimonious theories apply.

4

GENDER DIFFERENCES IN POWER AND STATUS

"Size matters"

It is generally assumed that men have more power and status than women and that this advantage leads them to use violence against women (e.g., R. E. Dobash & R. P. Dobash, 1979; Koss et al., 1994). In this chapter, I attempt to show that the picture is much more complex. First, I discuss gender differences in coercive power, emphasizing the role of size and strength in violent encounters. Then I discuss the gender distribution of other resources and of status (or prestige), primarily in the United States. I review evidence that challenges the assertion that American men have more status than women or more power in their personal relations.

NATURE OF COERCIVE POWER

Coercive power involves the ability to force change in the behavior of others. It depends at least in part on the level of resources available to each party. Resources include physical size and strength, weapons, third-party support, and anything else that enables one person to harm another successfully, with tolerable costs. Also included are resources that enable one party to reward another, as the withdrawal of rewards produces harm.

The greater the dependence of one person on another for rewards, the more power that other has over the person. Emerson (1972) described this relationship in a formula: the dependence of B on A = the power of A over B. People are more dependent and therefore less powerful when they have few alternative relationships available to them (Thibaut & Kelley, 1959).

The interdependence of men and women is critical in discussions of gender relations (e.g., Eagly & Mladinic, 1994; Guttentag & Secord, 1983). It is not clear which gender is more dependent on the other. Women tend to be more economically dependent, but men may have as much emotional dependence and greater sexual dependence. Men need women at least as much as women need men, and much of what men do is to attract women. Men's and women's dependence on each other and their attempts to impress each other are not characteristic of other group relations. Gender is very different from race and socioeconomic status for this important reason.

Power is a characteristic of the relationships between people, rather than a characteristic of individuals. As a result, power in one sphere of life does not necessarily transfer into other spheres (Etzioni, 1968). For example, a homeless man lacks economic power and political influence, but if he is large and threatening, he may still intimidate the middle-class person he confronts on the street. The head of a corporation has power over his employees but not necessarily over his wife or anyone else outside his workplace.

Power in one sphere can sometimes transfer into other spheres, however. The CEO's economic clout may give him some advantage in his relationship to his wife—his status and income increase her interest in him and makes him more attractive to other women and therefore less dependent on her. However, the power he derives from this dependence factor may be offset by his psychological or sexual dependence on her, his ties to his children, and the financial costs of divorce (see Lips, 1991; McManus & DiPrete, 2001). In addition, high-status men tend to marry women who also have high-status characteristics, so they lose their power advantage. For example, the wealthy man and his attractive wife both have alternatives available, and therefore neither has an advantage. The principles of exchange should lead to counterbalancing power in couples. Power and dependence are multifaceted and complex phenomena (see McDonald, 1980).

Research has failed to demonstrate that men have more power than women in American families. Studies showed that, even in the 1950s, wives were just as likely as husbands to make household decisions (e.g., Blood & Wolfe, 1960; see McDonald, 1980, for a review of this literature). The power equation in families in more traditional societies is apparently just as complex. According to Lips (1991), even when husbands and wives believe in male dominance, actual decision making often does not necessarily reflect the ideology.

Although some critics have claimed that husbands are more likely to make the major decisions, others have claimed that power is too difficult to measure. At any rate, the attempt to demonstrate that men dominated American families using data on decision making was largely abandoned. In addition, time diary data reveal that husbands and wives work a similar number of hours a week, counting both paid and unpaid work (e.g., Juster & Stafford, 1991; J. H. Pleck, 1985). Third, evidence from the National Violence Against Women Survey suggests that men are slightly more likely than women to report that their partners attempt to control their activities (Felson & Outlaw, 2002). Finally, no one has shown that husbands spend more family money on themselves than their wives do, the reverse may be true. In sum, whether one focuses on behavior or benefits in American families, men do not appear dominant.

Neither gender dominates the other in small groups, according to a meta-analysis of laboratory and field studies of leadership (Eagly & Karau, 1991). Although men are more likely to become leaders in short-term groups and in groups that do not require complex social interaction, women are more likely to become social leaders. In general, the greater structural power of men in patriarchal societies has limited effect on the dyadic power relationship of individual men and women (Glick & Fiske, 1999; Guttentag & Secord, 1983).

Group differences in power may affect individual behavior in violent encounters, but they should not be the center of analysis. Combatants in a violent confrontation are probably much more concerned about their relative physical capabilities than their group memberships. Clear and present danger focuses one's attention on the immediate situation. For example, a smaller person is likely to fear a larger person regardless of the relative economic and political power of their ethnic groups. The relative power of groups is more relevant for group conflict than for interpersonal conflict. Interpersonal conflict depends primarily on the relative power of individual antagonists, not the relative power of the groups to which they belong.

Coercive power is not fixed, and individuals can take steps to increase it. For example, to increase their power, they can lift weights, take courses in martial arts, arm themselves, walk in groups, or join gangs for protection. However, potential adversaries can counter these actions by increasing their own power. The process is demonstrated in research based on experimental games (e.g., Pruitt & Rubin, 1986). Enhanced resources or threats can lead to escalation or compliance by the other party, depending on the circumstances. In other words, the application of power sometimes deters aggression and sometimes instigates it. For example, arming oneself can provide safety and protection, or it can lead to an escalating arms race. As a result, the peaceful resolution of many social conflicts depends on the behavior of both adversaries and is difficult for one party to solve on its own. The choice between combativeness and conciliation in social conflict is a fundamental human dilemma.

AGGRESSION AND COERCIVE POWER

In general, people are more likely to use aggression against those who they believe have less coercive power than themselves (Kipnis & Schmidt, 1983; Lawler, 1986). (The discussion will focus on actual power, when in fact adversaries respond to perceived power. Individuals may over- or under-estimate their own power and the power of their adversaries.) Those with a power advantage are likely to anticipate lower costs and greater success when they use coercion against a weaker target. Lower costs are expected because retaliation is unlikely and should not be very costly if it occurs.

Several experimental studies show that a participant's coercive power relative to an antagonist is positively related to the use of aggression in competitive situations (see Tedeschi & Felson, 1994, for a review). As the magnitude of an available punitive resource increases, the frequency of its use increases (Fischer, 1969; Hornstein, 1965). For example, W. P. Smith and Leginski (1970) gave participants the opportunity to threaten their opponent with fines in a bargaining situation. They found that participants issued more threats as the magnitude of the fines they could assess increased.

Research on bullies shows that they tend to pair off with particular "whipping boys" (Olweus, 1979, 1984). These whipping boys tend to be socially isolated, anxious, passive, and afraid to defend themselves. Research on victims of peer aggression has found that a small subset of available children are consistently victimized (Patterson, Littman, & Bricker, 1967). The victims tended to reward the aggressive behavior of their attackers by giving in to their demands. In general, physically weaker boys are at greater risk for victimization.

The relationship between coercive power and overt violence is actually much more complex than the above discussion implies. At least six processes counteract the tendency for powerful parties to attack weaker parties. First, those with more power are sometimes less likely to actually attack an adversary because their threats are sufficient to gain compliance (Goode, 1971). Because they have a credible threat, they find it unnecessary to engage in an overt attack. In fact, Goode suggested that an attack on a family member is sometimes a sign of weakness: It is used when the threat of violence fails to influence a target. For example, a husband may rarely use overt violence against his wife, because his threat is sufficient to force her compliance. A coercive social relationship may therefore appear peaceful and cooperative because weaker parties are intimidated and careful to avoid offending their stronger adversaries. As a result, weaker people probably generate fewer grievances and therefore become involved in fewer conflicts that might lead to aggression than we might otherwise expect.

The tendency for greater coercive power to lead to lower levels of overt violence has been demonstrated in robbery. Offenders typically prefer vulnerable targets, although they sometimes choose powerful targets because they are more lucrative (Cook, 1976). They use weapons to give themselves an advantage when they confront victims with coercive power (e.g., potentially armed proprietors of commercial establishments). When offenders are unarmed, they are more likely to attack and injure the victim during the robbery than when they are armed, even when victims do not resist (e.g., Luckenbill, 1980). Armed offenders have a more credible threat and therefore more often find it unnecessary to actually carry out that threat.

A second factor that leads people to attack stronger parties is related to the identity aspect of aggression. An attack on a stronger party increases one's status more than an attack on a weaker party. Dominating a powerful person makes the person doing so appear even more powerful. According to this principle, we would expect a man attempting to demonstrate his power to attack another man, not a woman. From an identity perspective, a physical fight with a woman is a no-win situation: His image is tarnished whether he wins or loses. Perhaps, given the risks of retaliation, he will prefer to target a man who is slightly weaker than he is.

Third, weaker parties sometimes engage in preemptive attacks to deter or incapacitate more powerful adversaries whom they expect will become aggressive (Lawler, 1986; Straus, 1993). These preemptive attacks are sometimes attempts to communicate an unwillingness to give in to intimidation (Lawler, 1986) or tactical maneuvers designed to take advantage of surprise. During a violent incident, antagonists may kill more dangerous adversaries in a preemptive attack in the belief that they must "kill or be killed" (Felson & Messner, 1996).

Fourth, a power disadvantage invites intervention by third parties on one's behalf. Research on coalition formation shows that weaker parties are sometimes better able to attract allies (e.g., Gamson, 1964). The anticipation of third-party intervention may encourage weaker actors to use aggression because they expect to be protected. This "weakness is strength" principle has been supported in research on sibling aggression. Younger siblings are more likely to fight with an older (and usually stronger) sibling when they can expect a parent to intervene and punish the older sibling (Felson, 1983; Felson & Russo, 1988). The tendency of parents to protect and side with younger siblings gives them the courage to fight with their older siblings and leads to more sibling fighting. On the other hand, when parents do not intervene or when they give supervisory authority to the older sibling, siblings fight less frequently. Similar findings were reported for gender. When parents automatically intervene on behalf of girls, who are typically weaker than their brothers, the siblings fight more frequently.

The "weakness is strength" principle may have implications for mandatory arrest policies for couple violence. Although mandatory arrest may discourage some husbands from using violence against their wives, it may also encourage some wives to be more aggressive and violent if they think that the police will intervene on their behalf if their husbands become violent. This reasoning may help explain why arrest is an inconsistent predictor of recidivism when men are violent toward their wives (e.g., Sherman, 1992).

Fifth, social norms may discourage an individual from using violence against weaker adversaries. Groups develop norms to protect the weak from the strong and to counter strong adversaries' temptation to use violence (Thibaut & Kelley, 1959). For example, third parties may admonish the bully to "pick on someone your own size." Most men are stronger than their wives but unwilling to use physical violence because of a norm of chivalry—attacks on women are viewed more negatively than attacks on men (see chapter 5). Social norms, and the anticipation of costs associated with violating these norms, are likely to inhibit violence against weaker parties.

Finally, decisions made during aggressive interactions are often careless and impulsive. As indicated in chapter 2, individuals who are angry, stressed, or intoxicated sometimes fail to consider the costs of their behavior. Rationality and self-control decline in the heat of an argument, particularly when alcohol or other drugs are involved. Weaker parties under the influence of strong emotion or an intoxicating substance may attack stronger parties without giving much thought to the consequences of their actions. In addition, they are likely to misjudge the costs of using violence: They may overestimate their own coercive power or underestimate the power of their adversaries.

In sum, the relationship between power and violence is complex. Although individuals are generally more likely to attack weaker parties than the reverse, there are countereffects. The situation is complicated because threats make overt violence unnecessary, attacks on stronger parties enhance one's image, weaker antagonists engage in preemptive attacks, third parties intervene on behalf of weaker parties, and social norms act as inhibitors. Finally, the power equation has less impact on careless and impulsive decisions in which individuals either do not consider, or misjudge, the costs and the likelihood of success.

BIG PEOPLE HIT LITTLE PEOPLE

When violence is a possibility, physical power is a critical resource. Those who are bigger and stronger have an advantage over those who are smaller and weaker. The schoolyard bully understands this principle: He threatens children who are physically weaker and smaller (e.g., Olweus, 1978). Boys who are small and weak are painfully aware of their disadvantage. On the other hand, weapons can alter the power equation in violent encounters. Weaker parties can gain an advantage over stronger adversaries when they possess a firearm or knife. For this reason, a gun is sometimes referred to as an "equalizer." On the other hand, as indicated earlier, opponents may also arm themselves in anticipation of an armed attack.

The importance of size and strength should not be underestimated. In boxing and wrestling, weight is so important that it is necessary to classify contenders into weight divisions to produce a fair fight. Because there are no weight divisions outside the ring, there are many uneven contests. In addition, there may be no one to stop the fight before someone gets seriously hurt. The risks of physical violence against someone bigger and stronger are therefore high.

The importance of physical power is shown in a study in which respondents were asked whether they were bigger and stronger than their antagonists in violent disputes (Felson, 1996a). In incidents not involving weapons, the person who was bigger and stronger was much more likely to hit the weaker person than the reverse. In addition, the respondent was more likely to be injured if the antagonist was more powerful. In incidents involving armed violence, on the other hand, weaker antagonists were just as likely (and there was some evidence that they were more likely) to engage in armed violence. Relative physical power was unrelated to who was injured in the incidents involving weapons.

Based on the discussion above, one might expect big people to initiate unarmed violence more frequently. Although power characterizes relationships, not individuals, powerful people are likely to encounter more people less powerful than they are. I am not aware of any study of the relationship between strength and the initiation of violence, but there is evidence that homicide offenders tend to be heavier and taller than the general population (Hooton, 1939).

Gender Differences in Physical Power

The study showing that individuals usually hit smaller adversaries also examined the role of gender (Felson, 1996a). In the self-reported incidents of unarmed violence, men were stronger than their female antagonists in 81% of the incidents; they were larger in 74% of the incidents. The results showed that men were more likely to hit women than women were to hit men. However, the gender difference disappeared when differences in physical power were controlled. Size and strength completely mediated the gender effects. These results suggest that the gender difference was due almost entirely to the difference in physical power. A major reason why men hit women more than the reverse is that men are bigger and stronger.

In contrast to the survey research reviewed in chapter 3, men were more likely to hit women in these incidents. For various reasons, this survey tapped more serious incidents, where gender asymmetry is more likely to occur. The study also showed that when men use violence, they are more likely to injure their opponent than women are, even when gender differences in physical power are controlled. This gender effect may be due to the fact that men are more skillful at physical violence than women, probably due to their greater experience. Boys are more likely than girls to engage in rough-and-tumble play, giving them more practice at fighting (Aldis, 1975). Through fighting with other boys, they learn how to throw a punch and how to defend against an attack.

Women may also be less violent than men because they tend to be more fearful in aggressive situations. Faced with the same threatening situations in experiments, female participants are more likely than male participants to perceive themselves as risking danger if they retaliate (Eagly & Steffen, 1986). As a result of this gender difference in perception, women are less likely to respond with aggression (Bettencourt & Miller, 1996).

Men are also more likely than women to be willing to use violence, according to studies of gender differences in violent behavior (e.g., Bettencourt & Miller, 1996; Eagly & Steffen, 1986). The higher frequency of male violence is probably due to both gender roles and innate sex differences (see Kruttschnitt, 1994, for a review). Whatever its explanation, men's greater tendency to use violence, as well as their advantage in size and skill, can increase their power in conflicts with women. On the other hand, the tendency for people to be attracted to people like themselves should moderate the gender difference in propensity to violence. Violent people are probably more likely to choose mates who are also violent (see chapter 7).

Gender differences in size, skill, fear, and willingness to resort to violence are important in fights involving heterosexual couples. These fights typically involve a bigger person with some training in violence and a smaller one with little or no training. If men are willing to use violence against their partners, they have a tremendous advantage.

Offsetting Factors

Superior physical power or skill is not relevant if men are unwilling to use violence. Most men would probably not consider using violence against women (see chapter 5). They may have moral inhibitions about the use of violence and particular inhibitions about using violence against women. However, the norm that inhibits men from attacking women may encourage women to attack men, at least men they know. A woman may be more willing to confront or hit a man she knows, thinking that the man will not strike her back. However, once provoked by a woman's attack, a man's inhibitions about attacking a woman are likely to be reduced. Thus, Young, Beier, Beier, and Barton (1975) found that "traditional" men, who were less likely than men with more liberal attitudes about gender roles to hit women with a foam club without provocation, were just as willing to do so once the women hit them.

Women may counter the size and strength of their male adversaries with weapons. The widespread availability of firearms in the United States might give women an advantage in their violent conflicts with men were it not for the fact that men are much more likely to own and use firearms (J. D. Wright, Rossi, & Daly, 1983). Gender differences in gun ownership probably explain why men are more likely than women to use guns when they commit homicide. However, female homicide offenders are more likely to use guns against male victims than against female victims (Kleck & McElrath, 1991). In other words, when women are violent toward men, they tend to use weapons to counteract male physical size and strength. The use of weapons by women gives them an advantage and makes them more dangerous to their adversaries.

Most women are unwilling to use guns and knives for physical violence. Much more often, they use less lethal weapons. The image of wives hitting their husbands with pots and pans has an element of truth (Straus, Gelles, & Steinmetz, 1980). The humor associated with the image reflects the fact that we do not consider violence by women against men as very serious.

Woman may also engage in preemptive strikes against male adversaries. For example, a woman might kill her abusive husband in anticipation of later attacks. This scenario has sometimes been proposed in battered wife defenses, although its frequency is unclear (see chapter 3). The use of preemptive strikes to incapacitate powerful adversaries may explain why offenders are more likely to kill male victims than female victims during an assault (Felson & Messner, 1996).

Finally, women may counter male violence by seeking the protection of third parties, including the legal system. Evidence presented in chapter 6 shows that female assault victims are more likely to call the police than male assault victims, and victims are more likely to call the police on male offenders than female offenders. Women receive special protection from the police and other third parties because of a norm of chivalry (see chapter 5).

Men may fear the costs that their wives or the police might impose. However, men who assault their wives are often men who are lacking in either scruples or self-control. They are likely to commit other types of crimes, and they are likely to mistreat people of both sexes (see chapter 7). In situations in which an impulsive antisocial male is in an intense conflict with a person of lesser physical power than himself, we should not be surprised when he uses violence.

OTHER SOURCES OF POWER IN MARRIAGE

Physical power is not the only relevant power dimension in partner violence. The relative power of a husband and wife also depends on how dependent they are on each other for rewards. As indicated above, the greater one's dependence, the less one's power (Emerson, 1972). A dependent husband is less likely to assault his wife than a husband who cares little for the rewards she provides. If he needs her, he had better not hit her.

The threat of divorce or separation is one source of power. When divorce became easier and more acceptable, the power of women and their vulnerability to mistreatment probably declined. Although divorce is more financially costly for women (R. R. Peterson, 1996), it is still costly for men. The financial costs are likely to inhibit the extent to which men mistreat their wives. In addition, men risk loss of contact with their children through divorce, and that is an advantage for women.

Some commentators have suggested that because of their dependence, many women tolerate violence by their husbands: They stay in violent marriages, they do not call the police, and they refuse to cooperate in prosecution when the police do become involved (e.g., Pagelow, 1984; Walker, 1979). However, evidence suggests that women assaulted by their husbands are not particularly reluctant to call the police or sign complaints or particularly willing to protect the offender (see chapter 6). In fact, the evidence shows that women are more likely than men to sign complaints against offenders, particularly if the assailants are their husbands (Felson & Ackerman, 2001). Victims are also slightly more likely to sign complaints against male offenders than female offenders (see chapter 6). This evidence casts doubt on the idea that wives are particularly passive or tolerant of violence due to their dependence on their husbands.

Perhaps when women are economically dependent on their husbands, men have an advantage. She may be more willing to put up with his violence and less willing to divorce him, so he may be more willing to assault her. This reasoning would lead to the hypothesis that economically dependent wives should be less likely than economically independent wives to call the police on assaultive husbands. We found no support for this hypothesis using data on domestic assaults in the NCVS. Nonemployed married women were just as likely as employed married women to call the police in response to an assault (Felson & Ackerman, 2001). In addition, studies of the relationship between marital violence and gender difference in education and income, discussed in chapter 7, yield inconsistent results (see Ronfeldt, Kimerling, & Arias, 1998, for a review). Still, the economic dependence argument is a plausible one and should be the subject of further research.

Psychological or emotional dependence may be more significant than economic dependence. If a husband is more emotionally dependent on her than he is on him, she gains in power. His emotional dependence on her may inhibit him from using violence, whereas her emotional dependence on him may lead her to tolerate violence. Research is needed on these issues.

Some have argued that dependence is likely to depend on the alternative relationships available to people (e.g., Thibaut & Kelley, 1959). According to this perspective, marriage operates according to market principles, where individuals have certain resources that make them more or less attractive as mates. An attractive woman is less dependent on her husband than an unattractive woman because she has more options. She should be more likely to leave her husband if he mistreats her, and therefore he should be less likely to mistreat her. An attractive man also has more options, but his occupational prestige and income are also likely to be an important resource. He will be less concerned with getting her angry if he has high value in the marriage market. However, individuals with greater resources probably have higher standards or expectations. They expect a more desirable mate, and potential mates with the desired characteristics are more difficult to find and to attract. As a result, once they find such a mate, they are likely to be as dependent on her as are less desirable men. In general, objective characteristics are not likely to be good predictors of dependence.

Female sexual power can also counter male physical power. If a man hits his wife, for example, she may retaliate by withdrawing her affection or refusing to have sexual relations with him. Sexual deprivation is often available as a power resource for women because men typically desire sexual relations more often than women (see chapter 10). In other words, sex differences in sexuality provide women with a powerful weapon to use against their partners when they think they have been mistreated. Because the weapon can be used legitimately and covertly—she says that his misbehavior has destroyed her mood—it is not seen as aggression or as a crass form of punishment.

In sum, I have suggested that the relative power of husbands and wives depends on their personal situation, and that power is specific to relationships. The fact that the U.S. Senate is run by men is largely irrelevant to the private conflicts of individuals. Even a senator who has that power does not necessarily have power over his wife. If he is smitten, she has power over him. In general, the economic power of the average man and woman in society and the fact that our political leaders are male are not likely to be significant factors in violent spousal conflicts. From this perspective, dyadic power has much stronger effects on how spouses treat each other than structural power. It would not be too much of an exaggeration to say that "all conflict is local."

Gender and Status

The feminist approach assumes that women have lower status or prestige in society and implies that their devaluation plays a role in their victimization. I view women's status, and status generally, as more ambiguous and as dependent on context. People assign status to groups who excel in activities they value, but they do not necessarily agree in these judgments, and there may be ambivalence. It is difficult, for example, to determine the relative prestige of Jewish or Asian Americans: As a whole they are both respected and resented for their economic success. In addition, it is difficult to distinguish the status dimension from the related concept of prejudice. When sociologists or laypeople assign a group low status (e.g., African Americans), they may do so because they know that some people are prejudiced against the group and discriminate against their members in certain situations. In other words, assigning low status to a group may be another way of saying that some people are prejudiced against them.

The empirical evidence does not support the idea that in general American women have lower status than men or that they are the targets of greater prejudice. Eagly and Mladinic's (1994) review of contemporary research in the United States suggests that attitudes toward women are generally more favorable than attitudes toward men. They call this pattern the "women are wonderful effect," but it is better known as "putting women on a pedestal." For example, research shows that both male and female college students have more favorable stereotypes about women than about men. Perhaps the tendency for men to commit higher levels of violence and criminal behavior stigmatizes men and counteracts the status they gain from their achievement in public arenas. Cross-cultural research shows no overall gender bias in the evaluation of traits; women are evaluated more favorably in some countries and men are evaluated more favorably in others (J. E. Williams & Best, 1977).

Other studies present participants with information about a target person and manipulate the target person's gender using gender-identifiable names (see Eagly & Mladinic, 1994, for a review). These studies do appear to show some negative attitudes toward women and stereotypes in masculine domains such as male-dominated jobs. However, the studies provide limited information about target persons, increasing the likelihood of reliance on stereotypes. In addition, Kasof (1993) showed that these studies have a confound: They tend to use more popular male names than female names, and the popularity of the names predicts the participant's reaction to the target person. Perhaps the researchers consciously or unconsciously chose these names to confirm the hypothesis of bias against women. Perhaps the reviewers were biased. On the other hand, the explanation does not necessarily indicate ideological corruption of science. It is more difficult to publish null results in general. Studies with equally popular male and female names that did not find gender effects may never have been published.

If women do have lower status or are the target of prejudice, it is apparently restricted to masculine domains, such as in male-dominated jobs, according to the evidence reviewed by Eagly and Mladinic (1994). The effects are weak, but apparently women are evaluated more favorably than men on traits associated with their domestic role, whereas men are evaluated more favorably on traits associated with male-dominated occupational roles. Yet it is the family context where women are vulnerable to violence. Women are much less likely than men to be the target of violence in the public sphere— by strangers, for example (see chapter 3). In other words, women's victimization is relatively high in the context where their status is lower and their victimization is low in the context where their status is higher.

Males also do not appear to have higher status than females among adolescents and young adults, when sexual coercion is most likely to occur. Popular girls enjoy as much status as popular boys. Boys' physical advantage gives them higher status in sports, but girls perform better in school, are more likely to graduate, and are just as likely to play leadership roles (Sommers, 2000). The animosity that elementary school boys express toward girls does not seem to lead to violence: Boys typically target other boys. The obsessive concerns of young men (and women) with approval by members of the opposite sex do not indicate an asymmetrical status relationship.

Women as Property

Some commentators have suggested that women were or are treated as property in some cultures (e.g., R. E. Dobash & R. P. Dobash, 1979). As far as I can tell, the statement was a metaphor that has come to be taken literally. To say that women were in fact considered property is to imply that they were slaves. Slaves were human property in a literal sense: They could be bought and sold, people thought of them as property, and their status was codified in law. I am not aware of any societies that permitted women to be bought and sold or anywhere they were referred to as property. There are instances in which women (but not men) are or have been enslaved. For example, in Thailand, some rural families are paid to give their daughters up for prostitution. And instances of "white slavery"—the sale of women—have been reported in the United States and elsewhere. But these are deviant behaviors, not accepted practice.

Men dominate their wives in patriarchal families, and slaveholders dominate slaves. This similarity is probably the source of the metaphor. Another source of the metaphor may be the mistreatment of women. If men are treated better than women and people are treated better than property, then women are like property.

A subordinate, however, is not a piece of property. For example, parents dominate their children, particularly when they are young, but children are not property: Parents do not buy or sell children, nor do they consider them property. In an absolute monarchy, the monarch ruled over his or her subjects, but this did not mean that the citizens were property. Strong anticommunists accused the Soviets of enslaving their people because citizens lacked freedom and could only work for the state. However, citizens under Soviet communism could not be bought or sold, nor were they considered the property of the state. Strong metaphors make good political slogans, but not good science.

In some societies, women gave up control of their property to their husbands when they married, but they did not become property themselves.

Although arranged marriages involve economic exchanges (e.g., dowries and bride-prices) between families, neither sons nor daughters are considered property, nor can spouses be sold once these marriages take place (Harris, 1997). One could argue that the families who participated in these marriages treated their children like property, because there was an economic element to the exchange.

However, modern romantic marriages sometimes also involve an economic exchange. We do not refer to a man as property just because his wife was attracted to him because of his money or earning power. Bride-prices are much more frequent than dowries. Actually, wives have higher status in cultures where they occur; if the man's family must provide extra compensation to effect the marriage, the wife has higher value (Harris, 1997).

Applying the property argument cross-culturally is further complicated because the distinction between people and things is not necessarily made in non-Western societies. According to Hirschon (1984),

> Broadly speaking, our attitudes to property are associated with development of capitalism and with the notion of the commodity. Property for us is based on the idea of "private ownership" which confers on the individual the right to use and to disposal. Property is thus seen as valued good/objects which can be transferred between legally-constructed individuals. But what we take for granted—the idea of an individual actor having defined rights vis-a-vis others, and the notion of property as consisting in object or things—is far from being universal. On the contrary these concepts are historically and culturally situated in the western tradition. (p. 2)

Ethnocentrism and an egalitarian ethic influence Westerners' view of male domination in other societies. However, good science dictates that social scientists use clear and simple language for description. We should avoid polemical metaphors in our attempts to demonize hierarchical relations of which we disapprove. It is more reasonable to discuss whether men are dominant or have legitimate authority in their families or in the public sphere, and then determine whether their position affects the likelihood of violence against women.

CONCLUSION

Men have a substantial advantage over women in physical power and a greater willingness to put that power to use with violence. These gender differences are critical in understanding intergender violence. On the other hand, the male advantage in terms of status and other resources is much more limited in scope and degree, at least in the United States. Female victimization is much more likely in the family context, where women enjoy relatively high power and status. Men's economic power in their families is counteracted by their emotional and sexual dependence and by women's central role in this institution. Women's equal status and power in American families is indicated by evidence on stereotyping, family decision making, workload, and share of rewards. Men have an advantage in power and status in the public sphere, but they do not victimize women as often as they victimize other men in that arena. Whatever the gender differences in power and status, when push comes to shove, the size of one's body is much more important than the size of one's paycheck.

One might expect that women would have higher violence victimization rates than men as a result of sex differences in size, strength, and skill. The fact that women are at less risk of being the victim of violence than men is therefore a paradox requiring explanation. One explanation is that men are more likely to provoke their victimization through aggressive or deviant behavior. Another explanation is the norm of chivalry—a powerful norm that protects women from violence, and that is the subject of the next chapter.

5

CHIVALRY

Feminist scholars view male violence against women as normative behavior (e.g., Archer, 1994; Bograd, 1988; R. E. Dobash & R. P. Dobash, 1979; Koss et al., 1994). From their perspective, patriarchal societies allow husbands to use violence to control their wives and men to use violence to dominate women (Brownmiller, 1975; Cazenave & Zahn, 1992; Lips, 1991). The legal system, and the larger male-dominated society, tolerate and even support violence against women to maintain male domination.

I present evidence for the opposite point of view in this chapter. I suggest that violence against women is not only deviant behavior, but that it is perceived as much worse than violence against men. An attack on a woman is a more serious transgression than an attack on a man because it violates a special norm protecting women from harm. This norm—sometimes referred to as "chivalry"—discourages would-be attackers and encourages third parties to protect women. However, that protection is to some extent undermined by the fact that violence toward women often occurs in marriage and other intimate relations, where the impact of third parties is often limited. The privacy of intimate relations, not tolerance of violence against women, leaves some women vulnerable to male violence.

I am not arguing that women should (or should not) receive special protection. A norm protective of women may have various negative consequences, if one wants to reduce gender inequality. For example, the norm might limit women's opportunities by encouraging their dependence on men or by reinforcing stereotypes. Concerns about negative consequences, however, should not blind us to the possibility that the norm has the proximate effect of deterring violence against women.

Ambivalence about special protection for women is not new. For example, after the sinking of the Titanic, some women's groups complained about the priority given to women in access to lifeboats (Wade, 1992), and other women built a monument to honor the chivalrous men who died. Also, in Victorian England, women's groups differed in their attitudes toward breach of promise suits against men who proposed marriage and then reneged (Frost, 1995). Some objected to the dependence of women implied by these suits, whereas others were reluctant to take away the protection these suits provided.

I begin the chapter with a description of the chivalry norm and speculation about its possible origins. I then review evidence concerning whether participants in experiments and criminal justice officials are reluctant to harm women, and whether that reluctance is related to traditional attitudes about gender roles and the presence of an audience and mirrors. After discussing the double standard as an exception to the chivalry effect, I examine research on reactions to violence against women. I discuss the treatment of violence against wives historically and in other cultures and the implications of privacy concerns for that treatment. I postpone a discussion of the response of the police and the criminal justice system to violence against women and wives until the next chapter.

ORIGINS OF THE CHIVALRY NORM

The term "chivalry" originated as a description of a code of behavior for knights in the Middle Ages that included protective behavior toward women (see Keen, 1984). I use the term here in a more restricted way to refer to a norm requiring the protection of women from harm. "Chivalry" is not an ideal descriptive term, because it implies a norm that constrains the behavior only of men. In fact, the norm protects women from women as well as from men and from nonhuman as well as from human sources. For example, the maritime rule giving women priority over men in access to lifeboats protected women from death. Also, neither gender is willing to deliver shocks to women in some of the experiments cited later in this chapter. However, the norm emphasizes the forbidding of male violence against women. According to traditional gender role expectations, a gentleman should show special courtesies to women. In addition, because men engage in much more violence than women, the norm is probably most often applied to the protection of women from men.

The reason for the norm protecting women is unclear. One explanation is that chivalry is a response to the economic and physical vulnerability of women. Women are economically vulnerable because of the gender division of labor. For example, in breach of promise suits of the 19th century, the courts used the economic dependence of women in marriage to justify their decisions against men who reneged on marriage proposals (Frost, 1995). They are physically vulnerable because they tend to be smaller and physically weaker than men. Both physical and economic vulnerabilities may lead women or their kin to seek protection. Thus, chivalry could reflect an attempt by groups—particularly women's kin—to counteract the temptation for individuals to engage in violence against vulnerable women. According to Thibaut & Kelley (1959), groups develop norms to protect weaker parties and discourage the exercise of raw power.

A related explanation is that the norm developed out of an exchange process in which the vulnerability of women to male violence led them to trade submission for protection (see Brownmiller, 1975; Chesney-Lind, 1978; Visher, 1983). According to this perspective, chivalry is a form of "benevolent sexism" that provides a justification for traditional gender roles (Glick & Fiske, 1999). The argument implies that men withdraw their willingness to protect women who do not submit and who fail to conform to gender roles. Women are like vulnerable inmates in male prisons who agree to exclusive sexual behavior with a more powerful inmate in exchange for protection from other predators.

It should be noted, however, that the punishment of deviant women may have nothing to do with their gender or with any implicit exchange. People who engage in deviant behavior often lose social support, regardless of their gender or whether they violate gender norms or other norms (see also chapter 12). In addition, evidence reviewed later in this chapter suggests that we treat deviant women less, not more, severely than deviant men.

Another explanation is that chivalry developed to protect the reproductive and child-rearing role of women. Thus, chivalry may be an extension of the attempt to protect children, rather than a reflection of any special value attached to women. We may, for example, attach greater value to women's lives because a shortage of women limits a group's production and nurturance of offspring much more than does a shortage of men. A sociobiological perspective might suggest that the greater value attached to women's lives and the tendency to protect women is a part of our biological makeup. A man who protects the mother of his children or future children may be more likely to pass on his genetic material to future generations. However, the pattern may also reflect rational efforts to protect children by protecting their primary caretakers.

The protection of women from sexual predators may reflect efforts to protect children by avoiding bastardy. Traditionally, efforts were made to prevent sexual relations outside of marriage—whether forced or consensual—

primarily by regulating the behavior of women (Kertzer, 1993). These attempts to regulate sexuality were justified as protection of the woman's honor as well as the honor of her family.

The protection of mothers played a critical role in the development of the welfare system in the United States. Although welfare began as an attempt to help Civil War veterans, during the early 1900s it turned to the aid of mothers (Skocpol, 1992). Legislatures and courts refused proposals to turn benefits for Civil War veterans into more general benefits for laborers. Instead, "the federal government and most states enacted social spending, labor regulations, and health education programs to help American mothers and children along with women workers who might become mothers" (p. 526).

The child-protection explanation might be preferable to the vulnerability explanation because it can account for why we might attempt to protect women from women and nonhuman sources. Why should the economic and physical vulnerabilities of women lead us to rescue them from sinking ships first (unless we think the men are better able to swim to shore)? On the other hand, child protection cannot explain why we generally attempt to protect all women, not just mothers, and not just young women. Neither explanation can completely account for the chivalry norm, suggesting that child protection and female vulnerability both lead societies to protect women.

RELUCTANCE TO HARM WOMEN

Those who believe that violence against women is normative often point to the high level of violence against women in the United States or elsewhere. However, the fact that a behavior is common does not indicate that people approve of it. Norms vary in the degree to which they control behavior. The norm of reciprocity, for example, has an important impact on social behavior, but people frequently violate it.

The frequency of violence against women in the United States surely reflects the high level of violence generally, relative to many other countries (e.g., Messner & Rosenfeld, 1994). In addition, men who engage in violence against women tend to engage in other types of crime and deviant behavior as well (e.g., Fagan, Stewart, & Hansen, 1983). "Wife beaters" are breakers, not bearers, of society's norms.

Data presented in chapter 3 showed that men are more likely to be the target of violence than women. For example, Table 3.2 shows that in 1994, 57.4% of victims of criminal violence were men and 42.6% were women (Bureau of Justice Statistics, 1997a). This difference is observed in spite of the fact that women tend to be more physically vulnerable than men and thus less costly to attack. The gender difference in victimization may be due to chivalry. However, it could also be due to the greater tendency of men to provoke others or to the routine activities of men that put them at greater risk (M. Felson, 1998).

Experimental research is useful in controlling for provocation and opportunity and in isolating any normative effect of gender on victimization. These studies consistently find that participants are much more likely to deliver shocks to men than to women (e.g., Dengerink, 1976; Kaleta & Buss, 1973; Taylor & Epstein, 1967). Sixth graders deliver higher intensities of noxious noise to boys than to girls, suggesting that children learn chivalry at an early age (Shortell & Miller, 1970). The gender difference has been found in a large number of experimental studies using different procedures, different measures of aggression, and different participant populations (see R. A. Baron & Richardson, 1994).

Because chivalry reflects traditional attitudes about gender roles, one might expect traditional men to be less likely to use violence against women than nontraditional men. Conversely, a feminist approach suggests that traditional men are more likely to attack their wives because they devalue them or think that violence is appropriate in a dominance relationship (see chapters 4 and 7). At least three studies have found that traditional men are less violent toward women. First, Rosenbaum (1986) found that men with traditional attitudes about sex roles were less likely to report using violence against their wives. Second, Bookwala, Frieze, Smith, and Ryan (1992) found that traditional men were less likely to use violence against dating partners. Finally, a laboratory study showed that traditional men were less likely to hit women with pillow clubs than were men with more liberal attitudes toward gender roles (Young, Beier, Beier, & Barton, 1975). The difference between the two groups of men was reduced in the second bout, when the female confederate became more aggressive. Apparently, inhibitions about attacking women may be lower if women attack first (R. A. Baron & Richardson, 1994). As indicated earlier, people may be less inhibited about harming deviant targets regardless of their gender (Tedeschi & Felson, 1994).

Other survey research does not find that traditional men are less violent toward women than nontraditional men. Six of eight studies reviewed by Hotaling and Sugarman (1986) found no relationship, and two found that traditional men used more violence (see also Fagan & Browne, 1994). The inconsistent results probably reflect differences in the measurement of traditional attitudes. These measures may reflect, in varying proportions, traditionalism, hostility toward women, and antisocial attitudes.

In addition, it is difficult to be confident about the causal interpretation of correlations between attitudes and self-reported violence, given the possibility of response sets and reciprocal causation (see chapter 7). For example, men who engage in violence toward women may justify their behavior by expressing negative attitudes toward women or expressing dominance. Self-justification would produce a positive correlation between traditionalism and violence. Such an effect might offset the negative effect of traditionalism on violence.

Chivalry may also limit punishment of women convicted of criminal behavior. Its effect should be limited in this context because the discretion of police, juries, and judges is constrained by formal rules, and because those who violate norms sometimes lose normative protection. Still, according to a recent meta-analysis, about half of the 50 studies reviewed showed more lenient treatment for women than men, about one-quarter showed mixed effects, and one-quarter showed no effects (K. Daly & Bordt, 1995). These gender effects could in part reflect concern for the family obligations of female offenders (e.g., Steffensmeier, Kramer, & Streifel, 1993). However, the tendency to protect their child-rearing role could reflect chivalry as well. In addition, concern for family obligations cannot explain gender differences in the application of the death penalty in capital cases. Only 1.5% of prisoners under of sentence of death in 2000 were women, whereas in 1998, 10.5% of murder defendants were women (Bureau of Justice Statistics, 2001; Fox, 2001).

Chivalry effects are observed in spite of attributional processes that operate in the opposite direction. Our expectations are that women are much less likely than men to engage in criminal and deviant behavior. In addition, our stereotypes about women tend to be more favorable than our stereotypes about men (see chapter 4). Therefore, when a particular woman engages in deviance, we are more likely to attribute that behavior to her personal attributes rather than external factors. Although negative stereotypes about a group can increase the likelihood that a member of that group is judged guilty, once guilt is determined, the negative stereotype can lead to more lenient treatment. For example, a judge may decide that a delinquent girl must have serious problems, whereas "boys will be boys."

Experimental studies of helping behavior also demonstrate chivalry effects. A meta-analysis of these studies showed that women were consistently more likely to receive help from participants than men (Eagly & Crowley, 1986). In addition, male participants were consistently more likely than female participants to provide help, at least in short-term encounters between strangers. Gender differences in helping and being helped were stronger when an audience was present, suggesting that the gender effect is normative. Eagly and Crowley attributed gender differences in altruism to chivalry on the part of male participants.

The operation of chivalry can be seen in the content of humor. Most humor is at someone's expense. Jokes targeting men are a much more common comedic theme than jokes targeting women. Violence against men is considered humorous, whereas violence against women is not. For example, the scene in the motion picture *Nutty Professor II* (Brubaker & Segal, 2000) where a large hamster rapes the male college dean would not be tolerated if the dean were female. Although the gender difference has certainly been enhanced by recent attempts to avoid offending protected groups, it existed long before political correctness. Some feminists complained about Ralph Cramden's idle threats in the 1960s television series *The Honeymooners*— "One of these days, Alice. . . ." They did not mention Ralph's more severe threats and attacks on Ed Norton, who responded with pratfalls.

Effects of Audiences and Mirrors

A typical method of distinguishing normative from deviant behavior is to compare public and private behavior. People are more likely to engage in normative behavior in front of an audience and conceal their deviant behavior. Survey research shows that the presence of an audience inhibited violence in mixed-gender disputes but encouraged violence in conflicts between men (Felson, 1982). When men attack their wives or other women, at least in the United States, they prefer to do it when no one is watching. The reason violence against women is hidden is that it is deviant behavior (Frude, 1994).

Men may also attempt to conceal their violence against women from survey researchers. Thus, a study of high school students found that the frequency of boys' self-reported violence against girls was lower than the frequency of girls' reports of victimization by boys (Hilton et al., 2000). On the other hand, the frequency of self-reported violence against boys corresponds to the victimization rates of boys.

Experimental research also shows audience effects. Scheier, Fenigstein, & Buss (1974) found that men delivered less intense shocks to women in front of an audience than in a control condition. On the other hand, audience effects on delivery of shocks to men depend on the type of audience and the context (see Tedeschi & Felson, 1994, for a review).

Another method of examining whether behavior is antinormative is to place participants in experiments in front of mirrors. Evidence shows that mirrors direct people's attention to their internalized moral standards and thereby increase the likelihood of behavior consistent with those standards (Wicklund, 1975). Participants facing a mirror are particularly unlikely to deliver shocks to female targets (Carver, 1974; Scheier, Fenigstein, & Buss, 1974). Thus, these studies show that chivalry reflects internalized standards, not just public behavior. On the other hand, these same studies show that mirrors can increase or decrease shock delivery to men, depending on whether participants perceive the aggression as justified.

The "Double Standard" Exception

The "double standard"—the tendency to condemn women more than men for sexual promiscuity—is an exception to the chivalry effect. The double standard may explain why girls are sometimes treated more severely than boys for minor status offenses (Chesney-Lind, 1988). It may be an important normative pattern, because according to some scholars, the double standard affects the prosecution of rape (see chapter 12). Given that it is an exception to our tendency to punish men more severely, it seems unlikely to be attributable to some form of prejudice against women. Why would there be a double standard favoring men in regard to promiscuity and a double standard favoring women in regard to other types of deviance? Other explanations seem more likely. First, it may be more important for practical reasons to control female sexual behavior. A daughter's sexual behavior is of more concern than a son's, because she and her parents are more likely to suffer the consequences of unwanted pregnancy. In addition, because female promiscuity decreased confidence about paternity (at least before DNA testing), society has had a greater interest in controlling female sexual behavior than in controlling male sexual behavior. Evolutionary psychology would suggest that this sex difference has become part of our biological makeup. However, this is unlikely, as the double standard is apparently not a cultural universal. A survey of restraints on adolescent sexual behavior in 186 tribal societies found that the majority did not have a double standard (Barry & Schlegel, 1984).

Another explanation is that the double standard exists because female sexual behavior is more malleable and therefore easier to control (Baumeister, 2000). Baumeister reviewed evidence showing that female sexual attitudes and behavior are more variable across the life course and change more easily in response to education, religion, political ideology, and historical norms. The malleability of female sexual behavior could be due to greater male power, but this seems unlikely, given that many other female behaviors are not more malleable. Differences in expectations for men and women may also contribute to the tendency to attach a greater stigma to female promiscuity (as they do for female deviance, generally). If promiscuity is expected from men, individual men who engage in this behavior are less likely to receive a negative attribution.

Reactions to Violence Against Women

The evidence shows that, in general, we are reluctant to harm women. In addition, third parties respond more negatively to those who harm women than they do to those who harm men and in general are more likely to intervene on behalf of women under attack. Thus, combatants seeking allies in wartime emphasize the enemy's attacks on "women and children" in their propaganda. The publicizing of stories on rapes committed by Serbian soldiers in Bosnia and Kosovo is one recent example.

Survey research reveals strong moral condemnation of violence against wives. Rossi, Waite, Bose, & Berk (1974) found that respondents ranked beating up a spouse as a serious offense—more serious than beating up an acquaintance, but less serious than beating up a stranger. Rossi et al. reported a high level of agreement between men and women, and between Black and White respondents, in their evaluation of these offenses.

Other survey research indicates that most people disapprove of more mild forms of spousal violence, such as slapping, although many can imagine instances in which such behavior might be justifiable (Arias & Johnson, 1989; Greenblat, 1983; Straus, Kantor, & Moore, 1994). In these studies, respondents generally evaluated violence against wives more negatively than violence against husbands. The fact that some respondents may have given a socially desirable response only adds support to the notion that respondents consider violence against wives deviant behavior.

One might expect that men are more likely to justify violence against their female partners than the female victim. However, a survey of men and women in London suggests that men are *less* likely than women to say that male violence is justified in response to various provocations (Mooney, 2000). For example, 12% of men said they would be justified in hitting their partner if she had sex with a close friend, whereas 21% of women said their male partner would be justified in hitting them in this situation.

The tendency for people to evaluate violence against women more harshly than violence against men has also been demonstrated experimentally. Thus, participants judge men who aggress against a female target as less moral than men who aggress against a male target (Kanekar, Nanji, Kolsawalla, & Mukerji, 1981). Harris (1991) manipulated the gender of actor and target and their relationship to each other using a hypothetical scenario involving an argument. Participants evaluated aggressors who slapped women more negatively than aggressors who slapped men, regardless of whether they believed the adversaries were spouses, friends, strangers, or siblings.

It is possible that there are subcultures in which violence against women is normative, even though the behavior is perceived as deviant in the larger society. On the other hand, it may be that in these subcultures violence against men is also acceptable. This issue needs to be investigated by research.

Chivalry also affects how the gender of the victim of violent crime affects the offender's treatment by the criminal justice system. A recent study found that charges of first-degree murder are more likely to be reduced when the victim is male than when the victim is female, controlling for prior record, relationship of offender and victim, victim provocation, and other circumstances of the crime (Beaulieu & Messner, 1999). Sentences are, on average, 10 years shorter for wives convicted of killing their husbands than for husbands convicted of killing their wives, controlling for victim provocation (Bureau of Justice Statistics, 1995). Both the offender's and the victim's gender may produce this large difference in sentence length; a woman who kills her husband receives a more lenient sentence because she is a woman and because her victim is a man. (Note, however, that a study reviewed in chapter 6 found no evidence of chivalry in arrest decisions; Felson & Ackerman, 2001.)

Third-party intervention plays an important role in protecting women from violence in smaller-scale societies (e.g., Baumgartner, 1993; Chagnon, 1977; Landes, 1971; Levinson, 1989). Typically, a woman's kin or other third parties intervene on her behalf when her husband has assaulted her. In some cases, the group designates a brother or some other man as the wife's protector at marriage. In some societies it is reported that the farther wives live from family support, the more likely they are to be the victims of violence by their husbands. For example, among the Yanomamo, a particularly violent tribe, women abhorred being married to men in distant villages (Chagnon, 1977). They knew that their fathers and brothers could not protect them if they lived too far away. Among the Ojibwa Indians of North America, newly married couples moved to distant areas with virtually no neighbors and no way of communicating with family members (Landes, 1971). Ojibwa women living in these arrangements were at risk of physical violence by their husbands.

In sum, the evidence for a norm of chivalry is overwhelming. Women are less likely than men to be harmed by participants in experiments, by criminal offenders, and by agents of the criminal justice system. Audiences and mirrors, which are known to inhibit antinormative behavior, inhibit violence against women more than violence against men. In experiments, in opinion surveys, and in the criminal justice system, third parties react more negatively to those who commit violence against women. They condemn violence against wives as well as violence against women outside the family. Finally, participants in experiments are more likely to provide help to women than men, particularly when an audience is present.

TREATMENT OF DOMESTIC VIOLENCE HISTORICALLY

Some feminists have argued that in the past (if not in the present), men's violence against their wives was condoned (e.g., R. E. Dobash & R. P. Dobash, 1979; Eigenberg, 2001). From their perspective, the approval, or at least toleration, of men's violence against their wives was based on beliefs in male dominance. As the head of the family, the man was viewed as having the right to use various means, including violence, to control those under his authority. Just as parents were permitted to physically punish their children, husbands were permitted to physically punish their wives. Perhaps if they went too far, the court would intervene, but minor forms of violence were tolerated to permit men to carry out their role as head of the family.

Presumably, in the not too distant past, most Americans approved of male dominance in the family. However, approval of male dominance in the family does not necessarily imply approval of violence to maintain that dominance. People do not necessarily condone violence against subordinates. Many people approve of parents hitting their children, but they do not condone violence by employers against employees.

Historical research in Western societies has shown that societies have taken special steps to protect women from their husbands. There have been special laws prohibiting violence against wives in the United States, and sometimes severe punishments, since the 1600s (Gordon, 1988; E. H. Pleck, 1979, 1989). By 1870 there were specific laws forbidding violence against wives in most states. Before special laws existed, the courts could punish husbands using general laws prohibiting assault and battery.

E. H. Pleck (1979), the leading historian on this topic, argued that attitudes toward violence against wives in 19th-century America were similar to current attitudes, but control was more extensive and punishment was more severe. In the 19th century, punishment was usually informal. Vigilante groups sometimes beat up, whipped, or publicly shamed offenders. The Ku Klux Klan—better known for its attacks on black Americans and other ethnic groups—also engaged in vigilante justice against men who hit their wives. Ritual public shaming was also applied to offenders in 19th-century England (R. P. Dobash & R. E. Dobash, 1981). In 1905, Portland, Oregon, instituted a law that prescribed flogging for men who assaulted their wives (Peterson del Mar, 1996).

Some societies have apparently tolerated minor forms of violence by husbands. In ancient Rome, for example, a husband had the right to use moderate levels of physical discipline with his wife (E. H. Pleck, 1987). Castan (1976) reported that mild forms of physical chastisement by husbands were allowed in 18th-century France. Male dominance was part of the rationale for chastisement: Because the husband was accountable for his wife's behavior, he had the right to control her behavior.

Some appellate courts in 19th-century America tolerated minor spousal violence. For example, in a case in North Carolina in 1864, a man seized his wife by the hair, pulled her to the floor, and held her there. She had taunted him, accused him of visiting a prostitute, and called him a hog thief. Because he did not hit or choke her, the state supreme court overturned a lower court ruling, deciding that he had not committed assault and battery. This opinion was atypical, however, according to E. H. Pleck (1979). Most court rulings in England and America rejected the idea of tolerating any form of physical violence.

A common claim is that a "rule of thumb" permitted men to hit their wives if they used a stick no bigger than a thumb (e.g., Eigenberg, 2001). Apparently, this interpretation of the rule of thumb is a myth (Kelly, 1994; Sommers, 1995). Jurists in the 19th century mistakenly attributed the rule to earlier times, and modern-day activists repeated the error. Blackstone (1836), the famous jurist to whom this idea is sometimes attributed, was actually an advocate of intervention in family disputes.

Blackstone also referred disparagingly to earlier historical periods when he claimed that unenlightened people condoned violence against wives. He also misinterpreted the historical record, assuming toleration of violence against wives that did not exist (Kelly, 1994). Blackstone is, of course, not alone in viewing people from earlier historical periods as barbaric and from his own as enlightened.

The general consensus regarding mild forms of physical violence is difficult to determine from the historical record, given the absence of opinion surveys. The fact that mild forms of domestic violence were rarely prosecuted does not necessarily mean that violence against women was viewed as acceptable behavior (Fagan & Browne, 1994). Violence by wives against their husbands was not prosecuted either. Wives are just as likely as their husbands, at least today, to engage in these mild forms of violence (see chapter 3). It is impossible to determine without a statistical analysis of historical records whether violence against wives was less likely to be prosecuted than other forms of family violence.

PRIVACY AND DOMESTIC VIOLENCE

E. H. Pleck (1989) argued that historically, the privacy of family life obstructed efforts to protect wives from their husbands (and children from parents). Her work suggests that the conditions under which the government, the church, or other outsiders should intrude in family matters has been the subject of enduring controversy. In the 17th century, an Englishman coined the phrase "a man's home is his castle" in an attempt to discourage the government from interfering with family life (E. H. Pleck, 1987). The Puritans, on the other hand, believing neighbors and the church had a duty to regulate family life, instituted the first special laws against wife abuse in the Western world in 1641. According to E. H. Pleck (1989), state intervention on behalf of wives and children in the United States has been episodic, depending largely on attitudes related to domestic privacy. For example, she attributed the decline of interest in family violence from 1830 until reforms in 1875 to "the growing distrust of government interference in the family, the increasing respect for domestic privacy, and the waning zeal for state enforcement of private morality" (p. 30).

The privacy issue is expressed in the judicial decisions she reviews. Most courts rejected the privacy argument, but there were exceptions. In North Carolina in 1868, for example, the state supreme court reviewed a case in which a man gave his wife "three licks with a stick the size of one of his fingers." It upheld a lower court ruling finding the husband not guilty. The court based its decision on the principle of privacy in minor cases of violence and rejected the notion of male authority as justification. It acknowledged that its decision not to intervene in such cases was inconsistent with court rulings from other states that advocated intervention and therefore required extensive justification. The following excerpt illustrates the judges' thinking:

> It will be observed that the ground upon which we have put this decision is not that the husband has the *right* to whip his wife much or little; but that we will not interfere with family government in trifling cases. We will no more interfere where the husband whips the wife than where the wife whips the husband; and yet we would hardly be supposed to hold that a wife has a *right* to whip her husband. We will not inflict upon society the greater evil of raising the curtain upon domestic privacy, to punish the lesser evil of trifling violence. Two boys under fourteen years of age fight upon the playground and yet the courts will take no notice of it, not for the reasons that boys have the right to fight, but because the interests of society require that they should be left to the more appropriate discipline of the school room and of home. It is not true that boys have a *right* to fight; nor is it true that a husband has a right to whip his wife. (*State v. Rhodes*, 1868)

Black (1976) described the privacy issue in terms of "relational distance," or the degree of intimacy between adversaries. From his perspective, nonintervention in domestic violence reflects the more general effect of relational distance. The closer the relational distance between adversaries (or between offender and victim), the less likely outsiders will intervene in their disputes. Thus, he argued that violent disputes between strangers are most likely to activate a legal response, whereas disputes between intimates are most likely to be handled privately (see also Gelles, 1983).

The effect of relational distance on third-party intervention in violent disputes has important implications for the protection of women, because women are much more likely than men to be involved in violent disputes with people they know (e.g., Browne & Williams, 1993; A. J. Reiss & Roth, 1993; Wolfgang, 1958). If disputes between intimates are not reported to the police, or if the police take a laissez-faire approach, women cannot receive the protection of the legal system.

It is possible to test the dominance and privacy explanations of why violence against wives is sometimes tolerated. The empirical issue is whether men's violence against their wives is more likely to be tolerated than women's violence against their husbands or any other form of family violence. If family violence is treated leniently, then a privacy explanation is supported. If only violence against wives is tolerated, then the dominance explanation is favored. In addition, privacy effects should occur without regard to gender. If privacy is the issue, then outsiders should be reluctant to interfere in any family matter, whether it involves husbands and wives, parents and children, or siblings. Thus, the fact that tort law has traditionally been held to be inapplicable to family relations supports the privacy, not the dominance, argument. In addition, evidence regarding police intervention in the United States, presented in chapter 6, supports the privacy argument.

REACTIONS TO DOMESTIC VIOLENCE IN OTHER CULTURES

The survey evidence reviewed earlier in this chapter shows that most American men do not approve of violence against wives. Similar results have been reported in Canada (M. D. Smith, 1990), Australia (Mugford & Mugford, 1989), and Singapore (Choi & Edleson, 1996). For example, fewer than 6% of respondents in Singapore agreed that "sometimes it is all right for a husband to use physical force against his wife."

On the other hand, much more approval of violence against wives appears to be present in some non-Western societies. A survey of 45 matrilineal societies found that 34 showed tolerance of violence against wives (Schlegel, 1972). High levels of acceptance of violence against wives have been reported in an Australian Aboriginal population (Kahn, 1980) and among people from rural areas in Papua New Guinea (Morley, 1994). None of these studies compares toleration of violence against wives with toleration of other types of violence. The former may reflect general attitudes about violence.

High levels of toleration of violence against wives in some tribal societies do not indicate group consensus. Dispute over the issue is indicated by discussions of the importance of third-party intervention in protecting women from violence (e.g., Baumgartner, 1993; Chagnon, 1977; Landes, 1971; Levinson, 1989). In general, it appears that although some men in such societies may believe that it is legitimate for them to use violence against their wives, their wives' kin often do not agree.

Studies of Palestinian husbands and Arab men living in Israel have also found high levels of approval of violence against wives under certain circumstances (Haj-Yahia, 1996, 1998). For example, only 41% of Palestinian men agreed with the statement that "there is no excuse for a man beating his wife." Seventy-one percent agreed with the statement that "a sexually unfaithful wife deserves to be beaten."

The role of dominance in violence against wives is expressed in the Koran. On one hand, the Koran teaches that men and women are created as mates and should treat each other with affection and compassion within the bonds of matrimony (Marsot, 1984). On the other hand, the Koran includes the following passage:

> The men are placed in charge of the women, since God has endowed them with the necessary qualities and made them bread-earners. The righteous women will accept this arrangement obediently, and will honor their husbands in their absence, in accordance with God's commands. As for the women who show rebellion, you shall first enlighten them,

then desert them in bed, and you may beat them as a last resort. Once they obey you, you have no excuse to transgress against them." (Sura 4:34).

The passage legitimates wife beating as the response of last resort when wives resist their husband's authority. It may help explain the survey evidence showing that many Arab men approved of violence against wives in restricted circumstances. It appears that in Arab societies, violence against wives has some legitimacy as a means for men to maintain dominance over their wives.

Unfortunately, the statistical studies do not report attitudes toward women hitting husbands or men using violence against people who are not their wives. In addition, they do not rule out the possibility that male dominance is used as a justification for violence by husbands who have other motivations. For example, a husband might use violence against his wife to get his way or save face in response to an insult, and then attempt to legitimate his behavior by citing the Koran. Still, the studies are a striking contrast with studies of Western societies, and they show a substantial amount of support for violence against wives in some societies. They suggest the possibility that violence against wives is related to dominance in some non-Western countries and that it may have been a factor in the past in Western countries before the development of egalitarian gender roles.

CONCLUSION

Individuals and societies have always tolerated or approved of violence in some circumstances. People who engage in antinormative violence sometimes receive lenient treatment or evade punishment altogether. Violence against women is no exception. However, violence against women is treated more severely than violence against men because it violates a powerful chivalry norm that inhibits men from attacking women. The evidence for the effect of the norm comes primarily from recent research in the United States, but one suspects that the norm was even stronger in more traditional societies of the past. The normative protection of women was undermined by the fact that their assailants were often partners or family members, and societies were reluctant to intervene in conflicts among intimates. Male dominance in the family may have been a counteracting factor leading to at least minor forms of violence against wives. Male dominance may also lead to violence in some non-Western countries in modern times.

Currently, the legal system treats violence against wives more leniently than in the past, provides more procedural safeguards, and orders counseling as well as punishment for offenders. Of course, crime and deviance in general are treated less severely today than in the past. The change in response to violence against wives may reflect this general trend rather than anything special about society's response to women.

The conflict between the concern for protecting family members and the concern for privacy is still a factor in the jurisprudence of family violence (Zimring, 1989). The concern for family privacy continues to inhibit state intervention in family conflict. Thus, verbal attacks and mild forms of physical violence against children elicit a legal response only if they occur outside the family. Recent legal reforms have attempted to increase state intervention in various forms of domestic violence at the expense of privacy concerns (Zimring, 1989).

Chivalry has implications for the argument that there is an epidemic of violence against women (see chapter 3). Violence against women is certainly frequent relative to general societal expectations about how men should treat women. Chivalry leads one to expect much lower levels of violence against women than exist in U.S. society, which has high levels of violent crime. Because of chivalry people respond with greater emotion to violence against women than against men. However, a feminist perspective considers the idea of chivalry as paternalism and an insult to women. The egalitarian ethic and the reluctance to promote negative stereotypes about women make it difficult to admit that chivalry is the rationale for the special distaste for this form of violence. The desire to treat women favorably also contributes to a reluctance to assign women negative stereotypes. We want to protect women, but we do not want to admit they need protecting. Ironically, chivalry, as well as political correctness, inhibits the discussion of chivalry in relation to violence against women.

6

PRIVACY AND POLICE INTERVENTION

Homes as castles

The conventional wisdom is that domestic violence, particularly incidents involving violence against wives, is hidden from authorities. Both metaphorically and literally, domestic violence occurs "behind closed doors" (Straus, Gelles, & Steinmetz, 1980). This assertion is critical to the argument that there is an epidemic of violence against wives—its frequency would be apparent were it not hidden from view. Family violence researchers and feminists both take this perspective, although they differ over whether the epidemic involves men's violence against female partners or domestic violence in general.

Before the legal system can respond to violence, the offense must be brought to the attention of the police. The police rarely observe crime or violence themselves—they typically become involved when citizens call them (e.g., A. J. Reiss, 1971). Therefore, to understand police intervention in couple violence, it is important to consider factors that affect whether victims and third parties call the police.

In this chapter, I present in some detail the results of studies that examine whether the police or those who call the police respond differently to male violence against partners than to other types of violence. The first two studies examine whether victims and third parties are reluctant to report violent assaults involving couples. The third study examines the reasons victims give for reporting or not reporting violence committed by their partners and others. The fourth study examines whether the police show leniency in the case of partner violence when incidents are reported. The fifth study examines gender effects on the reporting of partner violence and the response of the legal system when partner violence is reported.

REPORTING VIOLENT INCIDENTS TO THE POLICE

It is important to be clear about the comparison being made when hypothesizing about the reporting of violence against wives and female partners to the police. It is not enough to show that violence against wives is often unreported, because violence in general is often unreported. A more informative approach is to examine whether the violence of men against their female partners is less likely to be reported to the police than other types of violence.

To examine this issue, it is also important to disentangle the effects of gender and social relationship on reporting. Research shows that violence against women is much more likely than violence against men to involve a family member (e.g., Browne & Williams, 1993; A. J. Reiss & Roth, 1993; see chapter 3). In addition, women are more likely to call the police than are men (Gottfredson & Gottfredson, 1980; Greenberg & Ruback, 1992). If gender and the social relationship between an offender and victim are related to each other, and if both affect reporting, then a multivariate framework is necessary to distinguish between their effects. Gender of offender, gender of victim, and a measure of their social relationship must be included in equations.

It is also necessary to consider the possibility of statistical interactions between gender and social relationship. Discussions of domestic violence imply that victims are particularly unlikely to call the police when the victim is a woman and the offender is her husband or male partner. This pattern would be expected if women have special concerns about abusive male partners. Some commentators suggest, for example, that wives may be particularly reluctant to call the police on their husbands because of fear of reprisal (e.g., Frieze & Browne, 1989; Pagelow, 1984). Others suggest that women are reluctant to report their husbands to the police if they are emotionally or economically dependent (e.g., Pagelow, 1984). Such women may fear that reporting the incident will reduce their husband's capacity or willingness to provide financial support. In addition, violent husbands supposedly "sweet-talk" their wives, promising never to repeat their violent actions. These arguments imply a statistical interaction between the offender's gender (male), the victim's gender (female), and the relationship between the offender and victim (intimate partner). They imply that when women are assaulted by their male partners, they should be less likely to report the incident to the police than victims of other types of assaults.

When examining whether an incident is reported to the police, it is also necessary to consider the tremendous variation in the seriousness of violent incidents. Violent incidents include everything from a push, a shove, or an idle threat to injury-producing assaults and homicide. The historical literature reviewed in the last chapter suggests that the response to minor offenses is likely to be very different from the response to more serious attacks. In addition, there may be statistical interactions involving seriousness. Serious assaults may be reported to the police no matter how close the offender is to the victim and regardless of the gender of the victim or assailant. An assault in which a family member is severely injured, for example, is unlikely to be viewed as a private matter. On the other hand, citizens are likely to use more discretion in reporting relatively minor assaults, such pushes, shoves, or unarmed threats. They may consider these incidents private matters when they involve family members.

I examined gender and relationship effects on whether the incident was reported to the police using the 1980 Albany data described in chapter 3 (Felson, 2000). Respondents were asked to recall the last dispute they were involved in that involved violence (but no weapons) and to indicate whether the police became involved. The results showed that gender and relationship had additive effects—incidents involving men's assaults on their wives were not special. There was evidence that disputes involving couples were much less likely than incidents involving strangers to be reported to the police (see also R. Block, 1974). However, violent disputes between men and women were more likely to be reported to the police than violence between men, particularly when a witness was present. On the other hand, incidents were less likely to be reported if a woman engaged in a physical attack. Chivalry does not apply to the violence of women unless there is fear that she may be subject to retaliation. In addition, people tend to view women's violence as less serious than men's violence (Feld & Robinson, 1993; Straus, 1993).

In analyses where measures of relationship are left out of the equation, the intergender effect disappears, suggesting that the effects of relationship on police involvement offset the effects of gender. That is, when women were involved in violent disputes, their adversaries were more likely to be partners, and violence between partners is less likely than stranger violence to be reported to the police. The offsetting effects are depicted in the causal diagram in Figure 6.1.

We also found that the police were more likely to be called when there were witnesses present during the assault. In addition, third parties were much less likely to witness incidents involving couples than incidents involving people in other relationships. For example, witnesses were present in 84.6% of incidents involving strangers but only 27.1% of the incidents involving couples. The results suggest another indirect effect of gender on reporting (see Figure 6.1). Because violence involving women is more likely to involve couples and family members, it is less likely to be witnessed by third parties,

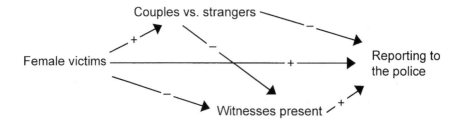

Figure 6.1. Mediators of gender effects on reporting assaults to the police.

and this factor decreases the likelihood that it is reported to the police. In other words, third parties are less likely to witness the domestic disputes in which women are often involved, and their frequent absence means that violence involving women is less likely to be reported to the police than other types of violence and that third parties are unavailable to intervene.

In sum, the effects observed in this study are consistent with an extensive literature showing that people perceive violence against women as more negative than violence against men. The study shows statistically how chivalry's impact is limited because violence against women usually occurs among couples and others who know each other. Third parties, including the legal system, tend not to get involved in what are seen as private squabbles. The privacy of the family limits the extent to which society can protect women. The results show how we can perceive violence against women as evil and, at the same time, have difficulty controlling it. In other words, privacy to some extent undermines the effects of chivalry.

REPORTING CRIMINAL ASSAULTS TO THE POLICE

A second study was based on data collected from 1992 to 1994 by the National Crime Victimization Survey (NCVS; Felson, Messner, & Hoskin, 1999a). The NCVS collected information on victimizations from a nationally representative sample of households in the United States. Incidents in which victims reported having been attacked or threatened by a single offender were selected for analysis.

We attempted to determine whether gender and the victim's relationship to the offender affected whether victims and third parties called the police. We controlled for the seriousness of the incident and other relevant factors. The results (summarized in Table 6.1) show that victims were just as likely to report an assault to the police when the offender was their partner or another family member as when the offender was a stranger. These results are contrary to the results for the Albany sample reported in the previous section (see also R. Block, 1974). The discrepancy may be due to the fact that violence surveys focus on minor violence, whereas the NCVS is a criminal vic-

TABLE 6.1
Selective Summary of Results from an Analysis of Reporting to Police

	Dependent variables		
Comparison	Victim reporting	Third party reporting	Witness presence
Partner vs. stranger	ns	−	−
Other family vs. stranger	ns	ns	ns
Male offender–female victim vs. male offender–male victim	+	+	ns

Note. Data are from National Crime Victimization Survey. + = positive relationship; − = negative relationship; ns = nonsignificant relationship.

timization survey. The discrepancy may also be due to change over the past 25 years in the tendency for victims of domestic violence to call the police.

Although the NCVS interviewers encouraged respondents to report nonstranger assaults even when the respondent was uncertain about the criminal status of the incident, it seems likely that some censoring still took place. Respondents probably did not fully report incidents they did not perceive to be crimes to NCVS interviewers. Many of these excluded incidents likely involved conflicts between intimates in which neither participant called the police because neither believed that a "real" crime had occurred. Some of the excluded incidents may have been extremely minor or may have involved violence by both parties.

These results, therefore, are best understood as pertaining to incidents in which respondents believed they had been (or may have been) crime victims. They suggest that if people believe that they are possibly the victim of a violent crime, they are not inhibited from calling the police by the fact that the offender is a spouse or someone else they know. I shall attempt to explain this surprising finding later in this chapter.

The offender–victim relationship generally did not affect third-party reporting, unless witness presence was left out of the equation. The results suggest that third parties were less likely to report assaults involving couples than assaults involving strangers because they were much less likely to witness such assaults. The tendency for violence involving couples to occur "behind closed doors" lowers the likelihood that third parties report the incident.

Much stronger effects on third-party reporting were observed when we restricted our analysis to relatively minor incidents involving unarmed threats. In these minor incidents, the offender made a verbal threat but did not actually attack the victim or threaten the victim with a weapon. For these incidents, third parties were much less likely to report the incident if the offender was a spouse or other relative than if the offender was a stranger. Some of the effect remained when we controlled for whether a witness was present. This direct effect indicates that third parties are reluctant to call the police when they observe intimate partners or other relatives threaten each other.

The reluctance of third parties to report minor couple violence is consistent with experimental evidence. In a series of studies, participants observed a staged fight in which a man attacked a woman (Shotland & Straw, 1976). The bystanders were much more likely to intervene in the fight if they believed the antagonists were strangers than if they thought the fight involved a married couple. Virtually all participants who did not intervene in the fight involving the couple said they felt the fight was "none of their business." Participants did not intervene for other reasons as well: They were less likely to believe the woman wanted help if the man was her husband than if he was a stranger; they were more likely to assume that the husband's attack was less damaging to the woman; and they thought that if they intervened, the husband was more likely to stay and fight, whereas a stranger would run away. In general, the studies show that when couples are fighting, bystanders perceive the need for intervention as low and the costs as high.

We also observed gender effects on victim and third-party reporting. The results (summarized in Table 6.1) show that victims and third parties were more likely to report incidents when men assaulted women than when men assaulted other men. As in the previous study, the effects of gender to some extent offset the effects of social relationship on third-party reporting. Third parties are more likely to report male violence against women, but they are less likely to report domestic violence. As a result, the ability of police to protect women from male violence is limited, because those who assault women are often their partners or family members. Police intervention is also limited by the fact that men's violence against women is less likely to be witnessed by third parties who might report the incident.

Finally, our results showed that the effects of gender and relationship are additive. The absence of any significant interactions between gender and relationship shows that incidents involving assaults on women by their male partners are not particularly likely to escape police attention. Neither victims nor third parties were particularly reluctant to report these incidents.

In sum, victims are not inhibited about calling the police on their husbands or partners when they believe they have been assaulted. They report these assaults as often as they report assaults by strangers. Third parties, on the other hand, are less likely to report assaults involving couples both because they are less likely to witness them and because they are reluctant to report more minor assaults involving couples. If no one has actually been attacked, and if no weapon has been drawn, third parties are less likely to report domestic violence to the police. However, their reluctance to report minor violence is not due to their tolerance of male violence against women or wives. In fact, police intervention is more likely when men assault women, presumably because of chivalry.

MOTIVATIONS FOR REPORTING AND NOT
REPORTING ASSAULTS

It is surprising that victims are just as likely to report criminal violence committed by partners as they are to report criminal violence committed by strangers. Perhaps there are characteristics of partner violence that motivate as well as inhibit victim reporting. Moreover, the inhibitory factors cited by researchers concerned with partner violence may play a role in the reporting of other violence as well. We explored these issues using NCVS data (1992 to 1998), excluding incidents in which third parties called the police or in which the victim reported the incident to some authority other than the police (Felson, Messner, & Hoskin, 1999a). In this survey, assault victims who reported an incident to the police were asked why they did so, and assault victims who did not call the police were asked to explain why they did not.

A frequency distribution of the main reasons victims gave for reporting and not reporting these assaults is presented in Table 6.2. The most frequent reasons for calling the police involved self-protection. Respondents who called the police were most likely to say that they wanted to either protect themselves from future attacks or stop the incident from continuing. The most frequent reasons for not calling the police were that the incident was trivial or a private matter. Fear of reprisal and desire to protect the offender were cited much less often as reasons for not reporting the incident to the police.

For both reporters and nonreporters, we examined the victim's stated motivation as a function of the offender's gender, the victim's gender, and the relationship of the victim to the offender. We controlled for whether the victim was injured, the offender was armed, and other relevant factors. Our multivariate results show that the effects of gender and relationship are generally additive, implying that women who are assaulted by their male partners did not have special incentives or inhibitions regarding calling the police. For example, women were not particularly likely to be fooled by their "sweet-talking" husbands after the assault. They also were not particularly likely to avoid calling the police on their male partners because they feared reprisal.

The results from the additive analyses are summarized in Table 6.3. Partners and family members are combined because the results are similar. The results suggest that three factors inhibit victims from calling the police on partners and family members (versus strangers): (1) the greater concern for privacy, (2) the stronger desire to protect the offender, and (3) the greater fear of reprisal. The concern for privacy is a particularly important inhibitory factor. Two factors encourage victims to call the police on partners and family members: (1) the greater concern for self-protection when the victim will see the offender again and (2) the perception of family violence as more serious than stranger violence. These offsetting factors help explain why victims of violence in the NCVS were just as likely to call the police when the offender was a partner as when the offender was a stranger.

TABLE 6.2
Frequency Distribution of Reasons for Calling and Not Calling the Police

Variable	Category	Percentage
Reason for calling the police (N = 1598)	Protection from future attack	29.1
	To stop the incident	22.0
	Protection of others from future attack	10.9
	To punish the offender	8.6
	Duty to tell the police	5.8
	To catch the offender	5.0
	Other	22.9
Reason for not calling the police (N = 3760)	Private matter	30.7
	Trivial matter	25.4
	Not important to the police	7.1
	Fear of reprisal	4.9
	Protecting the offender	4.2
	Other	42.4

Gender also plays an important role in the victim's decision whether to report the incident to the police. The results show that women are more likely than men to call the police for three reasons: (1) They are more likely to desire protection, (2) they are less likely to think that the violence is a private matter, and (3) they are less likely to think the incident is trivial. Only one factor—greater fear of reprisal—inhibits women from calling the police. The factors encouraging women to call the police are much stronger than the single factor that discourages their calling. As a result, women are more likely than men to call the police when they have been assaulted. Note that the gender of the offender also played a role in the decision whether to report the incident to the police, although its effects were smaller. The most important gender effect was on fear of reprisal. Victims were more likely to fear reprisal from men.

In sum, scholars have focused too much on factors that inhibit victims of domestic violence from calling the police and ignored factors that might encourage their reporting. Victims' greater concerns for protecting themselves from future domestic assaults and their perceptions of these assaults as particularly serious events offset concerns for privacy and other inhibitory factors. In addition, domestic assaults are more likely to involve women, and women are more likely to call the police for protection because they view their victimizations as more serious and less a private matter. These factors help explain why victims are just as likely to report domestic violence to the police as violence committed by strangers.

POLICE RESPONSE TO DOMESTIC VIOLENCE

Some scholars have accused the police of showing special leniency toward offenders, particularly male offenders, in domestic assaults (Buzawa,

TABLE 6.3
Effects of Social Relationship and Victim's Gender on Reasons for Reporting and Not Reporting Assaults

Characteristic	Reason for Reporting	Reasons for Not Reporting			
	Protection	Trivial	Private Matter	Protect Offender	Fear of Reprisal
Partners and family members vs. strangers	+	−	+	+	+
Female victims vs. male victims	+	−	−	ns	+

Note. + = positive relationship; − = negative relationship; ns = nonsignificant relationship.

Austin, & Buzawa, 1995; R. E. Dobash & R. P. Dobash, 1979; Martin, 1976; Roy, 1977a, 1977b). They suggest that the police fail to make an arrest when the circumstances warrant it and that this laissez-faire approach—the failure to respond more aggressively to domestic assault—leads to its perpetuation (Buzawa et al., 1995). Police reluctance to make arrests for domestic violence is attributed to beliefs in male dominance, hesitation to intervene in family matters, or the reluctance of victims to cooperate in prosecution (see Elliott, 1989, for a review). Women assaulted by their husbands are sometimes unwilling to assist in prosecution, according to some research (Elliott, 1989; Schmidt & Hochstedler, 1989). Mandatory and proarrest policies were designed to counteract the police tendency toward leniency (Bachman & Saltzman, 1995).

A number of studies have found that assaults involving domestic violence are less likely to lead to arrest than assaults between strangers (Black, 1971; Buzawa et al., 1995; Fyfe, Klinger, & Flavin, 1997, Vera Institute of Justice, 1977). Other studies have found that police respond just as vigorously to domestic assault as nondomestic assault (Faragher, 1985; Feder, 1998; D. A. Smith, 1987). In addition to the mixed evidence, it is not clear from these studies whether the police show special leniency when men assault their wives, that is, whether there is a statistical interaction between gender and intimacy. Nor is it clear whether the response to assaults involving couples is different from the response to assaults involving family members or other nonstrangers.

In a recent study we examined the leniency hypothesis using NCVS data on incidents that were reported to the police (Felson & Ackerman, 2001). We examined whether the likelihood of arrest when an assault was reported to the police depended on the relationship between the offender and victim, the gender of each, the seriousness of the assault, whether the victim signed a complaint, the presence of witnesses, and various social and demographic factors.

The evidence suggests that the police are less likely to arrest someone who assaults an intimate than someone who assaults an identifiable stranger. However, leniency does not depend on gender: Police were just as likely to arrest men who assaulted their wives as they were to arrest women who assaulted their husbands. We found no evidence of a chivalry effect. Arrest was slightly more likely when either the offender or victim was male, although only the latter was significant. Nor was there a statistical interaction between gender and relationship: The police did not show special leniency toward men who assaulted their female partners.

Leniency was most likely to be shown when the victim knew the offender but the offender was not an intimate or family member. We suspect that the proarrest laws offset the tendency toward leniency in domestic violence. This research provides some evidence, then, that these policies are having their intended effect on police behavior.

The offender–victim relationship had stronger effects on arrests for verbal threats and minor attacks than for more serious assaults. The police were particularly likely to show leniency in the case of minor attacks by someone the victim knew. In other words, the police were less likely to treat a push or a shove as a serious matter deserving of arrest if the parties knew each other. In these incidents, we found a strong tendency for the police to show leniency toward offenders who attack intimates as well. On the other hand, the police did not use their discretion in incidents involving weapons or injury; in these instances, the offender's relationship to the victim did not affect whether the police made an arrest.

We also found that the response of the police to domestic and other violence depended to a large extent on evidentiary concerns. In a large number of these assaults (45%), the victim was unable to identify the offender. This factor lowers the likelihood of arrest of strangers and counteracts any tendency to treat nonstrangers more leniently than strangers. In other words, the fact that domestic offenders can be identified is one factor that makes arrest more likely for domestic violence than stranger violence, offsetting any tendency toward leniency.

Another important evidentiary factor leading to arrest is the presence of witnesses. The police are not able to determine guilt in many incidents of violence, particularly when the participants give different versions of the event. Witnesses, who are one source of information, are much less likely to be present during intimate assaults. This factor decreases the likelihood of arrest in assaults involving intimates.

Victims are also an important source of evidence for prosecuting cases, and they are reluctant to sign complaints when they know the offender. This reluctance decreases the likelihood of arrest in assaults involving intimates. However, victims are reluctant to sign complaints against anyone they know, not just their intimate partners. Thus, our research questions the idea that women are particularly unlikely to cooperate in the prosecution of their assaultive husbands and partners. We do observe gender differences, but these differences do not point to a reluctance to cooperate on the part of women. Rather, women are more likely than men to sign complaints against their assailants, particularly if the assailants are their husbands. Thus, we observe a statistical interaction between gender and relationship, but the sign is opposite to conventional wisdom, consistent with the literature showing that women are more likely than men to express complaints and anger (see chapter 5). In addition, victims are more likely to sign complaints against male offenders than female offenders. The causal arguments suggested by these analyses, with the exception of the statistical interaction, are depicted in Figure 6.2.

EVIDENCE FROM THE NATIONAL VIOLENCE AGAINST WOMEN SURVEY

A recent national survey confirms some of our findings on partner violence (Tjaden & Thoennes, 2000). In the National Violence Against Women Survey, victims of violence by intimate partners (current and former dates, spouses, and cohabiting partners) indicated whether the incident was reported to the police and how the police responded. The study found that incidents involving violence against female partners were almost twice as likely to be reported to the police as incidents involving violence against male partners (26.7% vs. 13.5%). Incidents reported to the police were three times as likely to lead to arrest if the victim was the female partner (36.4% vs. 12.3%). Of those arrested, male perpetrators of violence against female partners were almost seven times as likely to be prosecuted as female perpetrators of violence against male partners (7.3% vs. 1.1%).

Unlike our studies, this study was restricted to couples, and it did not control for other factors that might affect reporting to the police or the police response, such as the seriousness of the incident. For example, some of the effects might be due to the fact that women were twice as likely as men to be injured (41.5% vs. 19.9%). Still, the findings cast further doubt on the idea that violence against women is more likely than violence against men to be hidden from authorities or to be treated more leniently.

CONCLUSION

The response of victims, the police, and other third parties to men's violence against their wives is complex. To understand the response, it is necessary to disentangle the effects of gender and social relationship. It is important to determine whether the response to partner violence, domestic violence, or violence between anyone in an ongoing relationship is different

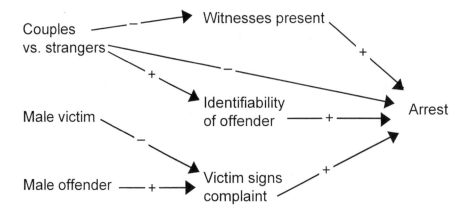

Figure 6.2. Determinants of arrest for assault.

from the response to stranger violence. The reactions also depend on whether the violence is minor or serious.

A careful analysis suggests that sexism does not lead to leniency toward violence against female partners. When gender effects are observed, they tend to involve more intervention on behalf of women. There is a tendency to treat minor acts of violence more leniently if they involve partners rather than strangers, but this leniency is related to attitudes toward privacy, not attitudes toward women. One might even conclude that sexism works to the benefit of female victims, if we associate chivalry with sexism. On the other hand, the norm of chivalry may also lead men to target women in private, out of the sight of third parties who might intervene or call the police.

7

CONTROLLING WOMEN

He: "Quit nagging me." She: "You need to be nagged."

Some scholars, particularly those taking a feminist perspective, attribute violence by men against their wives or female partners to a control motive (Browne, 1987; R. E. Dobash & R. P. Dobash, 1979; Dutton, 1988; for reviews, see Archer, 1994; Fagan & Browne, 1994; M. P. Johnson, 1995; Koss et al., 1994). Men try to control their wives, the argument goes, because they have been socialized in a patriarchal society to believe that men are expected to be dominant in the family (R. E. Dobash & R. P. Dobash, 1977–78; M. D. Smith, 1990; Yllö & Straus, 1984). Their belief in male dominance leads them to attempt to control their wives and girlfriends, and their desire for control leads them to use violence. I shall examine the second argument first—that the control motive leads to violence against partners. Later in the chapter I will address the issue of whether the control motive is related to beliefs in male dominance.

Although the control motive is one of the central themes in the feminist approach to violence against women, statistical evidence is virtually nonexistent. The theme of male control is prominent in a number of clinical studies (see Koss et al., 1994, for a review) and in a few statistical studies of motives in dating violence (Follingstad, Wright, Lloyd, & Sebastian, 1991;

Sugarman & Hotaling, 1989). These latter studies, however, are based on self-reported motives and limited samples, and they do not compare couples and noncouples to examine the relative frequency of the control motive. In addition, they have yielded inconsistent results. The lack of statistical evidence on the control motive probably reflects the difficulty of measuring offender motivation, particularly in naturally occurring events.

PATRIARCHAL TERRORISM

M. P. Johnson (1995) provided the most systematic statement of the feminist position on the control motive. In an influential article, he described sexist men who use violence to control their wives as "patriarchal terrorists." He distinguished these men from men and women who engage in "garden variety" domestic violence that tends to be less serious, less likely to involve continual abuse, and more likely to involve violence by both husband and wife. The patriarchal terrorist increases his level of attack against his wife, sometimes to the point of killing her.

This argument has had great appeal because it seems to reconcile the literature on domestic violence with the feminist literature. The literature on domestic violence relies on statistical survey data that show that wives hit husbands at least as often as husbands hit wives (see chapter 3). The feminist literature often relies on qualitative reports from activists working in shelters for battered women (M. P. Johnson, 1995). They describe the women in these shelters as nonviolent and passive, often suffering from battered wife syndrome. Their husbands are particularly nasty and violent—that is presumably why the women come to the shelter. From these reports, Johnson identified the patriarchal terrorist and his innocent victim. The scientific value of the activists' interpretation is questionable, however, because their views are based on subjective impressions rather than systematic data collected from representative samples.

In addition, Loseke (1992) described the tendency of the staff at these shelters to impose their interpretation of wife battering on their clientele. The staff is skeptical of clients whose experiences do not fit the feminist theme, and they assume these clients are in some form of denial. They sometimes refuse to admit these women to the shelter. Women who, for example, describe their own provocative behavior are perceived as irrationally blaming themselves. The staff is unwilling to recognize the possibility that the woman's behavior can play a causal role in assault because that would be blaming the victim. They confuse cause with blame and treat blame as a fixed quantity—they want all blame attributed to the husband (see chapter 12). Of course, sometimes the woman's behavior does not have a causal effect, and sometimes she is completely innocent of any wrongdoing. But in a realistic analysis of partner violence, it is not possible to maintain victims' causal and moral purity.

Even political terrorists usually believe they are responding to some offense or provocation. For example, on April 19, 1995, Timothy McVeigh bombed the federal building in Oklahoma City apparently in retaliation for the incident at Waco, Texas. From his point of view, he was punishing the government for its immoral actions against the Branch Davidians. Whether the perceptions of terrorists are accurate, debatable, or delusional, their perceptions govern their actions. Their attempts to control or harm their targets are frequently in response to a perceived wrong.

I suspect that violent husbands (like other offenders in assault and homicide) are typically responding to what they believe are provocations. What most distinguishes violent offenders generally is not that they engage in completely unprovoked violence; they do not choose their victims randomly. Rather, violent offenders are people who overreact to often minor provocations; that is, their violent responses are disproportionate to whatever offends them (Toch, 1993). Thus, many homicides involve reactions to what an observer would describe as a trivial provocation (Wolfgang, 1958), and most cases of child abuse occur during discipline situations (see Tedeschi & Felson, 1994, for a review). Most of us would respond with some irritation in these situations, but offenders respond with violence or with a strong verbal attack that elicits an aggressive reaction, to which they then respond with greater violence. In addition, because of the tendency for people to marry people like themselves, one would expect that women who marry violent husbands are more likely than other women to have personal problems or to be violent themselves. Thus, women who have been the victims of violence by their husbands are more likely to have experienced violence as a child or adolescent (see Hotaling & Sugarman, 1986, for a review). Apparently, women who seek help at shelters often have drug and other problems that precede their victimizations (Loseke, 1992).

M. J. Johnson (1999) recently presented statistical evidence for his typology based on evidence from the National Violence Against Women Survey. He examined the relationship between a scale supposedly measuring control behavior and various outcomes. The measure of control behavior is problematic, however, because it includes items measuring verbal aggression as well as controlling behavior. At any rate, he found that this measure was positively related to frequency of violence, severity of injury, and the victim's psychological problems. An alternative interpretation is that men who mistreated their wives in one way were likely to mistreat them in other ways (e.g., verbally attack them and boss them around).

We recently performed an analysis of this same data set and found that both men and women who engaged in controlling behavior toward their spouse were more likely to be violent toward them (Felson & Outlaw, 2002). Bossiness is associated with violence for both men and women. In addition, as reported in chapter 4, men are slightly more likely than women to report that their partners attempt to control their activities.

It seems unlikely that violent husbands can be neatly divided into two groups, one composed of violent controlling men, the other of ordinary guys who get in occasional violent altercations with their wives. Typologies exaggerate the differences between different types of behavior. Even if one could establish that the control motive was related to severity, frequency, or presence of provocation, it is doubtful that the correlations would be strong enough to justify a typology that treats them as part of a single syndrome.

Another problem is that a single incident involving a man's violence against his wife cannot be neatly categorized according to motive because it is likely to involve multiple motives. Physical violence is almost always preceded by verbal conflict (see chapter 2). An offended party attempts to control or punish someone and a verbal contest over saving face develops, sometimes escalating to physical violence. Physical attacks are likely to be a response to insults and to occur during the escalation of verbal conflict (Felson, 1984). This pattern characterizes violent incidents regardless of the gender of the antagonists or their social relationship.

In addition, there are no strong theoretical reasons to expect an association between the control motive and whether attacks are severe, repeated, or unprovoked. Mild forms of aggression and violence may be just as likely to involve a control motive. The threat of verbal attack, for example, may enable a quick-tempered family member to intimidate and dominate others. In addition, offenders' use of violence for social control implies that they are attempting to deter behaviors they find offensive; one might expect that the control motive is more likely to be involved in incidents where there is provocation.

I am not arguing against the idea that men sometimes use violence to control their wives. In fact, I present evidence later in this chapter that the control motive is more likely to be involved when men assault their wives than in other violent circumstances. However, I am skeptical that these assaults are more serious, more likely to be repeated, or more likely to be unprovoked. In addition, I do not think a typological approach is useful even if a statistical association could be established between motive and other variables. Finally, I suggest that a man's use of violence to control his wife is not necessarily related to sexism or patriarchy.

PRESENT VERSUS FUTURE INFLUENCE

Before evaluating the empirical validity of the control motive in violence against female partners, it is necessary to interpret and clarify what such an assertion might mean, because the literature does not do so. One ambiguous aspect of assertions about the control motive is the actor's time frame: He may be interested in influencing current behavior or future behavior. A robber, for example, is interested in influencing current behavior—his goal is immediate compliance. The goal of self-defense is also immediate influence—the assault victim wants to incapacitate the aggressor and stop the attack in progress. An actor may also use violence to influence future behavior. He may use violence to deter the target from repeating a specific behavior. He may also use violence to encourage obedience and to make the target submissive and compliant. One might describe the attempt to produce general long-term compliance in a relationship as an attempt to establish dominance.

An example might help clarify the distinction between the desire for dominance and other motives for punishment, i.e., aggression in a social control situation. For example, a mother tells her son to pick up his toys, and he disobeys. She has four reasons to punish him: (1) for retribution for his disobedience, (2) to encourage him to pick up the toys, (3) to encourage him to pick up his toys in the future, (4) to encourage him to be obedient. The last motive reflects her concern for dominance, a concern that may be greater than her concern about his messy room.

Similarly, during a conflict, a man may attempt to persuade his wife to do things his way in a particular conflict. If his attempts at persuasion fail, he may use violence. On the other hand, one can assume that some men use violence against their wives to achieve dominance. He threatens her or hits her to intimidate her and to make her docile and compliant. He cares more about the issue of obedience than about getting his way on a particular issue. He wants to show her that he is "the boss."

It seems unlikely that dominance and long-term influence are the goals of men who kill their wives. Homicide does not maintain dominance in the relationship, because she will be gone and he will probably be in prison. He could be interested in short-term influence: He kills his wife to prevent her from leaving him or to prevent her from continuing a relationship with another man. It would seem more rational for him to kill the rival, because then he has a chance of remaining with her; in fact, men kill rivals much more often than they kill partners in love triangles (see chapter 8). In general, homicide can be used to prevent unwanted behavior, but it does not increase one's future influence with the deceased. However, it can make the offender appear powerful, which may increase his influence with the living.

In general, when homicide involves a control motive, it is probably oriented to immediate compliance. For example, offenders sometimes kill their victims to prevent retaliation. During an assault, offenders are more likely to kill male victims than female victims, presumably because of a greater fear of retaliation (Felson & Messner, 1996). From this perspective, the control motive may be more important in homicides when the victim is male than when the victim is female.

A STATISTICAL STUDY OF THE CONTROL MOTIVE

The assertion that men who assault their wives are attempting to control them is an overstatement, because it is implies that violence against wives always has this motive. Perhaps the statement means that men who assault their wives are sometimes trying to control them. This is certainly true. Controlling others is one of the motives for using violence (see chapter 2). When husbands and wives are involved in a conflict, they are likely to attempt to influence each other to get their own way. Because men are stronger and have a greater proclivity to use violence, it is not surprising that some of them use violence as a means of influence. Women want to control their husbands as well, but they are less likely to choose violence as their method.

Perhaps the statement about husbands' motives refers to a comparison between the frequency of control as a motive to the frequency of other motives. Men who assault their wives may be more likely to have a control motive than any other motive or all other motives combined. If the control motive is involved in more than 50% of incidents, one could say that for the majority of assaults on wives a control motive is involved.

Other comparisons are possible. It could be that when men assault their wives, the incidents are more likely to have a control motive than when wives assault their husbands. It could also be that a control motive is more likely when men assault their wives than when they assault other people or when they assault women who are not their wives. These statements imply statistical interactions between gender and relationship.

Other assertions imply additive effects of gender. There is some evidence that men tend to seek dominance more than women (Pratto, 1996; Whiting & Edwards, 1988). Gender differences in dominance—whether due to biology or socialization—would lead men to use violence to control people of both genders. It is also possible that women are perceived as more vulnerable to influence and are more likely than men to be the target of violent control attempts by both men and women.

Fortunately, statistical techniques provide a way out of this morass. It is possible to disentangle the effects of the offender's gender, the victim's gender, and the offender–victim relationship to determine if there is anything special about husbands' motives for violence against their wives. We recently attempted such a study using data on assaults from the NCVS (Felson & Messner, 2000). We assumed that offenders who threatened victims before assaulting them were more likely to have a control motive than offenders who did not make any prior threat. The person issuing a threat communicates a contingency: The target will be harmed unless he or she complies with some demand. Theory and research suggest that the communication of a threat is the typical control tactic (Luckenbill, 1980; Milburn & Watman, 1980; Pruitt & Rubin, 1986; Tedeschi, 1970).

The issuance of a threat of physical harm is admittedly an indirect and imperfect indicator of a control motive on the part of an aggressor. The use of an overt threat does not always indicate that the offender is attempting to control the victim's behavior. Offenders sometimes communicate a threat without a contingency in an attempt to harm the target rather than achieve compliance (Tedeschi & Felson, 1994). In addition, threats are not necessarily stated overtly. For example, when parents use punishment, they communicate to their children that future misbehavior will also be punished, even if the parents do not explicitly articulate contingencies. The threat of future harm is ultimately the basis for the use of punishment as a deterrent. Still, the social psychological literature suggests that threats are a reasonable measure of the control motive.

Our sample included 3,317 assaults involving a single unarmed offender and a single victim. Armed assaults were omitted because a weapon implies a threat whether the offender is explicit about it or not. The relationships among threats, gender of offender and victim, and relationship are presented in cross tabulations in Table 7.1. The table reveals support for our hypothesis about the control motive in partner violence. Assaults involving a couple relationship, male offenders, and female victims are more likely than other assaults to be preceded by the issuance of a threat. Analyses not presented reveal a strong two-way statistical interaction between couple relationship and gender of victim; the three-way interaction is not statistically significant. However, there are very few same-sex couples in the data set, which makes it difficult to determine whether these incidents differ from those involving men and their female partners. Therefore, we cannot say conclusively that threats are more prevalent when women are assaulted by their male partners than when victims are assaulted by same-sex partners, even though a visual inspection of this table suggests that this is the case.

The results of this study suggest that there is an element of truth to the feminist assertion about the control motive in violence against wives. However, we must be careful not to overstate the case: The control motive is more likely to be involved in men's attacks on their partners than in other violent circumstances. Its frequency is still unknown. In addition, it is premature to make even this comparative statement with confidence. This is the only statistical study of the issue ever done, and it relies on an indirect measure of the control motive. Bold statements about the control motive in partner violence are not justified.

SEXISM AND THE CONTROL MOTIVE

Why might male assaults on female partners be more likely than most other kinds of assaults to entail a control motive? Attempts to use violence for control are likely to depend on the desire to exert influence and the rela-

TABLE 7.1
Incidents of Assault Preceded by Threat, by Gender and Relationship of Antagonists

Offender's Gender	Victim's gender	Noncouple (%)	Couple (%)
Female	Female	40.3 ($N = 360$)	37.5 ($N = 8$)
Female	Male	28.2 ($N = 71$)	27.0 ($N = 63$)
Male	Female	31.9 ($N = 436$)	54.6 ($N = 507$)
Male	Male	45.0 ($N = 1,141$)	18.2 ($N = 11$)

Note: $N = 2,597$. Base figures for percentages are reported in parentheses.

tive coercive power of adversaries. Men may have a greater desire to influence their female partners because they believe that dominance is their right (i.e., they believe in a patriarchal family structure). On the other hand, men and women may both have the desire to influence their partners, but women may lack the physical resources to use violent means successfully. The desire to control may have nothing to do with gender, sexism, or ideology.

Although some American men believe that they should dominate their wives, it is not clear how many actually achieve this purpose. For example, studies of decision making in the 1950s found that wives were as likely as husbands to make family decisions (see chapter 4). It appears that, in the United States at least, male influence is greater in the public sphere but not in the private sphere.

Violence does not necessarily follow from male dominance or beliefs in male dominance. Some relationships involving dominance produce violence (e.g., parent–child), whereas others do not (e.g., employer–employee). In addition, the evidence reviewed in chapter 5 suggests that traditional men are, if anything, less likely to be violent toward their wives. Perhaps the tendency for sexist men to use violence to establish dominance is offset by chivalry. These men think their wives should obey them, but they do not think men should hit women.

Studies of the relationship between marital violence and gender difference in resources (e.g., education, income, communication skills) yield inconsistent results. Some have found that husbands are more violent when they have more resources than their wives, some have found that they are less violent, and some have found no relationship (see Ronfeldt, Kimerling, & Arias, 1998, for a review). Coleman and Straus (1986) found that both male-dominant families and female-dominant families were more violent than egalitarian families if the couple disagreed about the prevailing power structure. Similarly, dating violence is associated with satisfaction with one's power position rather than perceptions of who has more power (Ronfeldt et al., 1998). These studies suggest that conflicts over decision making, not dominance or male dominance, lead to violence. Another study found that both husbands and wives were more violent in families in which either party made most of the decisions than when decision making was shared (Straus, Gelles,

& Steinmetz, 1980). Apparently, couples fight more if either the husband or wife is selfish or bossy. Finally, a review of 52 case-comparison studies concluded that violent and nonviolent couples did not differ in measures of sex role inequality (Hotaling & Sugarman, 1986).

As indicated in chapter 5, even if a relationship could be established between belief in dominance and violence, it does not necessarily mean that the beliefs caused the violence. Perhaps men who assault their wives for other reasons use the principle of male dominance to justify their actions. People who engage in deviant behavior often develop attitudes that "neutralize" or justify that behavior (Sykes & Matza, 1957). Thus, research shows that young men who engage in violent behavior are more likely to develop attitudes later on that are supportive of violence (Liska, Felson, Chamlin, & Baccaglini, 1984). In addition, the relationship between attitudes and behavior may be spurious. For example, perhaps selfish men tend to commit violence and also tend to express support for self-serving principles. Self-interest would lead them to prefer male dominance because it says they should get their way. Analyses of longitudinal data are needed to sort out the causal relationships between attitudes and behavior.

Perhaps the tendency for men to use violence to control their female partners has nothing to do with their beliefs in male dominance. An alternative explanation focuses on gender differences in coercive power and spousal interdependence rather than sexism. It suggests that men and women are similar in their desire to influence their partners, but men are more likely to have the physical capabilities necessary to use violence successfully against women for this purpose. In other words, it is possible that interdependence between partners promotes a desire to control each other's behavior, but men are more likely to use physical means against their female partners, because they are usually bigger and stronger. This is a less parsimonious explanation for the pattern than the feminist explanation. However, it is more consistent with the unpublished data reviewed early which suggests that women are actually slightly more likely to use nonviolent means to control their partner's behavior.

The evidence on complaining and anger expression also suggests that women are more likely than men to attempt to control the behavior of others (see chapter 2). Complaints and expressions of anger are important methods of control. Women are apparently more likely than men to complain to their spouses about the spouses' behavior. In a study in which couples were videotaped discussing their disagreements, the women complained about and criticized their spouses more often than the men did (Stets & Burke, 1996). As indicated in chapter 2, women may have more to complain about in their marriages. Because men engage in antisocial behavior more often than women, wives may have more grievances—more occasions in which they want to change their spouse's behavior. The stereotype of the nagging wife, like many other stereotypes, has an element of truth. Of course, it is a pejorative label favored by husbands. But it reflects the husband's defense of himself, not sexism. When a man tells his wife to quit nagging him, and she responds that he needs to be nagged, they may both be right.

It is important to avoid attaching value judgments to the control motive, whether attempts at control involve complaining, displaying anger, or violence. Controlling the behavior of others is sometimes legitimate and necessary. In addition, I do not wish imply that women complain too often or that men do not complain often enough. For example, men have been criticized for their reluctance to see a physician when their medical situation warrants it, and women have been criticized for seeking medical attention when it is unnecessary to do so.

Male provocation is only part of the explanation for gender differences in complaining, however. A meta-analysis of a large number of experimental studies suggests that women complain more often than men across a wide variety of situations, not just those produced by their husbands (Kowalski, 1996). In addition, women are more likely to express anger in a nonaggressive way when they have a grievance, according to research reviewed in chapter 2. A display of anger usually involves a complaint about some perceived wrong. The emotion expressed encourages the target to take the complaint seriously.

The evidence on gender differences in complaining and anger casts doubt on the idea that men's violence against their wives reflects a greater desire to control them. Women apparently attempt to control others more than men do. This gender difference may be due to men's stoicism: When a man has a bad experience, others might admonish him to "take it like a man." Being tough sometimes means not complaining. The evidence is more consistent with the notion that men and women differ in the methods they use to control others: Men are likely to use violence, and women are more likely to use peaceful means. The evidence is also consistent with the notion that women play a "civilizing" role in society (e.g., Courtwright, 1996), which suggests that women are more likely than men to serve as informal agents of social control, not just with their children but also with their spouses.

Gender differences in control behavior should not be exaggerated. Both husbands and wives attempt to influence each other. They both use persuasion, and if that fails, either may resort to coercive methods. Because men have a greater proclivity to engage in violence and greater size and strength, they are more likely to use violent forms of coercion to influence their wives to do what they want. Women use minor violence against their spouses as much as men do (see chapter 3), but probably not as often for purposes of interpersonal control. It is difficult to use violence to force compliance when the target is bigger and stronger, unless one has a weapon. Women may attack their husbands for retribution or revenge, but they are likely to use other methods to achieve influence and control.

THE SPECIALIZATION ARGUMENT

To understand whether men who engage in violence against wives are sexist or just violent men, it is useful to examine whether they engage in other types of violence or crime. If men who engage in violence toward their female partners are typically sexists, then one would expect many of them to specialize in violence against women. On the other hand, if they are men with a general proclivity to commit violence or crime and no preference for female victims, one would expect them to be versatile offenders, committing violence or crime when the opportunity arises. Marvell and Moody (1999) reviewed a large number of studies showing that men who engaged in violence against their partners typically had criminal records (see also Ageton, 1983). Moffitt, Krueger, Caspi, and Fagan (2000) found that many, but not all, people who mistreat their partners also engage in general criminal behavior. On the other hand, other research suggests that many men who engage in violence toward their wives do not report violence outside the family (Saunders, 1992; see Holtzworth-Munroe & Stuart, 1994, for a review). Clearly there are men who use violence against their wives (and perhaps their children) but never target anyone outside the family. These specialists may be sexists, but it also possible that they are men who commit more marital violence, or family violence generally, as a result of the high level of conflict and opportunity associated with these relationships (see chapter 3).

If these specialists are sexist men attempting to control their wives, they would be expected to have more sexist attitudes than generally violent men. They do not, according to a study of men reporting for treatment for marital violence. Saunders (1992) determined from self-reports whether these violent husbands were violent outside their families as well. He found that men who specialized in violence toward wives had more liberal attitudes about gender roles than men who were generally violent. This study suggests that to the extent there is specialization in violence against wives, it is not the result of sexism. It is consistent with evidence that traditional men are, if anything, less likely to engage in violence toward women (see chapter 5). Still, there may be some offenders whose sexism plays a causal role in their violence toward their female partners, but too few to produce a statistically significant correlation between attitudes and violence.

CONCLUSION

A central feminist argument is that when men engage in violence toward their female partners, their motive is to control them. Their desire to control their wives stems from their beliefs in male dominance. Johnson modified this approach claiming that only some men—whom he called "patriarchal terrorists"—have this motive. The empirical evidence is limited, but what is available suggests a different picture. As predicted by a feminist approach, men who are violent toward their wives are more likely to issue a threat before they attack than people who commit violence in other circumstances. This pattern suggests that violence against wives is more likely to involve a control motive. However, the following evidence on individual differences suggests that the control motive does not derive from sexism.

- Men who commit violence against their wives tend to commit violence against other people as well, and those who specialize in violence against their wives tend to be less, not more, traditional in their attitudes.
- Although the evidence is mixed, it appears that traditional men are less, not more, likely to engage in violence against their wives.
- Evidence regarding complaining and anger expression suggests that wives engage in more, not less, controlling behavior than husbands.
- Controlling women as well as controlling men are more likely to use violence against their partners. The association between bossiness and violence in marriage is no stronger for men.

8

LOVE TRIANGLES

Both evolutionary psychologists and feminists suggest that male violence stemming from love triangles reflects "sexual proprietariness," or a male desire to control female sexuality. They suggest that when women cheat on their male partners or attempt to leave them, men respond with violence as a method of control. However, the perspectives differ in their identification of the source of the control motive in love triangles. From a feminist perspective, sexism and patriarchy are the source of the desire to control (e.g., Websdale, 1999). From the perspective of evolutionary psychology, on the other hand, male desire for sexual exclusivity and control of female sexuality has an evolutionary basis (D. M. Buss, 2000; M. Daly, Wilson, & Weghorst, 1982; Lips, 1991). This perspective suggests that men are more upset by their partners' infidelity than women because of their concerns for paternity.

For evolutionary psychologists, sexual jealousy is a major factor in male violence and a more important motive for men than for women (M. Daly & Wilson, 1988). In addition, there are gender differences in the source of jealousy: Men are more concerned about their mate's sexual involvement with rivals, whereas women are more concerned about their mate's emotional involvement (D. M. Buss, 2000).

An alternative approach suggested in this chapter is that both men and women are proprietary. Both men and women feel possessive about their intimate partners and respond strongly when their relationships are threatened. In other words, love triangles create conflict between intimate partners and between rivals, regardless of gender, and this conflict sometimes results in violence.

I argue that the motivation for violence in love triangles is similar to the motivation for violence generally. The offended party uses violence to deter his or her partner or rival, to punish injustice, and to protect his or her social identity. However, the relative importance of different motives may depend on gender. Before addressing this issue directly, I discuss research that examines gender differences in the frequency of aggression and gender differences in the extent to which homicide stems from love triangles. These statistical patterns are relevant to a discussion of motive.

GENDER AND FREQUENCY

To analyze minor forms of aggression in love triangles, I collected data from college students. I asked students in an introductory class in sociology ($N = 276$) to remember a situation in which a person with whom they were romantically involved became involved with someone else. Over half the respondents (55.8%) reported that they had experienced such an incident. Women were significantly more likely to have been the offended party than men (63.9% vs. 48.0%). This gender difference could be due to the greater selectivity of women than men in their sexual behavior or to the general tendency of men to engage in more deviant behavior. It should be noted, however, that Feldman and Cauffman (1999) found no gender difference in the frequency in which college students experienced love triangles.

Gender differences in the characteristics of these love triangles and the reactions of respondents to them are presented in Table 8.1. The results show that men were more likely than women to report aggressive behavior in these circumstances; they were more likely to report that they attempted to "get back" at both the partner and rival, although the gender difference in aggression toward the rival was not statistically significant. These results are consistent with those of Feldman and Cauffman (1999), who found that men were more likely to use violence in response to a sexual betrayal. The results appear to support M. Daly and Wilson's (1988) evolutionary argument that men are more likely to engage in aggression in response to jealousy and love triangles. However, men are more likely than women to engage in aggressive behavior generally, so the finding is open to other interpretations, which I explored in a study of homicide and I describe in the next paragraph.

M. Daly and Wilson (1988) used an evolutionary psychological approach to understand the motive for homicide. They suggested that love triangles are a common motive for homicides committed by men and that homicides committed by male offenders are more likely to stem from love triangles than

TABLE 8.1
Gender Differences in Reactions to Love Triangles

Reaction	Men (%)	Women (%)
Had experienced situation	48.0	63.9*
Was very or somewhat angry at partner	69.6	86.7*
Was very or somewhat angry at rival	68.1	64.0
Considered it cheating	78.6	67.1
Placed a lot or some blame on partner	73.2	86.8*
Placed a lot or some blame on rival	67.1	71.1
Placed a lot or some blame on self	23.9	25.0
Was very or somewhat upset over betrayal	70.4	82.9
Partner hid affair	57.1	59.2
Relationship was very or somewhat serious	61.4	60.5
Rival was aware of relationship	71.8	61.8
Rival was a friend	26.8	25.0
Rival was acquaintance	40.8	26.3
Aggressed against partner	47.9	26.7*
Aggressed against rival	27.1	18.7
Intimidated partner	25.7	20.0
Intimidated rival	30.0	14.7*
Was very or somewhat humiliated	49.3	52.0
Was very or somewhat upset over embarrassment	54.9	52.6

Note. *$p < .05$.

homicides committed by female offenders. I examined these issues using homicide data collected in 1988 from a national sample of 33 urban counties. The sample included 2,060 homicide incidents involving a single offender and victim. The data set allows incidents to be coded for up to three motives based on prosecutors' files. The multiple coding addresses Daly and Wilson's concern that the frequency of love triangles is underestimated in homicide data sets because some incidents are coded as arguments or domestic quarrels.

Gender differences in the percentage of homicides that were identified as motivated by either love triangles or jealousy in prosecutors' files are presented in the first two columns of Table 8.2. The percentages are combined in the third column. The results show that these motives are not that common in homicide. They are consistent with Wolfgang (1958), who identified jealousy as the motive in 11.6% of homicides in Philadelphia. In addition, the results show that when women kill someone, they are almost twice as likely as men to be motivated by jealousy and love triangles. Thus, sexual jealousy is actually a more important motive in female violence than in male violence. These results contradict M. Daly and Wilson's (1988) argument that sexual jealousy is a major motivator for male violence and more important than for female violence. The results also contradict the feminist assertion that male homicides reflect a special interest in controlling female sexuality.

TABLE 8.2
Percentage of Homicides by Male and Female Offenders That Involved
Love Triangles or Jealousy

Gender of Offender	Triangle	Jealousy	Triangle or Jealousy	N
Male	2.4	4.2	6.6	1810
Female	4.5	8.1	12.6	246

The importance of love triangles may be exaggerated in this data. First, incidents involving multiple offenders and victims are omitted, and such incidents are less likely to involve love triangles. There were only a few cases in which an offender killed both the lover and rival. Second, incidents that did not result in an arrest because no offender could be identified are not included in the data file. This exclusion is likely to lead to an undersampling of violence involving strangers, because these cases are comparatively difficult to solve, and an oversampling of homicides involving couples, which are relatively easy to solve. This bias could, in turn, lead to an overestimation of the frequency of love triangles, as love triangles are more likely to involve people who know each other.

These results do not imply that women are more likely than men to kill out of jealousy. Men are more likely than women to kill because of jealousy and a host of other reasons—they are simply more likely to commit homicide. Thus, 88% of the total sample of offenders are men. It is necessary to control for the fact that men are more violent by examining love triangles as a proportion of the total number of homicides for each gender. Earlier research findings that jealousy was more likely to motivate men to kill than women did not control for the fact that men are more likely to engage in homicide (M. Daly & Wilson, 1988).

I also examined gender differences in the role of love triangles in a sample restricted to homicides involving heterosexual couples. Incidents in which a spouse, lover, or ex-lover was killed were selected. I identified 192 cases in which a male offender killed his female partner and 115 cases in which a female offender killed her male partner. The percentage of incidents in which the homicide stemmed from jealousy or love triangles was about the same for male and female offenders (19.3% for men vs. 18.3% for women). Thus, love triangles are just as important in motivating women to kill their partners as they are in motivating men to kill their partners. Again, there is no support for the idea that male violence is more likely to be oriented toward the control of a partner's sexuality.

CONTROL MOTIVE

A love triangle, like other deviant behavior, is likely to elicit a social control reaction from the offended party, whom I call the "protagonist." The protagonist may use coercive means to deter future dalliances between the partner and rival. He or she may use physical violence or threats of physical violence to intimidate the partner or rival. The protagonist may even kill the rival or partner to prevent the relationship from continuing. At a less serious level, jealous lovers may express anger at any flirtatious behavior by their partner to discourage more intensive developments (Bringle & Buunk, 1991). The expression of anger can be both a punishment and an implied threat.

The role of the control motive was revealed in the study of love triangles among college students. Respondents were asked whether they attempted to intimidate their partner or rival to prevent the relationship from continuing. Intimidation implies the use or threat of physical violence in order to control the behavior of the target. Men were more than twice as likely as women to use intimidation to deter the rival from continuing the relationship (see Table 8.1). However, no gender difference was observed in the tendency to intimidate partners. The results suggest that men are more likely than women to have a control motive when they use violence in love triangles, but the violence is directed at other men—their rivals—not their female partners.

The choice of victim in homicides stemming from jealousy and love triangles also contradicts the idea that male offenders are attempting to control women. Data on victim choice from the urban counties data set are presented in Table 8.3. They show dramatic differences between men and women in their choice of victims in homicides motivated by heterosexual cases of jealousy and love triangles. Approximately two out of three men killed their rivals, and two out of three women killed their partner. These results suggest that to the extent that male violence in triangles reflects a control motive, it is directed at men. Male offenders were much more likely to kill their male rivals in a love triangle than to kill their female partners.

There have been a few other studies of target choice in homicide but they are based on small samples. A study of 48 cases in Miami found that men were slightly more likely to kill their rival than their partner, but the authors did not perform a statistical test (Wilbanks, 1984). A study of 47 homicides from Detroit found that men were just as likely to kill the partner as they were to kill the rival (M. Daly et al., 1982).

The tendency to attack men rather than women is interesting, given the greater risk of physical retaliation (see chapter 4). One interpretation of the finding is that target choice reflects a reluctance to attack women based on the chivalry norm. It is also possible that male partners and rivals are more likely to react violently when they are challenged by the protagonist and thereby provoke a homicidal response. Alternatively, protagonists may be more likely to anticipate a violent response from a man and to therefore "finish him off," consistent with the evidence that offenders are more likely to kill male victims than female victims during an assault (Felson & Messner, 1996). On the other hand, it seems more likely that protago-

TABLE 8.3
Gender Differences in Choice of Target in Homicides Involving
Jealousy or Love Triangles

	Victim		
Gender of Offender	Lover (%)	Rival (%)	N
Male	34.5	65.5	116
Female	67.7	32.3	31

nists would avoid challenging men in the first place because of the greater risks involved.

It is likely that in some cases the homicide victim was actually the protagonist in the triangle and the offender was either the partner or the rival. M. Daly et al. (1982) reported that a woman (or her kin) killed a jealous man in 11 out of 47 homicides precipitated by the jealous man. Perhaps in some of these cases, the jealous man attacked the woman and the woman killed the man in self-defense. To examine this possibility, in our data we eliminated homicides involving heterosexual couples in which self-defense was identified as a motive (11 male offenders and 1 female offender). The gender patterns were similar when these cases were omitted from the analyses.

Violence is not as likely to be useful as a control tactic with partners, because it might drive them further away. Violence against rivals is more likely to be a successful control tactic. In addition, as indicated in chapter 7, there is a logical problem explaining homicides targeting unfaithful partners in love triangles to dominance or long-term control. Killing unfaithful partners does not maintain dominance in the relationship, because the partners' death terminates the relationship. However, it is possible that the homicide offender intended only to injure and not to kill the victim.

Research on gender differences in stalking behavior also casts doubt on the idea that men are more likely to respond to rejection with control behavior. Stalking tends to occur during the breakup of dating and marital relationships (Frieze & Davis, 2000). Research shows that women are just as likely as men to engage in unwanted pursuit behavior, but male stalkers are more likely to be physically threatening (Langhinrichsen-Rohling et al., 2000; Logan et al., 2000). The pattern points to gender differences in tendencies toward violence, not the desire for control; method differs, not motive.

RETRIBUTIVE JUSTICE

The protagonist's violence may reflect concerns for justice rather than control. Infidelities are usually perceived as transgressions (Lieberman, 1988), and they are likely to lead the offended party to feel angry and aggrieved at the partner. The phrase "she done him wrong" reflects this sentiment. Offended parties may believe that they have been abandoned, deserted, or betrayed. They may terminate the relationship or confront the partner, seeking an explanation or reconciliation (see Feldman & Cauffman, 1999; Roscoe, Cavanaugh, & Kennedy, 1988). On the other hand, the offended party may attempt to punish the partner verbally or physically.

The protagonist may also be angry and aggrieved at the rival. Because people often treat their relationships to loved ones as proprietary, they may blame rivals for the trespass. This possessiveness is reflected in phrases such as "he stole her away" or that "he is taken" or "accounted for." A man with a reputation for being an interloper used to be called a "cad" or a "louse," reflecting the view that his behavior was offensive. More recently, college students call such a person, whether male or female, a "ho"—for whore. On the other hand, the moral culpability of the rival may be ambiguous. The phrase "all is fair in love and war" implies that the rival's behavior is sometimes exonerated. Protagonists may have an equivocal response to rivals if they believe that rivals are morally justified in competing for their partner's affection.

Equity restoration (or redistributive justice) may also help explain a jealous attack on the rival (Nacci & Tedeschi, 1977; Tedeschi & Felson, 1994). If protagonists believe that the partner or rival has benefited at their expense, they may harm either or both of them to create a more just distribution of outcomes, whether they blame them or not. Still, from the theoretical perspective presented in chapter 2, the attribution of blame should be a key issue in explaining aggression toward the rival.

To explore issues of blame and injustice, I analyzed the data on love triangles collected from college students. Table 8.1 reveals that both male and female respondents were more likely to be aggressive toward their partner than toward their rival. Paul, Foss, and Galloway (1993) found similar results, but de Weerth and Kalma (1993) found less supportive evidence when they asked college students how they would react to a hypothetical scenario involving infidelity. However, their use of hypothetical scenarios and the word "abuse" may have affected their results.

The greater tendency to attack partners may reflect the fact that respondents assigned more blame to the partner than the rival. The pattern occurs despite the protagonist's psychological interest in blaming the rival rather than the partner. Protagonists who blame partners must acknowledge that their partner has lost interest in them or that their relationship with the partner is tenuous. Blaming the rival, on the other hand, allows protagonists to delude themselves about their precarious position.

The greater likelihood of attacking partners than rivals may reflect opportunity as well as preference, however. Protagonists may not have an opportunity to attack the rival, if the rival was difficult to identify or locate. In addition, an attack on the rival may require a search, and therefore impulsive attacks are less likely. The partner, on the other hand, is likely to be readily available, and if their relationship continues, the protagonist will have many opportunities to mete out punishment. Infidelities may be forgiven, but they are not likely to be forgotten, and the grievance over the infidelity may be resurrected during conflicts over other matters (Tedeschi & Felson, 1994).

As already indicated, Table 8.1 suggests that men are more likely than women to engage in aggression toward the partner. The table also shows that the gender difference in aggression against partners does not reflect a greater tendency of men to blame or be angry with partners. In fact, female protagonists were significantly more likely than male protagonists to blame their partners and to be angry with them. Feldman and Cauffman (1999) also found that women experienced more anger than men, but the difference was not statistically significant, possibly due to the relatively small sample size. Blumstein and Schwartz (1983) found that women were more likely to indicate that they would be troubled if their partner had sex with someone else. Presumably, the gender difference in aggression in triangles reflects the tendency for men to engage in more aggression generally, whereas the gender difference in anger in triangles reflects the tendency for women to experience more anger generally (see chapter 2).

I also examined some of the protagonists' reasons for assigning blame in love triangles. The results show that in most cases, the respondents perceived the partner as "cheating" and were upset over having been lied to and betrayed; often the partner hid the affair (see Table 8.1). Lies told to avoid detection are additional offenses that may elicit an aggressive response (see Bringle & Buunk, 1991). Results not shown suggest that there is also a relationship between deception, on the one hand, and blame, anger, and aggression, on the other. Respondents whose partners concealed the affair responded more negatively to both the partner and rival.

Table 8.1 shows that respondents usually believed that the rival had initiated the affair. Results not presented show that respondents who believed that their rivals initiated the affair were more likely to attribute blame to them and be angry and aggressive toward them. Presumably, they attributed more personal causality for the affair to more active rivals. There was also a tendency for women to attribute less blame to the partner when the rival initiated the affair. It appears that women attribute less blame to their male partners if they believe that the partners were seduced by female rivals.

Respondents usually believed that the rival was aware of their ongoing relationship with the partner, according to Table 8.1. Women reacted more negatively toward the rival if they thought the rival had been aware of the partner's relationship with the respondent. Women assigned more blame and were more angry at rivals who they believed were aware of the relationship, although this belief did not affect their aggression toward the rival.

IDENTITY CONCERNS

Social identities are likely to be threatened in love triangles. First, the liaison between the partner and rival represents a defeat for the protagonist. The protagonist has been "put down" or "made a fool of" by losing out to the rival. Second, the partner's affair implies rejection or a loss of interest in the protagonist. The protagonist experiences humiliation because he or she has been spurned by the partner. Rejection can produce a loss of face even when there is no rival. Identity concerns are likely to be particularly salient for the protagonist when third parties know about the triangle. The humiliation may be even greater when the protagonist is "the last to know," that is, when, on discovering the affair, the protagonist learns that others have known about it all along.

Identity concerns are likely to affect men and women differently. Men may feel more humiliated than women because they are more concerned about appearing powerless and vulnerable, which is inconsistent with the male social identity. The term "cuckold" reflects the negative identity assigned to the offended male in a love triangle; there is no equivalent term for offended women. To counter the image of weakness, men may be more likely to respond to the loss of face with anger and aggression. Offended men may be particularly likely to attack their male rivals in these identity contests (Katz, 1988; Luckenbill, 1977). Evidence suggests that conflicts between men are particularly likely to involve identity concerns (Felson, 1982).

I examined the effects of the love triangle on the social identities of the college students. About half of the respondents reported feeling at least somewhat humiliated by the experience or at least somewhat upset over "looking bad" (see Table 8.1). They were not as likely to be upset over the loss of face as they were over the betrayal, however.

Evidence presented in the table does not support the notion that men are more concerned about their image than women in love triangles. Women were just as likely as men to feel humiliated and to be upset over a loss of face. (It is possible, however, that men experienced more humiliation than women but were less likely to admit it.) However, there were gender differences in the reaction to a loss of face. Analyses not presented show that men who experienced a loss of face were more likely to be aggressive toward the rival. Female aggression was unaffected by loss of face. This statistical interaction suggests that men's aggressive reactions in love triangles are more likely than female's aggressive reactions to involve concerns for identity. These identity concerns may help explain why men typically kill their rivals in homicides involving love triangles. Identity competition is likely to be particularly intense between two men (see chapter 2).

CONCLUSION

Love triangles are just one of many types of conflict that can lead people to kill each other. Love triangles are more likely to motivate homicides committed by women than homicides committed by men, and they are equally likely to motivate men and women to kill their partners. These results suggest that evolutionary psychologists have exaggerated the importance of love triangles as a motivator of male violence.

The greater propensity of men to engage in aggression, particularly physical violence, was apparent in both the homicide data and the college student data. Men were much more likely than women to commit homicide. Among the college students, men were more likely than women to be aggressive toward their partners and to use intimidation to deter the rival from seeing the partner again. However, the college student data indicated that greater male aggression was not due to greater male anger; in fact, more women than men were angry at their partners.

The greater tendency for female homicide offenders to kill in response to love triangles may be due, in part, to the fact that men are more likely to be unfaithful than women. The greater sexual infidelity of men—apparent in the college student data—offends their partners and sometimes elicits female aggression. The gender difference in sexual behavior is consistent with an evolutionary psychological approach. However, it is also consistent with the fact that men tend to engage in more deviant behavior than women generally.

Strong gender differences were observed in the choice of victim in homicide. When women killed someone in response to a love triangle, it was much more likely to be the partner than the rival. Men, on the other hand, were much more likely than women to kill their rivals. This gender difference may be due to an inhibition against attacking women, but it may also be due to the identity concerns of male protagonists in love triangles. The loss of face experienced by men may lead them to retaliate against their competitors. This explanation is supported by the finding that male college students were more likely to be angry and aggressive toward the rival when their self-image was threatened. Although female protagonists in love triangles were just as likely as men to experience humiliation, they were less likely to respond to their humiliation by attacking the rival.

The results from the college student data also show that grievances and the desire for retribution play an important role in anger and aggressive behavior resulting from love triangles. Protagonists in love triangles are usually angry with the person or persons they hold responsible, and sometimes they seek retribution. Women were more likely than men to feel aggrieved toward their partners, although they were less likely to act on these grievances than men.

A crucial aspect of grievances in love triangles is the protagonist's perception that he or she has been lied to and betrayed. Thus, protagonists attributed more blame, and were more angry and aggressive, when the partner attempted to hide the affair. Attributions of personal causality also played a role in the grievance. The grievance with the rival was greater when the rival initiated the relationship and when the rival knew that the partner was already involved with the respondent. These behaviors made the rival more blameworthy.

I have argued that both male and female protagonists in love triangles are angry because they believe they have been mistreated and humiliated. Their aggression toward partners and rivals reflects their attempts to restore justice, save face, and deter the offensive behavior. For men, the loss of a face is important in their decision to engage in aggression against (and sometimes kill) the rival. The evidence does not support the notion that the control motive is particularly important in explaining why offended men attack their female partners.

In general, aggression (and sometimes violence) is likely when there is interpersonal conflict. Conflict is inevitable when people have illicit liaisons or lose interest and pick new partners. The conflict resulting from divergent romantic and sexual interests can result in aggression and violence, regardless of gender.

III

RAPE AND SEXUAL COERCION

9

COERCIVE VERSUS CONSENSUAL SEX

"Stingy with their genitals" (complaint about women among Mehinaku men of Brazil; Gregor, 1990).

In earlier chapters I suggested that spousal violence stems from social conflict rather than sexism. In this and later chapters I make a similar argument in regard to rape and sexual coercion. I suggest that sexual coercion is based, in large part, on differences in sexuality between men and women and the conflict that results from those differences. Because women tend to be more selective in their sexual activity than men, many situations arise where men want to engage in sexual activity and women do not. Sometimes men use coercion and other means to influence women to comply.

In this chapter I define sexual coercion and describe the situational factors associated with its occurrence. Definition is an important issue in estimating the frequency of sexual coercion and in evaluating the arguments that there is a rape epidemic in this country and that the legal system tolerates the offense. In addition, it is important to consider the events leading up to an incident of sexual coercion because they reveal information about causes and motives. In chapter 10, I present evidence concerning whether sexual coercion is sexually motivated. In chapter 11, I examine the role of sexism, power, and hatred of women as motivating factors in sexual coercion. Finally, in chapter 12, I examine the response of the legal system to charges of sexual assault and the question of whether it treats this offense more leniently than it treats other crimes.

This chapter focuses more on sexual coercion involving people who know each other, because these incidents generate the most disagreement about definition and interpretation. In some instances it is difficult to determine whether the incident involves consensual sex or sexual coercion. In addition, the interaction leading up to these events can be complex. Sexual coercion involving strangers, on the other hand, is more straightforward. The issue of consent is much more easily established, because male offenders usually use overt force and because women rarely engage in consensual sexual activity with strangers.

DEFINITION

Sexual coercion can be defined as the use of contingent threats or bodily force to compel a person to engage in sexual activity. In the case of contingent threats, the source threatens the victim with harm if she does not comply. In the case of bodily force, an offender uses his superior strength to physically force sexual activity on an unwilling victim, or he takes advantage of a person in an incapacitated state.

Threats and bodily force must be intended by the actor for his behavior to be classified as sexual coercion (see chapter 1). The victim's perceptions are useful only insofar as they provide information about the offender's behavior and intent. If a man mistakenly believes a woman is willing and has consented, then he has not engaged in sexual coercion. If one accepts the claims of some convicted rapists that they believed their victims really wanted to engage in sexual relations (Scully & Marolla, 1985), then their behavior is not coercive. However, one must be skeptical of the excuses and justifications offered by criminal offenders. Why would these men use threats, weapons, and bodily force if they truly believed the women were willing participants?

Actors may threaten negative outcomes other than physical harm to force sexual compliance. For example, an employer may threaten to fire an employee if she refuses his advances. A young man may threaten to leave his date stranded or to end their relationship if the woman will not comply. A spouse may threaten to leave a sexless marriage or seek outside companionship. A husband may show anger (not just feel it) or pout when his sexual invitation is refused. A behavior is coercive if it implies a threat of future sanctions or has the intention of harming or punishing the target.

Some of these behaviors we find morally offensive; others we might think are appropriate in certain circumstances. For example, we might approve of the use of a threat to leave a sexless marriage. The definition of sexual coercion, however, should not be based on beliefs about its legitimacy or its legality. People view coercion and other influence techniques as legitimate or legal in some circumstances and not in others. In this chapter, I focus on the use of sexual coercion as a type of social behavior and attempt to ignore legal classifications and avoid moral judgments.

The legal system classifies incidents as attempted or completed rape, sexual assault, or sexual harassment, depending on the outcome of the incident and other factors. Much of the discussion in this and subsequent chapters will be about rape—forced sexual intercourse—because of its centrality in the literature and its seriousness. It is not, however, the most prevalent form of sexual coercion.

COERCIVE VERSUS CONSENSUAL ENCOUNTERS

It is sometimes difficult to determine consent in sexual encounters between people who know each other. Men who use coercion against women they know tend to use bodily force rather than the threat of physical violence (Koss, Dinero, Seibel, & Cox, 1988; Ruback & Ivie, 1988). Because of the limited amount of coercion, the target is likely to feel pressured rather than endangered and often does not consider herself a crime victim (Gilbert, 1991). Another complication is that the coercive behavior often occurs during consensual activity. For example, a study of 81 date rapes found that every incident occurred during intensive consensual sexual activity (Kanin, 1985).

Whether the recipient of an intimate touch perceives it as coercive or not depends in part on whether she sees the behavior as legitimate. The behavior will be labeled differently depending on whether it is performed by someone perceived as having a right to make a sexual bid. The same behavior may be labeled normal lovemaking, an annoyance, or a sexual assault, depending on the context. Further, women are likely to differ in their tolerance of persistence and pressure. When a woman believes a man has pushed too far, she may believe that she is being coerced or assaulted. Because of these subjective factors, it is sometimes difficult to determine whether physical force is involved in a particular sexual encounter.

It is important to distinguish sexual coercion from the noncoercive means that men use to influence unwilling or ambivalent targets. Men generally use these methods with people they know because such means would rarely work with strangers. The methods are similar to the methods used for any form of social influence: persuasion, deception, the exchange or promise of rewards, and various forms of self-presentation (Greer & Buss, 1994). For example, a man may ingratiate himself, or he may devote extra effort to improving his appearance in order to improve his sexual opportunities. He may treat his date to an expensive dinner or promise some future reward. He may attempt to increase the woman's interest by creating a romantic atmosphere or by using foreplay. He may express his love for the woman, whether he feels it or not. He may try to lower her inhibitions by encouraging her to become intoxicated, or he may badger her when she resists his advances. Greer and Buss found that the most effective male tactics for promoting a sexual encounter were investing time and attention and communicating love and commitment to a woman.

Waldner-Haugrud and Magruder (1995) studied sexual influence attempts in dating relationships among 422 heterosexual college students. They compared various techniques used to influence men and women to engage in sexual relations when they would rather not. The most common techniques were "the other person turned me on by touching me although I was uninterested" and "the other person got me drunk or stoned." Other methods included the use of lies, guilt, false promises, restraint, and threat of force. Women were more likely than men to be subjected to many of these forms of coercion: 83% of the women and 73% of the men reported that they had experienced some attempt to influence them to engage in sexual relations when they would rather not. This comparison probably underestimates gender differences because it does not take into account the frequency with which these events occurred for each respondent. Still, when one broadens the concept of coercion, gender differences in victimization diminish dramatically.

The line between voluntary exchange and coercion is sometimes difficult to determine, particularly when there is a power differential between the source and target. For example, a professor who threatens to assign his student a worse grade if she refuses his sexual overture is using coercion. On the other hand, a professor who gives a higher grade to a student in exchange for sexual favors is not engaged in coercion. She benefits if she complies but incurs no cost if she refuses. The quid pro quo situation is similar to the bribery of officials.

A sexual encounter based on mutual attraction is not coercive, even if there is an apparent power differential. A female student may be attracted to a much older male professor because of his high occupational status or power, and he may find her youth and physical attractiveness appealing. One might argue that in this situation young women have more power than the older men because older, higher status men are much more likely to be interested in younger, attractive women than these women are to be interested in older, higher status men. She has referent power—power based on attraction (French & Raven, 1959)—whereas he has reward and coercive power which he may not be willing to use, given costs and moral considerations. In addition, if he has a greater interest in keeping the affair secret, as is often the case, she possesses additional leverage and therefore coercive power.

APPEARANCES ARE DECEIVING

Overt behavior during the event does not necessarily enable one to distinguish coercive from consensual sexual activity. Thus, some incidents may be coercive despite the appearance of consent. An employee has engaged in sexual coercion if he initiates sex with his employee knowing that she will be afraid of repercussions if she turns him down. He may state his desire as a request, but requests are sometimes interpreted as commands in sexual and other encounters. If that is his intended meaning, then his behavior is coercive. Whether the target feels threatened or not is not the defining issue. The legal system might find his behavior actionable if it were to conclude that he should have known, applying the reasonable man standard. However, coercion from a social psychological perspective must involve intent. As always, when attempting to understand human behavior, one must look at the subjective point of view of the actor.

For some incidents, the social interaction appears to be coercive when it is actually consensual. Sometimes women resist when they are actually interested in sexual activity (Muehlenhard & Hollabaugh, 1988). This type of resistance has been called "token resistance": The women say "no" when they mean "yes" or "maybe." Sometimes they resist initially but later either change their mind or comply reluctantly. Muehlenhard and Hollabaugh found that 39% of college women reported that they had said no to sexual intercourse when they meant yes, and 68.5% reported saying no when they meant maybe. G. D. Johnson, Palileo, & Gray, (1992) found that 17% of the college women in their sample indicated that they always said no to sexual activity when they actually meant yes. Two out of three said that, on occasion, they said no when they meant yes.

The college women in Muehlenhard and Hollabaugh's (1988) sample gave a variety of reasons for engaging in token resistance. Ninety percent said that fear of appearing promiscuous was at least somewhat important; 92% cited practical reasons, such as fear of pregnancy or less than ideal surroundings. Approximately 77% cited inhibitions related to moral or religious reasons or not being emotionally ready. Game playing was also an important motivation: Over 75% wanted their partners to be more physically aggressive, to beg, to talk them into it, or to become more sexually aroused by the wait. Sixty-nine percent said they engaged in token resistance out of a desire to be in control of the situation.

This evidence suggests that women engage in token resistance either because they are ambivalent or because they can increase their power and status by not giving in too easily or by "playing hard to get." The greater restrictions on female sexual behavior—the double standard—may also lead women to play a more passive role in sexual encounters. Women may shift responsibility for sexual behavior to their partner by using token resistance.

Some couples pretend that they are involved in a coercive sexual encounter when their behavior is actually consensual. Their behavior is similar to play fighting. The controversial scene in *Gone With the Wind* (Selznick & Fleming, 1939) in which Rhett Butler carries Scarlett O'Hara upstairs to the bedroom, despite her protests, is a well-known fictional example. The frequency of pretend violence is suggested by Muehlenhard and Hollabaugh's finding that three out of four women reported that they had engaged in token resistance to encourage male aggressiveness or pressure. Sadomasochistic behavior is presumably an extreme example of play violence.

Coercive sex is a common theme in sexual fantasies. For example, Loren and Weeks (1986) found that about 39% of college students of both genders reported that they fantasized about forced sexual activity. A review of the literature on sexual fantasies shows that forced sex is one of the most common fantasies and that these fantasies are actually more common among women than men (Baumeister, 2000; Leitenberg & Henning, 1995). The fantasies usually involve men overcoming token resistance, leading to mutual satisfaction. These results do not suggest that women want to be forced to have sex, as researchers in the area have cautioned. They point out the importance of distinguishing mild levels of force from more violent forms of sexual coercion in both fantasy and real life. Thus, Laumann, Gagnon, Michael, and Michaels, (1994) reported that few women or men say that forced sex is sexually appealing—in this context, the respondents are probably thinking of violent forms of sexual coercion, not minor force in response to token resistance.

UNWANTED SEXUAL ACTIVITY

Coercive sex must be distinguished from unwanted sexual activity. People do many things they would rather not, out of obligation, to avoid embarrassment, or as a favor to others. Sexual activity is no exception. Studies that inquire about "unwanted sexual relations" are likely to include both coercive and noncoercive incidents.

Both men and women have reported that they have had sex when that was not their preference. In fact, Muehlenhard and Cook (1988) found that over 90% of men and women reported at least one instance where they engaged in sexual activity when they did not want to. The most common reasons that both men and women gave for engaging in unwanted sexual activity were that they had been enticed, they were engaged in an altruistic act for their partner, they were intoxicated, and they were inexperienced. For men, unwanted sexual activity was less likely to be related to their partner's verbal pressure or physical coercion.

The frequency of unwanted but consensual sexual activity was also revealed in a study of college students in committed dating relationships (O'Sullivan & Allgeier, 1998). Both male and female students kept a diary of their sexual interactions for two weeks. Thirty-eight percent of the students reported an incident of consenting to unwanted sexual activity during the period. The most common motives for engaging in this behavior were to satisfy the partner's needs, to promote intimacy, and to avoid relationship tension. Most participants reported positive outcomes from their unwanted consensual sexual activity.

How women respond to questions about unwanted sexual activity depends on the wording of the question and the context provided, according to unpublished research (L. Martin, personal communication, April, 1992). Women were much more likely to respond in the affirmative to a question about whether they engaged in unwanted sex when the question was placed with items about doing favors for people than when the same question was placed with items about coercion. The placement of the item did not affect men, many of whom had also engaged in unwanted sex.

Women are often ambivalent about whether they want to engage in sexual activity (Muehlenhard & Hollabaugh, 1988). This ambivalence may help explain why female resistance in most cases of unwanted sexual activity is minimal (Murnen, Perot, & Byrne, 1989). The level of coercion in incidents involving ambivalent women is also likely to be minimal.

MENTAL CONDITION OF THE TARGET

Another complicating factor is the target's ability to give consent. Consent may be difficult to determine when the target is underage, emotionally disturbed, or mentally impaired. A sexual encounter between an adult and a minor may be illegal or immoral, but it sometimes involves manipulation, deception, or the promise of reward rather than coercion. Thus, the law distinguishes between forcible and statutory rape. It is important to distinguish between consent from a legal perspective and consent from a behavioral science perspective.

Clearly an unconscious person cannot give consent, and any sexual activity with a person in this condition can be viewed as coercive—a form of bodily force. On the other hand, it is not coercive if the target consents while intoxicated because intoxication, unless at an extreme level, affects judgment, not free choice. For the same reason, the intoxicated offender who forces sex is still engaged in an act of coercion.

It is not always clear, however, when a person is so incapacitated that she cannot make choices, particularly given the fact that there are degrees of incapacitation. In addition, those who engage in antisocial behavior when they are intoxicated have an interest in saying that they did not know what they were doing or that they blacked out. The intoxicated woman may not want to admit she consented to sexual activity, and the intoxicated man may not want to admit he committed rape.

The ambiguity of some instances of sexual coercion is illustrated by a case in which a man confessed after he was accused of rape by a woman he did not know. His lawyer allowed me to listen to a 911 tape that came to his attention after the man was sentenced to a long prison term. In the tape I heard the victim telling the operator that she was being raped at that very moment and that the man was on top of her. Her voice was slurred and a baby was crying in the background. The operator told her that help was on the way. As the tape continued, the victim moaned with sexual pleasure and instructed the offender on how to stimulate her.

If this tape had come out in trial, the man might not have been convicted. She might have been seen as changing her mind during the event and consenting. Yet because he confessed, I suspect that he did intend to rape her and was therefore guilty. Evidently, both the offender and victim were under the influence of alcohol or drugs. He was so disoriented that he did not notice the victim calling 911 during the act, and she was so disoriented that she became involved in consensual sex during the rape.

This incident is unusual, but it illustrates the ambiguous nature of some coercive sexual encounters. Victims may be so intoxicated that it becomes unclear what is coercive and what is consensual. Victims may change their mind during the incident and participate fully once resistance becomes futile. They may also become sexually aroused due to an involuntary biological response. Male victims of sexual assault have reported that they experienced an involuntary sexual response about which they felt guilty, according to a small clinical study (Sarrel & Masters, 1982). Perhaps involuntary arousal contributes to the self-blame that some female victims of sexual assault apparently report. In addition, without arousal, forced intercourse is likely to produce physical pain and injury, so victims have an interest in becoming lubricated. Perhaps some rape victims face a dilemma: They must choose between sexual arousal and physical torture.

SEXUAL SCRIPTS

As indicated above, many incidents of sexual coercion involving people who know each other occur during consensual sexual activity. To understand sexual coercion, it is therefore necessary to consider the norms of consensual sexual interaction. Consensual sexual activity usually follows a sexual script that encompasses certain expectations about the proper sequence of behavior in a sexual interaction (Gagnon, 1977). According to the sexual script, men initiate each level of sexual activity, usually without making any verbal request, and women either comply or resist. The woman often communicates consent with subtle verbal and nonverbal cues (Hickman & Muehlenhard, 1999). Men proceed to higher levels of intimacy according to a prescribed sequence until they meet resistance. The sequence is sometimes described using a baseball analogy: first base, second base, and so on.

The implicit sexual requests men make during these encounters are different from other types of requests. Other types of requests are stated either explicitly or indirectly, with a statement of need inviting the target to make an offer. In sexual encounters, the man proceeds with the activity, assuming that the woman is agreeable unless she resists. On the other hand, sexual requests are sometimes similar to other requests in that compliance is expected. Targets of sexual requests feel obliged to give an excuse or justification, as targets do for other requests, when they refuse the offer. Excuses and justifications are typically given when people engage in unexpected behavior (Scott & Lyman, 1968). If women who refuse sexual requests also give excuses or justifications, it would suggest that they believe compliance is expected.

The pressure to comply with sexual requests may reflect cooperative face work—that is, an attempt to protect the self-images of others in polite social interaction (Goffman, 1955). Politeness requires that individuals avoid behaviors that imply anything negative about the other person. A woman who refuses a sexual offer risks offending the man, because that behavior may be taken as personal rejection. She may comply in order to save his "face" and avoid an embarrassing scene.

Some sexual encounters involve a negotiation where men make an offer and women comply after initial resistance. Men may treat initial resistance as an opening bargaining position rather than as a final offer. This perception is not necessarily inaccurate, as indicated by the evidence that women engage in token resistance (G. D. Johnson et al., 1992; Muehlenhard & Hollabaugh, 1988). Knowing that women sometimes use these strategies, some men may continue sexual activity in the face of resistance.

Men may also continue sexual initiatives in the face of resistance because they believe that the women will become sexually stimulated and change their minds. They may engage in certain intimacies with the thought that women will become interested once aroused (Waldner-Haugrud & Magruder, 1995). This strategy is more likely to be effective when women are ambivalent about whether to engage in sexual relations as they often are (Muehlenhard & Hollabaugh, 1988).

It is interesting to examine sexual scripts in tribal societies for purposes of comparison. For example, the influence of sexual scripts on sexual coercion was apparent among the Gusii of southwestern Kenya (Levine, 1959). Unmarried young men and women from different clans often met at the marketplace. Frequently, young men used their social and musical skills to seduce young women. Gifts and flattery were provided in hopes of influencing the young women to have sexual relations. The young women sometimes behaved provocatively and encouraged young men in the early stages of courtship in order to enjoy their gifts and attention, but they may have had no desire for a sexual relationship. The women often made provocative and hostile sexual comments and attempted to prolong the period of pursuit. The men assumed that the women would resist even if they were interested in intercourse. This sexual script sometimes led to rape and claims of rape, according to the ethnographer.

Marital relations among the Gusii included an institutionalized form of pretend violence. Sexual relations were an aggressive contest in which the men used force and attempted to inflict pain and the women resisted and sometimes attempted to humiliate their husbands (Levine, 1959). On the wedding night, the groom, aided by his clansmen, forced the bride to engage in sexual intercourse. She put him to a severe test and took magical measures to thwart his performance, positioning her body to prevent penetration. Brides took pride in the length of time they were able to deter their husbands. If she failed to resist, she was thought to be promiscuous. In marital relations, wives never initiated sexual intercourse, and they generally engaged in token resistance. According to the ethnographer, the hostile relations in part were a pretense and in part reflected the fact that the husband and wife are from different clans.

Men initiated most sexual interactions among the Mehinaku Indians of Brazil (Gregor, 1990). Men showed a much stronger proclivity than women to engage in sexual activity—they described unwilling women as "stingy with their genitals." The men attempted to encourage women to engage in sexual relations frequently by offering fish in exchange. Although there was a high level of promiscuity in the tribe, the women sometimes refused male overtures. On these occasions, the men sometimes used some level of coercion, described vaguely as "pulling," to force the women into the bush. Women did not view these incidents as traumatic events. These situations are not so different from many sexually coercive incidents on American campuses.

MEN'S SEXUAL EXPECTATIONS

Men are more likely to engage in coercion when they expect women to engage in some type of sexual activity and the women refuse. A man involved in a romantic relationship with a woman may believe that some level of sexual activity is appropriate. If she does not comply, he may attempt to influence her, and sometimes he may use some level of coercion.

A man's expectations may be based on previous sexual activity with the same woman. Perhaps expectations play a role in some incidents of marital rape and incidents involving estranged couples. Men may also develop expectations about more intimate sexual activity during a consensual but less intimate sexual encounter. These expectations may help explain why date rapes occur when women attempt to limit sexual activity (Kanin, 1985).

Expectations may also play a role in sexual coercion that occurs in the early stages of relationships. Because women often do not openly communicate their sexual desires, men develop expectations based on subtle cues or other information. For example, Goodchilds and Zellman (1984) found that men expected a woman to engage in sex if she had a reputation for having had sex with others, if she wore provocative clothing, and if she agreed to go to certain settings. Men also assumed a woman was interested in sex if she talked about sex or commented on her date's appearance. These sexual signals had similar meanings for both genders (see also Muehlenhard, 1988).

If women who are uninterested in sexual activity give sexual signals or engage in sexually provocative behavior, men are more likely to engage in sexual coercion. Evidence for this relationship was found in a study in which college women were asked whether they had ever been sexually aggressive and offended a male companion by their "forward or provocative behavior" (Kanin & Parcell, 1977). Approximately one out of four women answered affirmatively, and those who did were more likely to report having been the target of sexual coercion by men.

Exchange processes may also affect male expectations. Some men expect sexual activity when they have spent a large amount of money on a date or when they have given gifts to women. They may then feel cheated when the women refuse their sexual invitations and use force as a form of debt collection. Similarly, Black (1983) described some robberies between people who knew each other as a form of debt collection.

MISCOMMUNICATION ABOUT FEMALE SEXUAL INTEREST

Some instances of sexual coercion may be due to miscommunication about female sexual interest. Miscommunication is likely to occur in dating situations when men believe that women are interested in consensual sexual activity and they are not. In a study of female college students, over 50% of the acquaintance rapes and more than 20% of the stranger rapes were attributed to miscommunication by the victims (Koss et al., 1988). We must be careful in interpreting these statistics because they are based on incidents identified as rape by the researchers, not the victims, and they include incidents that did not necessarily involve coercion.

Miscommunication may lead women to perceive an event as aggressive and illegitimate when men believe they are involved in a consensual interaction. If a man does not view his own behavior as violent, the usual inhibitions about the use of coercion will not be activated. However, if she continues to resist strongly, it seems likely that he would realize that she is unwilling. A more detailed study of sexual interactions is needed to determine how important misunderstandings are in coercive encounters.

Misunderstandings occur, in part, because women often do not openly communicate about the level of sexual activity they desire. In addition, because women sometimes engage in token resistance, men may not believe that a refusal is sincere (Weis & Borges, 1973). Cooperative face work may contribute to misunderstandings if a woman does not express a firm refusal because she wants to avoid insulting her partner. Cooperative face work generally interferes with open communication in social interaction.

Research also indicates that men overestimate women's interest in sex. This tendency leads men to inaccurately interpret women's friendliness as sexual interest (Abbey, 1982; Muehlenhard, 1988; Shotland & Craig, 1988). Shotland and Craig attributed the gender difference in the perception of sexual intent to the "male's greater sexual appetite, which the male uses as a model for the attribution of the appetites of others" (p. 66). The tendency for men to assume that women have as much interest in a sexual relationship as they do is an example of the false consensus effect, which refers to a general tendency for people to assume that others act similarly and share their opinions (Ross, Greene, & House, 1977). The false consensus effect may also lead men to fail to fully appreciate the aversion of women to sexual coercion. In other words, men may not be as likely as women to view sexual coercion as a serious offense because of their tendency to view sexuality as recreational or body centered (Gagnon & Simon, 1973; I. L. Reiss, 1986; see chapter 10). In addition, they have a psychological interest in believing that women are sexually attracted to them when they are not.

There are at least two studies showing that men who misread female signals are more likely to engage in sexual coercion. In one study, men who engaged in sexual coercion were less able to discriminate friendly from seductive behavior (W. D. Murphy, Coleman, & Haynes, 1986). Another study shows that convicted rapists were more likely than other criminal offenders to have social information processing deficits that led them to misinterpret the cues they received from women (Lipton, McDonel, & McFall, 1987). It is unclear whether these are causal effects—that is, whether the misinterpretation of female signals played a causal role in sexual coercion.

IMPAIRED DECISION MAKING

It is difficult to determine how much offenders "plan" their offense. According to Gottfredson and Hirschi (1990), most criminal behavior is impulsive and involves little planning. However, Amir (1971) found that 71% of the rapes reported to the police were planned, although how much in advance is not clear. Glueck & Glueck (1956) found that 60% were committed on an immediate impulse and involved no planning. One problem is that the concept of planning is ambiguous; it can refer to how far in advance the offender decided to commit the crime and the amount of thinking devoted to how to commit the crime. We do not know how often rapists go out in search of a victim or decide to commit the crime when a situation arises or how calculating they are about method after they have decided to commit the crime.

One assumes that men choose methods, targets, and situations that increase their chances of success, even if these decisions are made impulsively or on the spur of the moment. Apparently, these calculations are often incorrect. In many instances of rape, as well as more mild forms of sexual coercion, the offender is unsuccessful in gaining compliance (Koss, Gidycz, & Wisniewski, 1987; McDermott, 1979). According to the NCVS, about half of attempted rapes are completed (i.e., result in intercourse; Bureau of Justice Statistics, 1997a). Rapes are less likely to be completed than robberies. Offenders fail because victims resist and for a variety of other reasons (Lizotte, 1986).

Men who commit sexual assault are often under the influence of alcohol. According to the NCVS, alcohol plays a much more important role in rape and sexual assault than it does in other violent crime. Rape victims have reported that offenders were under the influence of alcohol in 55.1% of incidents where they had some knowledge about the offender's alcohol consumption. In comparison, 39.3% of assault offenders were perceived to be under the influence of alcohol (Bureau of Justice Statistics, 1995). Surprisingly, some of our recent analysis of data from the NCVS indicates that men who rape strangers are more likely to be intoxicated than men who rape people they know. Perhaps offenders view rapes of strangers as more serious than rapes of people they know and are more likely to require the disinhibiting effect of alcohol to commit the crime.

The victims of sexual coercion are also frequently intoxicated (e.g., Muehlenhard & Linton, 1987; Scully & Marolla, 1984). Their impaired judgment can lead them to make careless decisions that play a causal role in their victimization. In addition, men are likely to perceive intoxicated women as more vulnerable to their influence, which is the reason they sometimes encourage women to drink. Finally, if men perceive women who are intoxicated negatively, their inhibitions about mistreating them are likely to be lower.

Research suggests that arousal from any source affects information processing and restricts one's focus of attention (Tedeschi & Felson, 1994). Sexual arousal, like arousal associated with anger, can interfere with careful judgment and self-control. If men become sexually aroused during consensual sexual activity or during the "negotiation" process, their inhibitions about using force may be lowered. They may give less attention to the feelings of their partner or to the long-range implications of the behavior and thus may fail to consider its costs or its moral implications. During the heat of passion, concerns for morality or the feelings of other people are not as likely to affect decisions. This is not to say that a sexually aroused offender is unable to control himself and is therefore not responsible for his actions.

ESTIMATING FREQUENCY

A good deal of the literature on sexual coercion is concerned with its frequency. Estimates are generally based on surveys in which women are asked about their sexual experiences with men. The researcher then, based on an interpretation of legal statutes, classifies the behaviors reported as rape or sexual assault without regard to how the respondent, herself, labels the event.

One source of statistics on sexual assault is the NCVS. The NCVS relies on extensive questioning to reveal whether the respondent has been the victim of a sexual assault. After asking respondents whether anyone attacked or threatened them, interviewers ask them specifically about "any rape, attempted rape, or other type of sexual attack." To broaden the net, the respondent is also asked about incidents involving people they know and incidents the respondent is not certain are crimes. Interviewers probe specifically for sexual assault using the following comment and question:

> Incidents involving forced or unwanted sexual acts are often difficult to talk about. Other than any incidents already mentioned, have you been forced or coerced to engage in unwanted sexual activity by someone you didn't know before, a casual acquaintance, or someone you know well? (Bureau of Justice Statistics, 1997a, p. 115)

According to the NCVS, one incident of attempted or completed rape occurred for every 270 women in the United States in 1994 (Bureau of Justice Statistics, 1997a). Of those incidents committed by lone offenders, 53% involved acquaintances or friends, 26% involved intimates, 18% involved strangers, and 3% involved other relatives (Bureau of Justice Statistics, 1995). The NCVS suggests that rape is relatively infrequent compared to other crimes against women. Only 8.7% of violence targeted at women involved rape. Because victims are probably less likely to tell interviewers about incidents of rape than about other types of violent crimes, these statistics probably underestimate the relative frequency of rape.

The NCVS reveals that about 6% of rape victims and over 99% of the offenders were male. Thus, when men get raped, it is typically other men who commit the crime. Most of the offenders are homosexual men, not heterosexual men committing hate crimes (Hickson et al., 1994). The NCVS may underestimate the percentage of rapes that involve male victims if men are unwilling to report these victimizations to interviewers. Rapes are humiliating to female victims, but they may be more humiliating to male victims, given male identity concerns and the added stigma associated with homosexuality and playing the passive role in anal sex.

These statistics do not include incidents that occurred in prison or in other institutional settings. Based on an anonymous survey in a midwestern state prison, Struckman-Johnson, Struckman-Johnson, Rucker, Bumby, and Donaldson (1996) found that 22% of men and 7% of women reported that they had been pressured or forced to have sexual contact against their will while they were incarcerated. Although some of the incidents involved persuasion, the majority involved coercion (see also Lockwood, 1980).

In a more recent national survey, respondents were asked about attempted and completed vaginal, anal, and oral sex (Tjaden & Thoennes, 2000). For example, women were asked "if a man or boy ever made you have sex by using force or threatening to harm you or someone close to you. . . ." Almost 15% of women reported that they had been coerced in that way at least once in their lifetime, while 2.8% had been the victim of an attempt to do so. (In contrast, only 0.3% of men reported being raped in their lifetime.) Seventy-six percent of the offenders were intimate partners, and 14% were strangers. No information is reported as to whether the respondents perceived themselves as crime or rape victims in these incidents.

Frequency of rape victimization has also been studied among college students. In the largest and most well known of these studies, respondents were questioned about their sexual experiences since they were 14 years old (Koss et al., 1987). The incidence of sexual coercion is close to its peak at the ages covered by this study, according to the NCVS. Nine percent of college women reported that they had engaged in sexual intercourse "because a man threatened or used some degree of physical force (twisting your arm, holding you down, etc.) to make you." Thirteen percent reported having engaged in an incident of sex play in response to physical force. About 44% of the college women reported that they had "given in to sex play (fondling, kissing, or petting, but not intercourse) when you didn't want to because you were overwhelmed by a man's continual arguments and pressure." These incidents more often involved persuasion than coercion.

Koss et al. (1987) also presented data based on college men's reports of their own sexually coercive behavior. These estimates are much lower than estimates that are based on women's reporting. For example, only 1% reported that they threatened or used some degree of physical force to get a woman to have sexual intercourse since the age of 14, whereas 9% of the women reported that they had been victimized in this way.

There are a number of explanations for the discrepancy. First, the responses may be truthful, and the rates accurate, if relatively few offenders commit multiple offenses. This pattern would lead to low frequencies based on men's self-report and a high frequency of victimization reported by women. Second, men and women may interpret some of the more ambiguous events differently due to miscommunication. He thinks the activity was consensual, and she thinks she was forced. Third, young men may underreport because they are unwilling to admit that they have engaged in these antisocial behaviors. Self-reports are frequently used in research on other types of crime and violence, and there is evidence supporting their validity (see Fagan & Browne, 1994, for a review). However, the stigma attached to male violence against women may lead to underreporting even on an anonymous survey.

Finally, it is possible that women overreport their victimization in sexual behavior surveys. Ambiguous situations are easy to interpret in self-serving ways. Labeling a sexual episode as coercive may also help young women avoid responsibility for behavior that they later regret. In addition, their interpretations of events may be affected by information they acquire from the media or from classrooms that draw attention to date rape. Finally, the victim label confers a special status that brings various social psychological rewards. It leads to sympathy and respect from others and offers a convenient explanation of any personal troubles one might be experiencing (Kanin, 1994). The woman is now identified as a "rape survivor," a label that makes her seem heroic and avoids the connotation of passivity associated with the label of "victim." In Koss et al.'s (1987) study, the cover page of the survey stated that the sponsor was *Ms.* magazine, and perhaps this association had an impact on the findings. The feminist sponsor may have led some women to exaggerate the level of coercion they had experienced or to reinterpret noncoercive incidents as coercive. It may have also have led men to underreport incidents, because they must have realized that their behavior was under scrutiny.

In another study (Sorenson, Stein, Siegel, Golding, & Burnam, 1987), data were obtained from 3,132 residents of Hispanic and non-Hispanic neighborhoods in Los Angeles. Men and women were asked about whether anyone had tried to pressure or force them to have sexual contact. About 17% of the women and 9% of the men reported that they had been pressured or forced to have sex during their lives. Persuasion was the most frequent method used, particularly in attempts to influence men. Women were much more likely to be the target of coercive behaviors such as threatened harm and physical restraint. Unfortunately, the authors did not provide information on the gender of the person who engaged in these behaviors, so it unclear from the data how often women used coercion against men.

Cross-Culture Comparisons

The claim that there is a rape epidemic in the United States implies that U.S. rape rates are higher than in other countries and that rape rates are higher than rates of other types of violence. Evidence from a study based on crime victimization surveys in 16 countries in 1989 does not support the idea that U.S. rape rates are particularly high (van Dijk, Mayhew, & Killias, 1990). The rates were higher for the United States, Canada, and Australia than for the Western European countries. However, the former also experienced higher levels of nonsexual assault. In a more recent survey (Mayhew & van Dijk, 1997), Switzerland, Sweden, and Austria had higher sexual assault rates than the United States.

Lottes and Weinberg (1996) compared rates of sexual coercion and noncoercive influence attempts (pressuring with continual arguments, getting the woman drunk, lying) for female university students in the United States and their counterparts in Sweden. They hypothesized that egalitarian gender roles in Sweden would lead them to have lower rates of sexual coercion. In support of their hypothesis (and in contrast to the evidence from the surveys of the general population), the American women reported higher levels of sexual coercion during their lifetime (28% vs. 15%) and higher rates of noncoercive tactics (69% vs. 41%). However, the researchers also examined noncoercive tactics used against men as well. The results showed that American men were more likely to be the target of noncoercive tactics than Swedish men. In addition, both men and women in the United States were more likely to engage in nonsexual violence against their partners than their Swedish counterparts. The conclusion is that, regardless of gender, violence is more frequent among American students than among Swedish students. In addition, American students engage in more noncoercive influence attempts than Swedish students, regardless of gender. The students in these countries apparently differ in levels of deviance and violence, not just in their levels of violent behavior toward women.

Evaluating the Evidence on Frequency

There are good reasons to be skeptical about estimated rates of rape or sexual coercion. Sexual coercion is difficult to measure, and accurate measurement is particularly important in determining frequency. Although there are clear instances of rape and sexual assault, there are also many ambiguous incidents between people who know each other that are difficult to classify. It is difficult to distinguish coercive from noncoercive incidents when a limited amount of coercion is involved and when targets are intoxicated, ambivalent, and comply reluctantly after initial resistance. The ambiguous meaning for respondents of the word "force" and the biases of both parties regarding who is responsible for what transpired in some of these incidents exacerbate the problem. These ambiguous incidents are common in frequency counts, because minor incidents always occur more frequently than serious incidents. As a result, many of the estimates of the incidence of sexual assault are probably inflated. On the other hand, it is also likely that some victims do not reveal incidents of sexual assault, even when surveys are anonymous. This factor should lead to estimates that are too low.

The ambiguity of some of these incidents is demonstrated by evidence on women's reactions to incidents that appear to meet the legal definition of rape. In Koss et al.'s (1987) study, the women did not view themselves as rape victims in 73% of the incidents the investigators defined as rape. In another study of college students, 88% of the women were not certain that what occurred in these incidents constituted rape (G. D. Johnson et al., 1992). In 42% of the incidents in Koss et al.'s study, the woman had consensual sex at a later time with the person who supposedly raped her. One interpretation is that many of these women were unaware that they had been raped. Gilbert (1991), on the other hand, rejected the idea that the discrepancy between the researcher and the target's perception is due to the target's ignorance. He suggested that "if reasonable people feel confusion rather than outrage, perhaps there is something to be confused about" (p. 60). Future research should elicit more detailed information on the social interaction that occurs during these incidents. We need to know more about the level of force, the level of resistance, and the participants' interpretations of what occurred.

The NCVS revealed much lower rates of rape and sexual assault than the other surveys. I suspect that the discrepancy is related to the fact that respondents perceive the NCVS as a crime victimization survey. Although the NCVS focuses on specific behaviors and encourages respondents to report incidents even when the respondent is uncertain whether they are crimes, it seems likely that some censoring still takes place. Incidents that are not perceived to be crimes by the persons attacked are probably not fully reported to NCVS interviewers. From this perspective, the NCVS underestimates the frequency of rape (see, e.g., Koss, 1992).

The definition of what constitutes rape, however, involves a value judgment. If we restrict the definition of rape to those behaviors that we believe should lead to a prison term, the NCVS might be viewed as an accurate measure. If a woman does not think she has been the victim of a crime, or if she was not so offended by the man's behavior that she discontinued the relationship, then perhaps the man should not be sent to prison. It seems reasonable to consider the victim's perspective in deciding the seriousness of an offense.

Gender differences are not as dramatic for more minor types of victimization. Surveys that cast a broad net and include many relatively minor incidents reveal incidents of persuasion and coercion directed at men as well. I am skeptical that many of the male "victims" in these incidents are traumatized or that legal action is called for. As discussed in chapter 3, a similar phenomenon occurs in estimating the frequency of couple violence: When minor incidents are counted, women appear to be as violent toward their partners as men.

Is there a rape epidemic in the United States? As in earlier chapters, I argue that is it is meaningless to talk about frequency without being explicit about the comparison. Rape rates correlate highly with rates of other violence. The United States has a high rate of violence, so one would expect it to have a high rate of sexual violence. In general, the evidence from the international victimization surveys and the study comparing Swedish and American students suggests that the U.S. sexual assault victimization rate is relatively high. However, these studies also suggest that national differences are related to cross-cultural variation in violence generally, not gender issues. The evidence does not support the idea that there is rape epidemic in this country.

Gilbert (1991) argued that feminist researchers have grossly exaggerated the frequency of rape, creating what he described as a "phantom epidemic." These "advocacy numbers" are useful for those who wish to demonstrate high levels of victimization of women by men for political reasons (see also Gutmann, 1990). This technique is common among "moral entrepreneurs" who attempt to influence the social construction of social problems (e.g., Best, 1995). Advocacy numbers may also be useful in promoting careers, because the work of researchers seems more important if the behavior they study is pervasive.

Frequency of Rape Proclivity

Malamuth (1981) argued that many men have a proclivity to rape and are inhibited only by the anticipated costs. He based this conclusion on a series of studies in which men (mostly college students) were asked to estimate the likelihood they would rape someone if they could be assured of not being caught and punished. Participants responded on a five-point scale ranging from 1 = not at all likely to 5 = very likely. Across his studies, Malamuth and his colleagues found that an average of 35% of college men answered 2 or above, and 20% answered 3 or above. Because a fair number of men did not absolutely rule out the possibility that they could commit this crime, he claimed that the data showed that many men have a proclivity to rape.

A measure based on respondents' estimations of how they would behave under hypothetical conditions must be viewed with great skepticism. Scores on these measures are either uncorrelated or only slightly correlated ($r = .15$) with a self-report measure of sexual aggression (Malamuth & Check, 1981; see also Greendlinger & Byrne, 1987). In addition, there is no attempt to compare the likelihood measure for rape to likelihood measures for other crimes to see if some men have a special proclivity to rape. Finally, it is unclear how participants interpreted the question. L. Martin (personal communication, April, 1992) found that responses to the likelihood measure depend on the context in which it is presented. He was able to replicate Malamuth's (1981) results when he placed the likelihood measure after items concerning sexual activity. When the measure was placed after items focusing on aggression and force, fewer respondents indicated any likelihood of engaging in rape.

The above results may be interpreted as indicating that a fair number of men—perhaps not as many as Malamuth (1981) suggested—are not so mortified by the thought of rape that they would rule it out completely. As indicated earlier, sex with some element of force is not so repugnant to some men and women that they do not fantasize about it. But it would be a mistake to take fantasies or responses to fantasy situations too seriously as evidence about human behavior.

OPPORTUNITIES FOR SEXUAL COERCION

The routine activity approach suggests that crime is more likely when the everyday activities of citizens create opportunities for crime to occur

(Cohen & M. Felson, 1979; M. Felson, 1998). Change in the crime rate over time reflects changes in opportunities for crime rather than changes in attitudes, legal sanctions, or the number of potential offenders. Crime rates are high in societies in which potential victims come into frequent contact with motivated offenders and the level of guardianship is low. The theory emphasizes the importance of the physical environment, supervision and surveillance, and the activities of youths, who contribute heavily to the pool of motivated offenders. Any activity that draws together motivated offenders and suitable targets in the absence of capable guardians increases the likelihood of crime.

The theory suggests that sexual coercion should occur more frequently when there is greater unsupervised contact between young men and women. For example, women who "date around" or who go out drinking more often are considerably more likely to be targets of sexual coercion (Kanin & Parcell, 1977; Lottes & Weinberg, 1996; Schwartz & Pitts, 1995). Rates of sexual coercion on college campuses may be higher because of frequent contact between young men and women in situations involving heavy alcohol use. The access of young adults to automobiles creates opportunities for both consensual and coercive sexual encounters because it enables them to evade parental supervision. Finally, consensual sexual activity creates opportunities for coercion because women sometimes attempt to limit the level of intimacy in locations where help cannot be summoned. In other words, sex play is a routine activity that puts vulnerable victims in contact with highly motivated offenders in the absence of capable guardians.

Activities that draw women outside the home, particularly at night, may put them at risk of stranger rape. Thus, McDermott (1979) found much higher rates of rape victimization among women who spent much of their time outside the home than among women who were homemakers. Amir (1971) found that the street is most frequently the contact point for the rapists and victims he studied and that most rapes occur at night. The risk of victimization by strangers is higher in urban areas in part because of the difficulties of identifying offenders.

According to Levine (1959), spatial segregation of the sexes and lack of opportunities for privacy are important inhibitors of rape in other cultures. Chaperonage, veiled seclusion of women, and separate schooling inhibit both consensual and coercive sexual relations. Levine attributed the increase in rape among the Gusii not only to low penalties but also to increased contact between unmarried people of different clans due to rapid population growth and British pacification. He suggested that when structural barriers preventing contact between men and women are lowered, socialized inhibitions become more important. If both men and women are uninhibited, then promiscuity results. If only women are inhibited, then rape is more likely to occur. He assumed that there are no cultures where women are uninhibited and men are inhibited, when there are apparently a few (Barry & Schlegal, 1984).

In contrast to Levine's assertion, the routine activity approach would predict higher rates of sexual coercion in cultures where both men and women are uninhibited about sex. Even though promiscuity is common when women are uninhibited, promiscuity does not necessarily imply that women are as indiscriminate as men in their sexual relations. Women will still avoid sexual relations with most men, creating an incentive for coercion. In addition, male expectations for sexual activity may be higher in cultures with high levels of promiscuity, which may increase the likelihood of coercion when women are resistant. Finally, and perhaps most important, consensual sexual activity creates opportunities for sexual coercion. The more frequent the involvement in consensual sexual liaisons, the greater the risk of coercive sex, because women sometimes attempt to limit the level of intimacy.

CONCLUSION

Many situations arise in which men want to engage in a particular sexual activity and women do not or are ambivalent. In these situations, men may try to influence women using various methods, some of them manipulative, some of them coercive. Male inhibitions are often low in these circumstances due to sexual arousal and alcohol and other drug use. Misunderstandings and unrealistic expectations are common because of the lack of direct communication. Men sometimes misinterpret women's politeness, miscalculate terms of exchange, and misread sexual signals. It is unknown to what extent these processes affect the likelihood of sexual coercion.

It can be difficult to determine whether incidents are coercive when women comply under pressure, when their mental state is impaired, and when they engage in token resistance or pretend violence. These factors make it difficult to estimate the frequency of rape and other forms of sexual coercion. Still, one can rely on victimization surveys to make comparisons across countries and over time, if one assumes minimal cultural and temporal variation in the interpretation and willingness to respond to survey questions. The research suggests that victimization rates for rape correspond to victimization rates for other violent crimes. Rape rates are not particularly high in the United States, given the high rate of violence, and they change along with other rates of violence. The evidence does not support the idea that there is a rape epidemic in the United States.

10

SEXUAL MOTIVATION

What do men want?

By definition, all acts of violence involve power, domination, and harm. When individuals impose outcomes on other people they are exercising power, and if they are successful, they dominate and harm their antagonists. However, the description of a behavior or its effect on victims does not necessarily identify its goal or motive. The goal refers to the desired outcome—the other outcomes may be incidental.

A completed incident of sexual coercion has three immediate consequences: sexual activity, harm to the victim, and the offender's domination of the victim. The question is, Which one of these outcomes is the goal of the offender, and which outcomes are incidental? For the past 25 years, feminists have asserted that sexual activity is not the goal—that is, that rape and sexual assault are not sexually motivated (e.g., Brownmiller, 1975; Medea & Thompson, 1974; Russell, 1975). The motivation, instead, is the offender's desire for power, fueled by sexism. This idea has become conventional wisdom. More recently, there appears to be some moderation in this stance. Koss et al. (1994), for example, suggested that sexual and aggressive elements somehow interact.

In this chapter I argue that most sexual coercion is sexually motivated. The offender dominates the victim and accepts the victim's suffering as a consequence of his actions, but neither domination nor harm is his goal. I suggest, however, that some men who use sexual coercion have a grievance with the victim and are more interested in harming her rather than in satisfying themselves sexually. In chapter 11, I discuss the role of the power motive and sexism in sexual coercion.

Certainly an offender could have multiple goals for a given offense. In fact, one response of my students to the evidence supporting sexual motivation is to suggest a compromise position on motive—both sex and power motivate the offender. It may be that these motives operate together, but assertions about multiple motives should be based on scientific evidence, not political compromise.

In principle, a single goal is sufficient to explain the offender's motivation in a particular incident. However, for a single offense, there may be secondary gains in addition to the primary goal. For example, when a couple is estranged, the man may feel both aggrieved and sexually deprived. He may use rape primarily to punish his ex-partner and secondarily for sexual satisfaction. On the other hand, sexual satisfaction could be the primary goal and punishment an added incentive.

External costs, attitudes regarding violence, internal inhibitions, and expectations of success are also important in decisions to engage in sexual coercion. If a man is tempted for some reason to commit the act, he may refrain because he fears punishment or because it violates his moral standards. In particular, notions of chivalry might inhibit him from using violence against a woman. On the other hand, if he is intoxicated or sexually aroused, he may not weigh the costs or think about the moral implications, as indicated in the last chapter. Also, a negative attitude toward the target or toward women generally may facilitate his use of violence.

I begin this chapter with a discussion of sex differences in sexual selectivity and evolutionary psychology's argument about its source. Whether this sex difference is due to biological or cultural factors, I suggest that it produces some of the conflict that results in sexual coercion. Then I discuss the logic of the sexual motivation argument and present evidence for it, bringing to bear the literatures on sexual deprivation, sexual aspirations, sexual arousal, preference for coercive versus consensual sex, the use of gratuitous violence, and target attractiveness.

GENDER DIFFERENCES IN SEXUALITY

Women almost never engage in rape. The gender difference in committing rape in part reflects gender differences in committing any type of physical violence. However, although men are approximately eight times more likely to commit violent crime, they are more than 100 times more likely to commit rape. Gender differences in the tendency to use violence can be only part of the explanation.

The gender difference in offending could also be due to bodily differences. Rape offending may be difficult for women because it would require male victims to be aroused. However, male victims can be aroused involuntarily during rape (Groth & Burgess, 1980; Sarrel & Masters, 1982), and they can be forced to engage in noncoital forms of sexual activity. Sex differences in physical strength may also play a role in gender differences in rape offending, but some women are stronger than some men, and weapons would provide potential female offenders with the necessary force. None of these factors can fully explain the fact that rape is almost exclusively a male offense.

There are good reasons to believe that gender differences in sexuality are critical in explaining why women almost never commit rape. Men are more likely than women to be indiscriminate and casual in their attitudes toward sexual relations and more interested in variety (e.g., D. M. Buss, 2000). Women, on the other hand, are more likely to insist on some commitment or closeness before engaging in sexual relations (Simpson & Gangestad, 1991). I. L. Reiss (1986) described male sexuality as body centered and female sexuality as person centered. Similarly, Gagnon and Simon (1973) suggested that men are more likely to view sexual activity as recreation, whereas women are more likely to associate it with romance.

Research on sexual attitudes and behavior reveals dramatic differences between men and women. Eysenck (1976) found that 61% of men and only 4% of women reported that they would take part in a sexual orgy. In an experimental study, 69% of male participants agreed when they were asked by a confederate of the opposite sex to engage in sexual relations; none of the female participants was willing (Clark & Hatfield, 1989). The large gender difference in the tendency to engage in casual sex has also been revealed in a meta-analysis of a large number of studies (Oliver & Hyde, 1993). A recent study of a large sample of identical and fraternal twins in Australia suggested that individual differences in interest in casual sex is at least partly genetic (Bailey et al., 2000).

Gender differences in sexual fantasies also suggest differences in sexuality. Sexual fantasies can reveal desires unfettered by opportunity and inhibition. Reviewing the empirical literature, B. J. Ellis and Symons (1990) concluded that "male sexual fantasies tend to be more ubiquitous, frequent, visual, specifically sexual, promiscuous, and active. Female sexual fantasies tend to be more contextual, emotive, intimate, and passive" (p. 529). In addition, men are much more likely than women to have sexual fetishes (Gregor, 1990). This difference may reflect gender differences in the tendency to disassociate sexual response from interpersonal relationships.

Men also have a stronger sex drive than women, according to an extensive literature. They masturbate more often, think about sex more often, report spontaneous sexual desire more often, desire sex more often, initiate sex more often, refuse it less often, rate their sexual urges as stronger, and are less likely to cite lack of interest and enjoyment as a reason for not having sex (see Baumeister, 2000, for a review).

Although men are less sexually selective and have a greater interest in sex, their opportunities are usually limited. Few women are promiscuous, even though their opportunities for promiscuity are virtually unlimited. In addition, women who are labeled promiscuous are probably still more selective than men. The girls with "bad reputations" in my high school were interested in sexual liaisons only with the popular boys. Because they were not popular themselves, they would not have attracted the interest of these boys if they had not been sexually available.

Even in a permissive sexual atmosphere, access to willing women is limited for most heterosexual men. From the male point of view, the demand exceeds the supply. The lack of opportunity explains why some men employ prostitutes if they have the financial means to do so, and it helps explain why some men use coercion. In addition, although men are not as sexually selective as women, they do have a strong preference for physically attractive women. Because the competition for these women is intense, most men's sexual access to attractive women is particularly limited. On the other hand, a man willing to use coercion has an almost unlimited choice of sexual partners.

Consensual heterosexual behavior reflects a compromise between the sexes. Gagnon and Simon (1973) suggested that young men attempt to socialize women to share their recreational perspective and young women attempt to socialize men to their romantic perspective. In addition, cultural changes since the 1960s have increased women's interest in recreational sex. Without these influences, gender differences in sexuality would be even greater.

Because homosexual liaisons do not require a compromise, they provide a window for viewing male and female sexuality (Symons, 1979). Comparisons reveal dramatic differences between gay men and lesbians in sexual behavior. A study of 151 lesbians and 581 gay men in Germany found that only 1% of the lesbians had engaged in sexual activity with more than 10 partners, but 61% of the gay men had (Schafer, 1977). (The AIDS epidemic has probably reduced this gender difference.) Gender differences in selectivity may also explain why there is a market for homosexual male prostitution but none for lesbian female prostitution.

The heterosexual prostitution market also reflects the substantial gender difference in sexuality. Many men are willing to pay women for sexual activity, but male prostitution serving a female clientele is extremely rare. The size of the gender difference in willingness to pay for sex may approach the size of the gender difference in rape offending. Perhaps no other gender differences in behavior are so strong as gender differences in rape offending and sexual behavior. It seems unlikely that these parallel differences are coincidental.

GENDER CONFLICT

Gender differences in sexuality inevitably lead to conflict between the sexes. Thus, research on conflicts between couples suggests that men are more likely to complain about the unwillingness of women to engage in sexual relations and women are more likely to complain about the sexual aggressiveness of men (D. M. Buss, 1989a). In addition, stress probably increases men's sexual desire but decreases women's desire, thereby exacerbating conflict among couples experiencing marital problems.

If men are less discriminating in choosing sexual partners, if they prefer variety, and if they have a stronger sex drive, then they should be more likely to attempt to influence women to have sex using a variety of tactics. The influence techniques that people use to influence others to have sexual relations were described in chapter 9. The evidence showed that men are much more likely than women to use persuasion and other noncoercive tactics to influence their partners. Perhaps this gender difference reflects gender differences in sexuality, whereas the tendency to engage in force reflects gender differences in violence as well.

Gender differences in sexuality also provide women with a resource that they can use to influence men. Women can exchange sexual activity for money, as in prostitution, or more favorable treatment from dates and husbands. They can advance their careers by engaging in sex with men in positions of authority. They can enjoy at least brief relationships with highly desirable men who otherwise would not be interested in them.

Gender differences in sexuality also allow women to withhold sexual relations as a form of punishment. They can use this resource to control husbands who might otherwise be inclined to mistreat them, for example. On the other hand, when men believe they have been treated unfairly, or when they resent the sexual refusals, they may force sex as a form of punishment. Gender differences in sexuality provide weapons for use in intergender conflicts because they increase the vulnerability of men and women to each other. Men are more vulnerable to sexual rejection, and women are more vulnerable to force. Men can produce much greater harm, of course, but most men are not willing to use this weapon.

Gender differences in power regarding sexual behavior are indicated by a study of long-term marriages (Ard, 1977). Wives indicated that their frequency of sexual activity corresponded to the amount of sex they wanted, whereas husbands reported a significant gap between the frequency they wanted and what they were able to have. One would expect that dissatisfied husbands use various means to influence their wives to engage in sexual relations.

BIOLOGICAL DIFFERENCES

Evolutionary psychology attributes sexual coercion to biological differences between the sexes in sexual behavior (L. Ellis, 1989; Shields & Shields,

1983; Symons, 1979; Thornhill & Palmer, 2000; Thornhill & Thornhill, 1983). In all mammals, it suggests, men and women have evolved different orientations toward the task of reproduction. Because of their evolutionary history, men are less discriminating, more promiscuous, and more assertive in their attempts to copulate than women are. In other words, men's desire for variety and women's desire for commitment have a biological basis. These evolution-based differences result in an inherent conflict between men and women over whether to have indiscriminate sexual relations and help explain why men sometimes use physical coercion to gain compliance.

According to the evolutionary argument, men have a limited investment in each of their offspring because of their ability to produce almost unlimited numbers. Men's uncertainty about parentage also reduces their investment. Women, on the other hand, have a strong investment in each offspring because the number they can physically produce is limited and because they are confident about parentage.

As a result of these differences, men and women have evolved different reproductive strategies. Traits evolved in men that increased their chances of inseminating large numbers of women. Traits evolved in women that led them to be careful in their choice of who will father their offspring. They developed a preference for men who would remain with them and help care for and protect their young. Women could increase the chances that their offspring would survive if they found men willing to make a parental "investment." This investment was particularly important to women in the human species because of the long period of infant dependency.

According to evolutionary psychology, tension between men and women is produced because of the disparity in reproductive interests. The result is a high degree of deception, negotiation, and compromise during courtship. Men use various means, including coercion and feigned commitment, to influence women to have sexual relationships. Women often resist, wanting some form of commitment before engaging in sexual relationships. They do not usually respond sexually until men exhibit evidence of willingness to commit.

The evolutionary psychologists support their argument using the evidence on sex differences in sexual selectivity. They claim that these differences are present in all cultures and that they produce rather than reflect gender roles. They also point to the fact that polygamy (multiple wives) is the most common marital arrangement (84% of cultures), whereas polyandry (multiple husbands) is almost never practiced (Ford & Beach, 1951). Frequency distributions based on compilations of ethnographic data indicate that there is considerable variation in heterosexual behavior in different societies, but it does not directly examine sex differences in sexual selectivity (Broude & Greene, 1976).

Evolutionary psychologists rely heavily on evidence concerning age and rape. They hypothesize that men prefer women at ages when their reproductive potential is highest (Thornhill & Thornhill, 1983). This preference explains why men are more sexually attracted to young women. The association between youth and sexual attractiveness for women is apparently a universal. In all 34 cultures D. M. Buss (1989b) studied, most men showed a preference for younger women (see also Thornhill & Thornhill, 1983).

The evolutionary approach also suggests that rape should be most likely at the ages prior to the usual age of marriage when competition for women is most intense. In support of this prediction, Thornhill and Thornhill (1983) cited *Uniform Crime Reports* data showing that the median age of rape offenders ranges from 20 to 23 and that this variable correlates positively over time with the median age at marriage. However, men are most likely to commit other types of offenses as well at these ages, and marriage inhibits criminal activity generally.

Evolutionary psychology does not indicate exactly what is programmed into the genes to explain sex differences in sexuality or the propensity to rape. It does not specify the relevant traits that are selected and the mechanism through which they affect sexual behavior (see Palmer, 1991). In a recent book, Thornhill and Palmer (2000) suggested that the tendency to rape itself may be represented in men's biological makeup.

It seems unlikely that a tendency to use sexual coercion—a social behavior—is programmed in the genes. It seems more likely that this behavior is a by-product of evolved sex differences in sexuality, and not an adaptation itself (Palmer, 1991; Symons, 1979). For example, perhaps sex differences in the quickness and frequency of sexual arousal have evolved, and that difference leads indirectly to conflict and coercion. Young men are much more likely than young women to report that they often think about sex and that they are more easily aroused (Eysenck, 1976).

It seems likely that evolution plays a role in sex differences in sexual response. It would be surprising if the biological responses of men and women to sexual stimuli were the same, given the difference in the physical appearance of the genitalia. In addition, sex differences in sexual response have very direct implications for reproductive potential. If evolution and biology influence any human behavior, sexual behavior is the most likely candidate.

SEXUAL MOTIVATION IN OFFENDERS

The evidence presented earlier in this chapter suggests that many situations arise—involving strangers, dating couples, or married couples—in which men desire sex and women do not. This ubiquitous conflict is likely to lead men to use various means to influence women to comply. Some sexually motivated men are willing to use threats or bodily force to gain compliance. In fact, given the inclination of young men to use violence, and given young men's strong sexual desire—sometimes approaching the level of obsession—it would be surprising if some young men did not use coercion to obtain sex.

The motive of men who use sexual coercion seems simple enough. If young men force women to have sex, one would assume they desire sex. The same common sense would lead one to attribute financial motivation to robbers. If robbers use violence to get money, one assumes that they want money, and evidence supports this assumption (Wright & Decker, 1997). It seems that the burden of proof should fall on those who claim that some more subtle motive is operating in robbery and rape.

Some of my students who reject the idea of sexual motivation for rape seem to be defining sex, at least implicitly, as intimate consensual behavior. Using this definition, rape is not really sex, and therefore its motivation cannot be sexual. These students do not understand why a man would enjoy forced sex as a sexual experience. In addition, they think that if a man wanted sexual release, he could masturbate, and that if he wanted a sexual partner and lacked access, he could hire a prostitute; a rapist must therefore have some other motive. Finally, these students are inclined to take the victim's perspective, and because the victim experiences domination and degradation, that must have been what the offender wanted.

Perhaps these students are projecting their own view of sexuality onto offenders. To understand the rape offender's (or anyone's) behavior, one must understand his point of view. He prefers sex with a partner to masturbation, but for him sex does not require intimacy. He could hire a prostitute, but a reasonably attractive prostitute is expensive and his financial means are likely to be limited. An attractive house prostitute is likely to cost at least a few hundred dollars, depending on the city and the services she performs. (J. Ackerman, a former police officer, provided this information in 2000 after discussions with police officers from various cities.) Furthermore, her attractiveness is lowered by the stigma attached to prostitution. A man can obtain the services of a streetwalker fairly cheaply, but she is likely to be physically unattractive, drug addicted, and possibly HIV positive. In addition, men who visit prostitutes run a risk of being robbed.

The rapist, on the other hand, can experience a sexual encounter with an attractive, high-status woman with no financial cost. His choice of women is almost unlimited. He can use threats to force her to simulate a consensual encounter and perform any sexual services he desires. Although he risks a long prison term, offenders are usually risk takers. In addition, offenders are often intoxicated and oblivious to the costs. For some offenders, the illegality and risk of the encounter may add to its excitement. Finally, it is clear that some men take great risks in the pursuit of consensual sexual encounters.

Sexual activity has other rewards besides physical pleasure. The motivation for sex—whether coercive or consensual—is at least partly based on nonsexual motives (Gagnon, 1977). Both coercive and consensual sexual activity could ultimately reflect quests for power, status, or self-esteem, for both men and women. For example, a man who has consensual sexual relations with an attractive woman may improve his status. Because sexuality in human beings is a social psychological as well as a biological process, it might be better to describe the goal of sexual coercion as "sociosexual" rather than sexual (Felson & Krohn, 1990). However, consensual sex seems much more likely than coercive sex to provide social psychological rewards. A man is more likely to gain status, feel powerful, and feel good about himself if he can gain the attentions of an attractive woman and satisfy her than if he uses force.

EVIDENCE REGARDING SEXUAL MOTIVATION

Palmer (1988) reviewed and criticized the arguments that have been made against the idea that rape is sexually motivated (see also Hagen, 1979; Shields & Shields, 1983; Symons, 1979; Thornhill & Palmer, 2000; Thornhill & Thornhill, 1983). In general, these arguments are based on spurious reasoning and the misreporting of evidence, in those few instances when any evidence is reported. The facts that force is used, that some rapes are premeditated, that some rapists experience sexual dysfunction, and that the victims are not always young have all been cited as evidence against sexual motivation. As Palmer pointed out, these facts say little or nothing about the motivation for rape.

In regard to sexual dysfunction, Groth and Birnbaum (1979) reported that 16% of the rapists in their sample experienced some degree of erective inadequacy during the incident, usually during the initial stage of the assault. However, one would expect some occurrences of sexual dysfunction because of victim resistance, the offender's alcohol use, and the offender's anxiety while engaging in a criminal act. In addition, it is odd that claims about sexual dysfunction among rapists have been used to argue that rape is power motivated rather than sexually motivated. If men anticipate experiencing sexual dysfunction, it is unlikely that their motive is to demonstrate power. The condition in which males are unable to perform sexually is called impotence—a term that probably describes their self-perception when this occurs as well.

In the discussion that follows, I review the evidence regarding the sexual motivation for sexual coercion. The focus is on factors that increase sexual desire and thereby increase the incentives for a sexually motivated man to use coercion. The factors include sexual deprivation, age, castration, sexual arousal, and the attractiveness of the target person. I also consider whether violence itself is sexually arousing for some offenders. Finally, I discuss how rapists treat victims during the crime for clues about motivation.

Sexual Deprivation

It is generally assumed that sexual deprivation heightens sexual interest. If this is true, and if sexual coercion is sexually motivated, then men who lack legitimate sexual outlets should be more likely to use sexual coercion. However, sexual desire is not likely to be related in any simple way to sexual deprivation. Although desire obviously declines immediately after orgasm, it is not clear how long that decline lasts; is desire greater after a week's hiatus than after a day's? In addition, the link between deprivation and sexual desire is limited by at least four factors: (1) Unlike the hunger drive, sexual desire is not driven by an internal aversive state (Singer & Toates, 1987); (2) external cues are important in stimulating sexual desire; (3) although men prefer to have a sexual partner, sexual desire is at least partially satisfied by masturbation; and (4) individual differences in expectations reduce the relationship between deprivation and desire, because those who have infrequent sexual relations have lower expectations than those who engage in frequent sexual relations.

Contrary to the deprivation hypothesis, Kanin (1967) found a positive relationship between the use of coercion and frequency of sexual experience among college men. Those who engaged in sexual coercion had more sexual experience, not less, than those who did not engage in sexual coercion (see also Lalumiere, Chalmers, Quinsey, & Seto, 1996). The coercive men also used noncoercive techniques more frequently than other men to obtain sexual relations. Together, these results suggest that men who engage in more effort to obtain sexual experiences are sometimes successful, and this leads to lower levels of deprivation. However, the longitudinal data that would be needed to evaluate a possible reciprocal relationship between sexual deprivation and sexual coercion are not presently available. As a result, it is unclear whether sexual deprivation leads to greater use of coercion.

Research has examined the relationship between sexual deprivation and physical coercion indirectly by examining the marital status of rapists. It was assumed that single men engage in sexual relations less frequently than married men and therefore experience more deprivation. The evidence shows that rapists are more likely than the general population to be single, but their marital status is similar to that of other criminal offenders (Alder, 1984; Amir, 1971).

I do not view evidence on marital status as informative about the motivation for sexual coercion. First, married men sometimes engage in sexually motivated behavior not involving their wives (e.g., masturbation, viewing pornography, extramarital affairs). As Symons (1979) suggested, "Most patrons of prostitutes, adult bookstores, and adult movie theaters are married men, but this is not considered evidence for lack of sexual motivation" (p. 279). Second, because many women are reluctant to have relationships with married men, married men may have less access to consensual relationships than single men do. Finally, whether married or not, men are often interested in variety (D. M. Buss, 1999).

If rape is related to sexual deprivation, then legalized prostitution may lower the incidence of rape, because it provides an alternative sexual outlet for men. In a longitudinal study, Barber (1969) found that rates of rape and attempted rape increased substantially following the closure of brothels in Australia. The increase was three times the rate increase for other violent crimes.

One location where heterosexual sexual access is either forbidden or severely restricted is in prison. Because many inmates are young and at the peak of their sexual interest, it is not surprising that homosexual relations occur among the heterosexual population. The use of sexual coercion in part reflects the fact that incarcerated men tend to be violent people. It may also reflect the reluctance of many heterosexual men to take the passive role in homosexual sex. A conflict results because many inmates are willing to play the active role and relatively few willing to play the passive role. Powerful inmates who seek sexual satisfaction are likely to force weaker inmates to play this role. This conflict is similar in some respects to the situation outside prison where there is a surplus of men and a scarcity of women interested in casual sex. Coercion is likely to be frequent in circumstances where demand exceeds supply.

Sexual deprivation apparently played a role in sexual coercion among the Gusii of southwestern Kenya (Levine, 1959). The sexuality of young men was limited by rules against sex within their own clan. Adultery and mastur-bation were forbidden, and bestiality was permitted only for the very young. Because of these restrictions, young men turned to unmarried women in other clans. Gusii men who did not have the economic means, the attractiveness, or the social skill to acquire a wife sometimes abducted women from another clan. Further, the ethnographers claimed that inflation in the brideprice (the number of cattle transferred from the father of the groom to the father of the bride) may have resulted in an increase in the incidence of rape. An increase in the cost of noncoercive means of obtaining a sexual partner apparently resulted in an increase in the use of coercion.

Sexual Aspirations

A better test of the role of sexual motivation in sexual coercion is to examine the effects of "sexual aspirations," or subjective sexual deprivation. Kanin (1965, 1967) found that sexual aspirations were positively correlated with the use of sexual coercion among college men. College men who were dissatisfied with the frequency of their sexual activity were more likely to engage in both coercive and noncoercive sexual behavior than those who were satisfied. Also, men who indicated that they needed a high frequency of orgasms during a week to be sexually satisfied were more likely to use coer-cion than those who required fewer orgasms. They also used noncoercive techniques more frequently than men with lower sexual aspirations.

More recently, a Canadian study of college students found that sexually coercive men expressed a greater preference for partner variety and casual sex than men who were sexually experienced but did not use coercion (Lalumiere et al., 1996). In addition, rapists who had been married reported a higher frequency of marital intercourse and extramarital affairs than nonoffending married men (Gebhard, Gagnon, Pomeroy, & Christenson, 1965; M. J. Goldstein, 1973; Le Maire, 1956). The only negative evidence comes from a study of Chinese students in Hong Kong, which did not find a relationship between desired frequency of orgasm and sexual coercion (Tang, Critelli, & Porter, 1993).

Kanin (1967) found that young men who engaged in sexual coercion devoted considerable effort to finding women who would engage in voluntary sexual relations and to influencing them to do so. For example, high school and college-aged men who used sexual coercion were much more likely to initiate "necking" and "petting" during the course of dating than noncoercive males. Their efforts were to some extent successful. As indicated above, those who used sexual coercion were likely to have more sexual experience, presumably because they engaged in more effort to obtain partners.

Social pressures apparently affect sexual aspirations among young men. Thus, Kanin (1967) found that the use of coercive sexual behavior was related to peer group pressure to have sexual experience. College men who were pressured by friends to find new sexual experience were more likely to use coercion than men who were not pressured. The men who used sexual coercion were also more likely to indicate that an admission of virginity would involve a loss of status with their friends.

One should not exaggerate the impact of the peer group on young men's sexual aspirations or sexual coercion, however. Evidence as to whether fraternity members have higher rates of sexual coercion than other college men is mixed at best (see Belknap, 2001, for a review). Baumeister (2000) reviewed evidence showing that the peer group has a stronger influence on women's sexual behavior than it does on men's. The privacy of most sexual activity may also limit the influence of peers. Finally, young men who are willing to use sexual coercion may choose friends with similar proclivities. Research shows that, in general, delinquents tend to choose delinquent peers as friends (e.g., Matsueda, 1988).

Research on the effect of castration on sexual coercion permits an examination of the effect of indirectly lowering sexual aspirations. Castration decreases the sexual interest of at least some adult men who have the operation (Ford & Beach, 1951). Evidence suggests that castration has a dramatic effect on the likelihood that sexual offenders continue to engage in sexual offenses. One study in Denmark showed that 15.6% of castrated sexual offenders, including rapists, continued these offenses, compared to 80.2% of offenders who were not castrated (Sturup, 1960). Castration may also have a slight effect on the commission of nonsexual offenses.

Sexual Arousal and Date Rape

Sexual desire is likely to vary across situations as well as individuals. If sexual coercion is sexually motivated, then sexual arousal should increase the likelihood that men use force in a sexual encounter. Evidence comes from a study of 71 college students who had committed rape (Kanin, 1985, discussed in chapter 9). In every instance, the rape occurred during an intensive consensual sexual encounter. Most of the incidents involved oral–genital sex, an activity more likely to produce high levels of sexual arousal than a desire for power. If date rape occurs in these circumstances, it suggests that a sexual goal is involved.

Men who rape in these circumstances are apparently interested in intercourse, whereas the women are interested in more limited sexual activity. Thus, Kanin's (1985) study suggests that date rapes typically involve a conflict over the level of intimacy rather than over whether to engage in sexual relations. As indicated in the last chapter, the incidence of date rape is likely to be high in social circumstances involving sexual freedom than when women have inhibitions about sexual intercourse. These inhibitions may be related to women's fear of pregnancy or disease or to special romantic meanings that women attach to intercourse.

In response to these data, some of my students have suggested that the motives for date rape and stranger rape are different. They acknowledge that men who rape someone they know are sexually motivated, but they assert that men who rape strangers are motivated by power. The students are unable to explain why they think the motives should be different. Perhaps they are interpreting stranger rape in terms of what they have learned in their classes—that rape is motivated by power. On the other hand, their interpretation of date rape is based on their personal experience of either pressure or mild forms of coercion by men they know. They are quite familiar with the strong sexual interests (and the arousal) of men they encounter in these situations and therefore are much more willing to entertain the possibility that these men are sexually motivated.

One could argue that acquaintance rape is more likely than stranger rape to involve sexual motivation because the men who rape acquaintances are much more likely to be sexually aroused beforehand. On the other hand, studies show that men who rape intimates and others they know well are more likely than men who rape strangers to injure the victim (e.g., Felson & Krohn, 1990), which implies that they are less likely to be sexually motivated (this issue will be addressed later in this chapter).

Further evidence of sexual motivation comes from an experimental study in which college student men were presented a scenario of a sexual encounter and asked how likely they would be to coax the woman to remove her clothes or to have sex with him even if she protested (Loewenstein, Nagin, & Paternoster, 1997). Participants who responded while being aroused through exposure to pictures from *Playboy* magazine reported a greater likelihood that they would use pressure or force than participants who viewed pictures without a sexual theme. Participants who had viewed the nude pictures the day before did not respond more aggressively, suggesting that the effect was due to sexual arousal, not to demand cues or to some message implied by the pictures. However, a nonsignificant manipulation check raised some question about whether arousal was successfully manipulated. In addition, the study is limited in that it used hypothetical scenarios and intentions, not actual behavior.

A sexually motivated offender is not overcome by passion or lust, although he may use that as an excuse. Sexual coercion, like other forms of coercion, involves decision making. However, as indicated in chapter 9, the decisions made under the influence of sexual arousal, like decisions made under the influence of alcohol, drugs, or anger, are often careless and impulsive. The offender's increased desire and his attention to that desire may distract him from considerations of morality and future costs. Sexual arousal reduces self-control, but it does not eliminate it.

Do Offenders Prefer Coercive to Consensual Sex?

Sexually motivated offenders should not have a special attraction or preference for coercive tactics. Rather, one would expect them to use a variety of means to achieve their sexual goal, at least when they know the target and therefore have reason to believe that these methods might be successful. An individual's use of multiple means to produce the same outcome is evidence that the outcome is that person's goal (Heider, 1958). In addition, when sexually motivated men use coercion with people they know, they should use it as a last resort, after other methods of influence have failed.

Kanin (1967) found that young men who used sexual coercion were more likely than noncoercive young men to use various methods to encourage young women to engage in sexual relations. For example, they were more likely to falsely profess their love for a woman and attempt to influence her to become intoxicated. Similarly, in male prisons, Lockwood (1980) found evidence that inmates tried noncoercive as well as coercive means to influence other inmates to engage in sexual activity. These results suggest that men who use sexual coercion have no special attraction for coercive sex because they use other means first.

Perhaps for some men physical violence itself is sexually arousing. Coercion may provide added excitement for these sexually motivated offenders. This issue is examined in laboratory studies in which penile tumescence is measured after subjects are shown films of either violent or consensual sex. The evidence shows that rapists are equally aroused by depictions of rape and depictions of consensual sexual acts (e.g., Abel, Barlow, Blanchard, & Guild, 1977; Quinsey, Chaplin, & Varney, 1981; see Nagayama Hall, Shondrick, &

Hirshman, 1993, for a meta-analysis). In other words, they show no preference for violent sex. Rapists do respond differently from control groups of nonrapists; the latter are less aroused by depictions of rape than by depictions of consensual sex. Further, when inhibitions are experimentally lowered—by blaming the victim, for example—the arousal levels of nonrapists to depictions of violent sex increases (e.g., Sundberg, Barbaree, & Marshall, 1991). These results indicate that rapists differ from other men in terms of their inhibitions regarding rape or violence, not in their preference for sexual violence (Marshall & Barbaree, 1984).

It is possible that rapists are more aroused than nonrapists by engaging in violent sex but not by watching it. Furthermore, if a small percentage of rapists were aroused by violence, it would not necessarily be revealed in the arousal studies, because they are based on relatively small samples. The evidence on sexual fantasies (see chapter 9) suggests that mild forms of coercive sex are arousing for some men (and women). Groth, Burgess, and Holmstrom, (1977) claimed on the basis of interviews with convicted rapists and victims that 4% to 6% of rapists are aroused by violence. Apparently only a small percentage of men who use sexual coercion derive sexual pleasure from the coercive aspect of these encounters; even these offenders are sexually motivated.

Are the Offender's Violence and Aggression Tactical?

In examining the goals of sexual coercion, it is useful to distinguish between the tactical use of force and gratuitous aggression during the incident. The tactical use of force—or coercion oriented toward immediate compliance—is involved in all incidents of sexual coercion. The offender uses contingent threats or bodily force, and if the victim complies no further force is necessary.

One would expect men whose goal is sexual compliance to use only tactical force. They would not physically attack or mistreat the victim unless it was useful to achieving compliance. On the other hand, if offenders harm victims during incidents of sexual coercion for reasons that are not tactical (i.e., if their violence is gratuitous), then it suggests that they value harm, not compliance.

An offender might physically attack (as oppose to "merely" threaten) the victim during the crime for a number of tactical reasons. The offender may attack the victim who resists, or he may engage in a preemptive attack to increase the credibility of his threat; these patterns are observed in robbery (Luckenbill, 1980). He may use a physical attack to frighten the victim and deter her from reporting the crime to the police. In some instances, offenders kill victims to prevent them from testifying in criminal proceedings (Felson & Messner, 1996).

Rape offenders may have a tactical reason for limiting the level of violence and threat they use as well. The rapist cannot injure the victim so much that she is incapable of complying with his commands. In robbery, offenders who require compliant actions by a victim—to open a safe, example—also limit their use of force (Luckenbill, 1980). In addition, the rapist, like the robber, must not frighten the victim so much that she freezes or panics and cannot comply with his commands.

Rape has some different tactical requirements than robbery, however, that could result in more violence. A rape requires more time, closer proximity, and greater bodily exposure than a robbery. These factors increase the rapist's vulnerability to identification and the intervention of third parties. In addition, victims are more likely to resist in rape than in robbery (Bureau of Justice Statistics, 1997a), probably because they view the costs as much greater. In addition, rape requires compliance from the victim for a series of acts, whereas robbery takes little time and a single act of compliance. Thus, rape victims sometimes report that offenders use violence to force them to take a more active role during the sex act (MacDonald, 1971). Koss, Dinero, Seibel, and Cox (1988) found that over 70% of rape victims reported that they resisted the rape by "turning cold" during the incident; rapists may try to counter this strategy with a threat or a physical attack.

In general, the evidence indicates that violence is used sparingly in incidents of sexual coercion (Amir, 1971). Ageton (1983) found that only a small proportion of adolescents used much physical force during incidents of sexual coercion. Studies of the National Crime Victimization Survey also indicate that rapes produce relatively few serious physical injuries (Bureau of Justice Statistics, 1997a). Finally, sexual coercion among college students rarely involves a physical attack (Koss, Gidycz, & Wisniewski, 1987).

A sexually motivated offender should not mistreat the victim in any way except to influence the victim's compliance. However, his behavior and language must be aggressive enough to maintain the credibility of his threat. On the other hand, if he engages in gratuitous insults or acts of humiliation or keeps the victim in captivity without a tactical reason, it suggests he has other motives. No one has ever systematically examined how men who engage in sexual coercion behave toward compliant victims. Holmstrom and Burgess (1979) reported 20 instances of "obscene names or racial epithets" and instances of "sexual put-downs" in a study of 115 victims of rape but did not obtain information on whether these were reactions to the victim's resistance. In 19 instances, the offender apologized to the victim, socialized with her, or attempted to help her after the crime was completed. MacDonald (1971) also reported incidents in which rape offenders engaged in acts of tenderness normally associated with consensual sex. In 91% of the rapes studied by Amir (1971), offenders let the victim go immediately after the rape; in the remaining cases, victims were usually held captive for tactical reasons.

In sum, it is difficult to distinguish tactical from gratuitous aggression and violence during rape. Behavior that might appear gratuitous might be tactical if it is designed to force full participation, increase the credibility of a threat, or deter resistance or reporting to the police. Still, the low level of force and injury in rape incidents is consistent with the idea that most offenders value compliance, not harm.

Target Attractiveness

If sexual coercion is sexually motivated, then physically attractive women should be at greater risk of victimization. This hypothesis assumes that men have preferences for attractive women, even though they are much more indiscriminate in their sexual choices than women. The relationship between attractiveness and the likelihood of being the victim of sexual coercion has never been directly examined. However, the effect of physical attractiveness has been examined indirectly in research on the age of victims. Men perceive younger women as more sexually desirable than older women, which explains why most female models, movie stars, and prostitutes are young women. The preference is strong and apparently exists in every culture (Buss, 1989b).

If sexual coercion is sexually motivated, then the victims should tend to be young women. In other words, rapists should prefer young women for forced sex for the same reason that men prefer young women as prostitutes and as models in pornography. Research confirms that young women are much more likely to be rape victims than older women. A comparison with other forms of victimization is useful because young people are at greater risk of crime generally. According to the NCVS, only 1.5% of rape victims were 50 years old or older, compared to 8.2% of robbery victims (Bureau of Justice Statistics, 1997a). Victims of rape also tend to be younger than female victims of homicide, aggravated assault, and property crimes (Ennis, 1967; Thornhill & Thornhill, 1983). The same pattern is apparent in the rape of male victims (Felson & Krohn, 1990), reflecting the strong sexual preference for young men displayed by gay men (Bell & Weinberg, 1978). The pattern occurs in spite of the fact that older men and women are weaker and more vulnerable than younger adult targets.

It is possible that victims of rape tend to be young because of the routine activity patterns associated with age (Cohen & M. Felson, 1979). Young women may be at greater risk because they are more likely to go out at night or to date young men (Ploughman & Stensrud, 1986). The comparison between rape and robbery victimization addresses the opportunity factor to some extent. Felson and Krohn (1990) examined the issue more directly by comparing crimes of robbery with crimes in which rape is committed in conjunction with robbery. During the robbery of women, the offender sometimes has the opportunity to rape her as well. Studying robbery victims holds opportunity to rape constant and allows a purer test of the hypothesis that rapists prefer younger women. The evidence shows that during a robbery involving a male offender and a female victim, a rape was more likely to occur if the victim was young. The average age of female robbery victims is 35, whereas the average age of female robbery–rape victims is under 28. This difference indicates that rapists have a preference for young women and that they prefer physically attractive victims.

Rapists have reported in interviews that attractiveness was an important factor in their selection of victims (Ageton, 1983; Queen's Bench Foundation, 1976). Chappell and James (1976) found that rapists preferred victims who were nice, friendly, young, pretty, and middle-class. On the other hand, Scully and Marolla (1985) found that some rapists preferred somewhat older women because they believed that they would be more sexually experienced.

Perhaps attacking a young woman gives the rapist a greater feeling of power or status than victimizing an older woman. Certainly, an older man gains status (and perhaps feels more powerful) if he has a consensual relationship with a younger woman. However, his status is likely to be enhanced because an attractive woman finds him desirable, which is not the case when the sexual relationship is coerced. Men might even lower their status if it appears that they must use force to gain a sexual partner. In addition, the power explanation cannot easily explain men's preference for young female models in pornography. They view these young women for the private act of masturbation, not for the enhancement of their social power or status.

Additional evidence for sexual motivation comes from a study of sexual coercion in a male prison (Lockwood, 1980). Lockwood found that most victims of prison rapes were young, slim, white males. Interviews with inmates suggested that men who were young and slim were preferred because they were viewed as more attractive and as more closely resembling women. Coercion was also more likely to be successful and less costly against these weaker targets. The inmates reported that white targets were more vulnerable, in part because they lacked the support that inmates from other groups enjoyed from fellow inmates who had lived in their neighborhoods. Weakness and vulnerability might also explain the preference for slim men who resembled women, but it cannot explain the age preference.

RETRIBUTION AND NONTACTICAL VIOLENCE

Sexual coercion, like other types of violence, can be used for retribution. A man who has a real or imagined grievance with a woman may force her to engage in sexual behavior as a form of punishment. A man with a justice motive values harm, not compliance. Perhaps his grievance is related to their sexual relationship. He may feel aggrieved if she has ended their relationship or if she resists his sexual advances. Just as some robberies involve debt collection (Black, 1983), some rapes might involve sexual entitlement. On the other hand, perhaps the grievance can be about anything.

To test the personal grievance explanation, it would be useful to determine whether men who commit acts of sexual coercion feel aggrieved toward the victim prior to the act. Men who engage in sexual coercion for retribution are likely to have been involved in a conflict with the victim beforehand. The social interaction is likely to be similar to homicides and assaults where verbal conflict escalates, culminating in physical and sexual attacks. No one, to my knowledge, has studied these issues.

The retribution motive is also indicated if the level of violence during the incident is greater than is necessary to gain compliance. If gratuitous, nontactical violence reflects grievance expression, then it should be more frequent during incidents of sexual coercion among estranged couples and others who know each other. A number of studies provide support for this hypothesis (e.g., Koss et al., 1988). Felson and Krohn (1990) found that victims were more likely to be physically injured in rapes committed by male partners. In most of these rapes, the husband and wife were separated (Finkelhor & Yllö, 1985). Presumably, the offender rapes and beats up his ex-wife or ex-girlfriend as an act of retribution.

Nontactical violence during the incident does not necessarily indicate an absence of sexual motivation. Sexually motivated offenders may become angry at the victim during the incident and engage in additional attacks. When rapists were asked how a victim made them angry, the most frequent responses were negative references to their masculinity (15%), threats to call the police (8%), threatened physical harm (6%), and sympathetic talking (5%) (Chappell & James, 1976).

Rapes involving older offenders are more likely to involve gratuitous violence (Felson & Krohn, 1990). The positive association between age and violence is striking, given that youths tend to be much more likely to use violence in other contexts (Gottfredson & Hirschi, 1990). A plausible explanation is that grievances are more likely to play a role in rapes committed by older offenders, whereas a sexual goal is more likely in rapes committed by younger offenders. Thus, incidents involving younger offenders with presumably greater sexual interests are less likely to involve less gratuitous violence. Another explanation is that a man committing rape at an older age is more likely to be a hardened criminal than a man who commits rape at a younger age.

One would expect offenders with sexual goals to choose younger victims because of the association between youth and attractiveness. Thus, the level of gratuitous violence should be higher against older victims than younger victims. In support of this line of reasoning, Felson and Krohn (1990) found that older victims were more likely to be physically injured during the rape than younger victims.

It is possible that men who use sexual coercion have grievances against a woman other than the target and that the incident is an instance of displacement. A rapist could be angry with his mother, his wife, or his girlfriend and displace his attack onto another woman. He displaces his aggression rather than attack the source of his grievance because he anticipates that an attack on the person he knows will be costly. Scully and Marolla (1985) reported that some of the rapists they interviewed attributed their attack against a stranger to their anger with a girlfriend (see also Groth & Birnbaum, 1979; Scully, 1990). It is difficult to evaluate this type of evidence because we do not know how frequently convicted rapists give this explanation. In addition, the accounts given by convicted offenders must be viewed with some skepticism.

CONCLUSION

It is not easy to establish the motive for violence or any other behavior. One can rely on offenders' explanations of their actions or their descriptions of their thoughts before and during the crime. One can examine the attitudes and behavior of men who engage in sexual coercion and compare them to the attitudes and behavior of men who do not. One can look at the types of situations that result in sexual coercion, at the choice of victim, or at how the offender treats the victim during the crime.

There is considerable evidence from these sources that sexual motivation is important in sexual coercion. Offenders have high sexual aspirations and almost always choose young women. Most of their violence during these events is tactical, not gratuitous. Offenders who know the victim typically use sexual coercion as a last resort after noncoercive techniques have failed. Some persist when the women resist them because they believe that the women are ambivalent or engaged in token resistance. Date rapes almost always occur when men become sexually aroused during consensual sexual activity.

Young men have sex on their minds, not the domination of women. It is safe to assume that on a Saturday night they aspire to find a sexual partner, not a woman to boss around. Their interest in attractive women is almost unlimited, whereas their opportunities for consensual sexual encounters with these women are extremely limited. Hence, it is not surprising that some unscrupulous men use violence to get their way.

11

SEXISM AND SEXUAL COERCION

Selfish or sexist

In this chapter I examine the whether male prejudice or desire for power and control lead them to engage in sexual coercion. I explore three arguments in regard to the motive of offenders: (1) Men use sexual coercion to make themselves appear powerful; (2) men use sexual coercion against women to control them; and (3) sexual coercion reflects certain sexist attitudes, including hatred of women, traditional attitudes about gender roles, or belief in rape myths. I conclude the chapter with a discussion of whether pornography influences these attitudes and behaviors.

DEMONSTRATING POWER

The idea that men use sexual coercion because it gives them a feeling or image of power is widely asserted but rarely discussed in any detail (e.g., Allison & Wrightsman, 1993; Deming & Eppy, 1981; Groth & Birnbaum, 1979). In addition, theorists do not relate power motivation in rape to power motivation in other forms of violence. Research discussed in chapter 2 shows that individuals sometimes use violence to demonstrate power to themselves or others. This motivation is implicated in bullying behavior and in violent responses to insults, particularly when audiences are present. Men show a stronger propensity than women to be concerned with their image as power-ful, presumably due to differences in gender roles. These concerns are par-ticularly strong when men are challenged by other men.

The relationship of the power motive to sexism is unclear. Perhaps male concerns for showing power stem from gender roles. If gender roles reflect negative attitudes toward women, then sexism is at least indirectly impli-cated in power-motivated violence against men and women. However, the appreciation of male physical power, embodied in the male gender role, may stem from the need for men to protect the community—to be informal body-guards, soldiers, and (in the past) hunters (Harris, 1997; see chapter 4). Men's desire to display power is more likely to be an attempt to attract women than a reflection of negative attitudes toward women.

The power argument implies that rapists are like bullies, in that bullies typically use violence without provocation to demonstrate power (e.g., Olweus, 1978). The schoolyard bully targets someone in front of an audience of supporters. He chooses a smaller child whom he can physically dominate, but it tends to be another boy. Presumably he would not enhance his status (or his self-image) if he targeted girls, because boys who use violence against girls are likely to be perceived as cowardly rather than powerful. A power-motivated male offender is likely to achieve the opposite image than the one he desires if he engages in violence against women. This image problem may explain why men who assault women, unlike bullies, commit their crime when no one is watching.

One could argue that group rape is an exception and that it is more likely to be image oriented. However, rape and sexual assaults are less likely than robbery and pure assault to be committed by multiple offenders. Ac-cording to the NCVS, less than 10% of rapes were committed by multiple offenders, compared to approximately 46% of robberies and 20% of assaults (Bureau of Justice Statistics, 1997a). This evidence suggests that rape is less likely to be motivated by image than other violent crimes, although there may be other explanations of the pattern.

People are much more likely to retaliate to avoid looking weak than to attack someone without provocation to assert power. Thus, experiments are unable to elicit aggression from participants without attacking them first. If sexual coercion is power motivated, then it should tend to be retaliatory like other forms of power-motivated violence. The offenders would use sexual assault as a method of retaliation when they have been verbally attacked by a woman. He believes that she has put him down, and he forces sex to put her down. In addition, when women reject a sexual overture, some men may perceive it as an attack on their identity and counterattack using sexual co-ercion. Men may also believe that their behavior is justified—that the women deserve to be punished—because of their belief in retributive justice. From this perspective, acquaintance rapes are more likely than stranger rapes to have a power motive, because they are more likely to involve a provocation.

The main study cited to support the power motive for rape is Groth, Burgess, and Holmstrom's (1977) clinical study of 133 convicted rapists and 92 victims. Based on descriptions of the assault, they classified 65% of the rapists as motivated by power and 35% as motivated by anger. (In other work, they separated a small number of "sadistic rapes" from the anger rapes.) The basis of their classification is not explicit, but it seems to be based primarily on whether the offender engaged in gratuitous violence and other abusive behavior during the incident. However, they gave no evidence to distinguish power from sexual motivation (see Palmer, 1988, for a critique of their classification). In many of the case studies, the rapists appear to this reader to be sexually motivated. In addition, it is difficult to determine the extent to which their sample is representative of rapists in the population and the extent to which interviewers may have influenced the rapists' response.

The power concerns of the majority of rapists stem from underlying feelings of inadequacy and powerlessness, according to Groth et al. (1977). The source of the power rapist's motive is low self-esteem, not sexism. However, research does not support the hypothesis that low self-esteem leads to violence (e.g., Baumeister, Smart, & Boden, 1996). Groth et al. attributed the anger rapists' motivation to negative attitudes toward women, but these attitudes seemed to stem from conflicts with mothers, girlfriends, and wives, not ideology. From their perspective, the attack on the rape victim is a form of displaced aggression due to some type of frustration–aggression mechanism. It is interesting that the work of Groth and his colleague is frequently cited to support the sexism argument, when in fact they focus on the rapist's psychological insecurity. It is also interesting that a study with such weak methodology has been given so much attention in the literature.

One method of studying the role of dominance in the motive for rape is to examine whether rapists are more concerned with domination over women than are other offenders. Malamuth (1986) found a relationship between scores on a sexual dominance scale and self-reported sexual coercion, but it was weak and appeared only when complex interaction terms were included in the regression equation. In addition, the sexual dominance scale includes items that appear to refer to sexual pleasure associated with dominance rather than social identities ("I enjoy the feeling of having someone in my grasp"). These may be men who are aroused by dominance rather than men who think of themselves as dominant. Finally, the causal interpretation of cross-sectional correlations between attitudes and behavior is always problematic.

To display power, a person must influence the target to do something he or she would not do otherwise. Therefore, sexually coercive men who are power oriented should show a preference for using coercion and overcoming resistance. They should initiate sexual activity with women whom they expect will resist. When initiating sexual relations with someone they know, one would expect these men to use coercive techniques as a first rather than a last resort. However, the evidence cited in chapter 9 shows that noncoercive techniques are used along with coercion in incidents involving people who know each other and that coercion is probably not used as a first resort. This evidence is more consistent with the hypothesis that most sexually coercive men are sexually motivated, not power motivated.

Another method for examining the power motive is to ask rapists about their motives. Most rapists do not mention dominance as their motivation for committing the crime (Feild, 1978; Yegidis, 1986). They are much more likely to mention sexual motivation or the desire for excitement. Scully and Marolla (1985) found that some rapists said that they enjoyed the power they exercised over their victims; however, they did not report percentages.

All studies based on rapists' accounts should be cautiously interpreted because they assume that rapists are aware of their motivations. In addition, one must be skeptical of offenders' accounts, because they often attempt to excuse and justify their behavior (Sykes & Matza, 1957). Finally, some convicted rapists with an eye toward gaining release may give the socially accepted explanation for their behavior.

One can also address the motive issue by asking rapists about what they wanted their victim to do during the crime. Interviews with rapists have indicated that they generally prefer acquiescence, rather than resistance, once they have made their intent known (Chappell & James, 1976). The overwhelming majority (78%) indicated that they desired the victim "to give up and agree to anything." On the other hand, 12% said that they preferred a woman to plead during the rape. This preference for submissive behavior could reflect a power motive among this subsample.

Power could be defined more broadly to refer to ego enhancement. Men could view their ability to attract women and gain sexual experience as a type of achievement. This type of thinking is reflected in the language of "scoring" and baseball (i.e., first base, second base, etc.) to represent the level of sexual activity . In this context it seems likely that men would view consensual, not coercive, sexual activity as an accomplishment. As indicated earlier, a man does not demonstrate his attractiveness to women if he must use coercion to find sexual partners—just the opposite. Although he could report a sexual liaison to his friends without mentioning the coercive aspect, he could just as easily lie about the sexual activity.

The achievement aspect of sexual relations for men is probably related to gender differences in sexuality. Because most women will not engage in sexual activity with men unless they have positive feelings for them, their decision to engage in sexual relations reveals those feelings and assigns him a special status (just as their refusal communicates a negative evaluation). A man is thus able to increase his status by having consensual sexual relations with women, particularly attractive women. This strategy is not as useful for women, because men are much less discriminating about sexual partners. A woman cannot assume or claim that a man holds her in high regard just because he is willing to have sex with her.

In sum, the main evidence regarding the power motive is based on the accounts of rapists: A relatively small percentage of rapists from an unrepresentative sample reported that they enjoyed the feeling of power when they committed the crime. Certainly, the state of the literature does not justify any bold assertions about the role of the power motive in rape. It is certainly plausible that sexual coercion is sometimes motivated by a desire to show power or to appear powerful. Because the power motive plays a role in violence, it probably plays a role in sexual violence, at least when that violence is in response to a (perceived) provocation. However, men do not display power or enhance their image when they use violence against women, and therefore the power motive is probably less important in sexual assault than it is for violence against men.

CONTROL OF WOMEN

Another popular feminist argument is that men use rape to control women who violate gender roles (e.g., Brownmiller, 1975; R. E. Dobash & R. P. Dobash, 1979; Koss et al., 1994). The rape is a form of punishment that serves as a deterrent for the offending women or other women who might consider violating gender roles and challenging patriarchal control. Its purpose is to "keep her in her place." In this chapter I discuss the possibility that social control motivates the rapist, and in chapter 12 I discuss the possibility that it motivates a lenient response of the criminal justice system to rape.

The control motive is different from the power motive in that the purpose of violence is to influence the behavior of women, not create an image. Although an image as powerful can lead to later influence, because it makes others fearful, it can also be an end in itself. Presumably, the rapist is similar to the violent husband who desires to dominate his wife (see chapter 5). However, it is not clear why a man who rapes a stranger or someone with whom he has a short-term relationship is concerned with long-term influence over the victim.

Some evidence suggests that men are more likely to use sexual coercion against women they consider deviant. Amir (1971) found that about 20% of the rape victims he studied had "bad reputations," and another 20% had police records, many of them for sexual misconduct. This pattern may simply reflect opportunity: Women who engage in deviant behavior are more likely to have contact with potential rape offenders. Their associations with deviant men put them at greater risk of victimization. In addition, they are more likely to engage in activities such as drinking, going to bars, and going out in the evening that bring them in contact with potential offenders.

Opportunity factors cannot explain evidence that men express a preference for deviant targets over other targets. Kanin (1985) asked college men how their best friends would respond if "they found out that you offended a woman by trying to force her to have sexual intercourse, during the course of which you used physical force and/or threats." Relatively few males (7% to 9%) believed that their best friends would respond favorably if the woman was a "more or less regular date." On the other hand, the percentages were much higher for "bar pickups," "known teasers," and "economic exploiters." Eighty-one percent of rapists and 40% of a control group indicated they would get a positive response from their friends if the woman was a "known teaser." Fifty-four percent of rapists and 16% of a control group indicated they would get a positive response from their friends if the woman was a "bar pickup." The rapists were also somewhat tolerant of sexual coercion toward promiscuous women. Twenty-seven percent of rapists and 10% of controls indicated that their friends would respond favorably to attempts to force women with "loose reputations."

A feminist explanation of these findings is that men condone the use of rape to punish women for violating gender roles. For example, men consider women who feign sexual interest in order to tease men or get their money as requiring correction, and they consider rape appropriate as a form of social control. However, there are other explanations. One alternative explanation is that the tolerance for using sexual coercion against deviant women reflects tolerance for harming deviants generally. Both men and women are more tolerant of violence if it is directed against deviant targets. Evidence for this argument is presented in chapter 12, which discusses the response of the legal system to rape. Another possible explanation is that some men feel justified in using at least some level of coercion against women who they believe have led them to expect sexual relations but then have not complied. They may perceive a woman who communicates sexual interest when she has none as duplicitous and as reneging on an implicit contract. They might believe they are entitled to have sexual relations with such women to carry out what has already been agreed on.

Rape and War

Some commentators argue that rape is used as a form of social control during war (e.g., Brownmiller, 1975). Rape may be a useful method for those who are attempting to terrorize a population because of women's fear of rape. In 1992 in Bosnia, for example, an occupying army used rape and other violence to terrorize the local population, encouraging them to leave (Lilly & Marshall, 2000). However, the goal of these "ethnic cleansing" operations is to force the evacuation of an area, not encourage traditional behavior in women. Men are also victimized, although with a more severe method of control—homicide. For example, the "rape of Nanking" (December, 1937 to January, 1938) included mass executions as well as mass rape. In general, an occupying army poses more danger to male civilians than female civilians—perhaps because of chivalry, perhaps because of the fear of future violence from those men who are spared. However, the occupied country emphasizes the victimization of female victims in its propaganda—even though female victimization may be lower than male victimization—to encourage resistance or to persuade sympathetic third parties to intervene.

Military leaders may encourage or permit the rape of enemy civilians in war zones for other reasons. During the Second World War, the Japanese military used "comfort women" to reward their soldiers for fighting and for long stretches of service. Even when rape is not a policy, it may be tolerated because of hatred of the enemy. For example, Stalin is alleged to have tolerated the rape of German women at the end of the Second World War (Lilly & Marshall, 2000). Rapes by American soldiers in the European theater targeted German women most frequently, and none of these soldiers were executed (Lilly & Marshall, 2000).

The rape of civilian women in war zones probably more often reflects the interests and opportunities of individual soldiers rather than the design of military leaders. Although punishment for rape in war zones is typically more severe than punishment for rape in peacetime, it is often more difficult to prosecute. In general, the frequency of rape is likely to be high when a large group of sexually deprived young men encounter women from a hated group in a situation where sanctions are not effectively applied.

Attitudes Toward Women

If sexism leads to sexual coercion, then men with sexist attitudes should be more likely to engage in sexual coercion. Rapists may hate women, may have traditional attitudes about women, or may have special attitudes regarding sex or forced sex. In this section I examine the evidence on attitudinal effects on sexual coercion.

If negative attitudes toward women do lead men to engage in sexual coercion, it is not clear whether they act as instigators or as facilitators. If a man who feels aggrieved toward women uses sexual coercion to punish them, his hostility instigates the attack. On the other hand, a man may have some other goal, and he may feel disinhibited about using coercion because of his negative attitude toward women (Malamuth, 1986). Thus, a correlation between sexist attitudes and sexual coercion is consistent with the argument that sexual coercion is sexually motivated.

If hostility toward women facilitates sexual coercion, then one would expect to find statistical interactions between attitudes and goals in their effect on behavior (Malamuth, 1986). A facilitator can have an effect only when there is already instigation. For example, one might predict that hostility toward women is more likely to lead men with high sexual aspirations to engage in coercion than men with low aspirations. On the other hand, if hostility alone is sufficient to motivate the crime, then hostility is probably an instigator rather than a facilitator. Support for the interaction model comes from Malamuth's finding that the effect of sexual arousal to rape scenes on sexual coercion depended on various attitudes of participants.

Numerous studies have examined whether men who use coercion are more hostile to women, more traditional, or more accepting of rape myths (Ageton, 1983; A. H. Buss & Durkee, 1957; Craig, Kalichman, & Follingstad, 1989; Kanin, 1969; Koss & Dinero, 1987; Lisak & Roth, 1988; Malamuth, 1981, 1986; Muehlenhard & Linton, 1987; Rada, Laws, & Kellner, 1976; Rapaport & Burkhart, 1984; Scully & Marolla, 1985). The evidence is mixed concerning the relationship between these attitudes and sexual coercion; some found a relationship, and others found none.

The inconsistent results may be due to measurement problems with some of the attitude scales. For example, much of the literature on attitudes and sexual coercion has focused on "belief in rape myths" scales (e.g., Burt, 1980). This is a strange way to identify a psychological scale, so it is not surprising that the scale has measurement problems. *Myths* are false but widely held beliefs. It is not clear from the research which of the beliefs are widely held (Burt, 1980), and not all of the beliefs included in these scales are false (Ellis, 1989). The scale creates what might be called meta-myths, or myths about myths. For example, there is evidence that both men and women believe that a woman who goes to the home of a man on a date where they will be alone is giving a signal that she is willing to have sex (Goodchilds & Zellman, 1984).

Finally, the scale is not unidimensional. Briere, Malamuth, and Check (1985) identified four factors in this scale through factor analysis: disbelief of rape claims, beliefs that the victim is responsible for rape, the perception of rape reports as manipulation, and the belief that rape only happens to certain kinds of women. It is unclear which beliefs are associated with sexual coercion and why they should lead to the use of coercion. For example, why should skepticism about rape claims lead someone to commit rape? Lonsway and Fitsgerald (1995) presented evidence that the scale actually measures hostility toward women. Given the ambiguity, the scale should be abandoned and attention instead focused on individual beliefs that may be conducive to rape.

The literature on the relationship between attitudes and sexual coercion is limited to cross-sectional data analyses. Even if a correlation between certain attitudes regarding women and sexual coercion could be established, the causal interpretation would be unclear. Attitudes may affect the likelihood of sexual coercion, but it is also possible that behavior affects attitudes. For example, men may express certain beliefs to justify coercive behavior already performed (Koss, Leonard, Beezley, & Oros, 1985). It is clear that people who engage in deviant behavior often give accounts for their behavior afterwards that either excuse or justify their actions (e.g., Sykes & Matza, 1957). For example, a rapist's claim that the woman enjoyed the experience serves to justify his behavior. It is also possible that men decide what their attitudes are after observing their behavior; if they think they have freely chosen to engage in a behavior, they may attribute their behavior to their personal attributes (Bem, 1972). I am not aware of any longitudinal research that examines the possibly reciprocal relationship between attitudes and coercive sexual behavior. However, a longitudinal study of other types of violent behavior among of high school boys found that attitudes and behavior had a reciprocal relationship (Liska, Felson, Chamlin, & Baccaglini, 1984).

A third interpretation of the correlation between negative attitudes toward women and sexual coercion is that it reflects a more general relationship between antisocial attitudes and crime. Criminal offenders are more likely than law-abiding men to express antisocial attitudes such as negative attitudes toward women and positive attitudes toward the use of force. To rule out this possibility, it is useful to show that the attitudes of rapists differ from the attitudes of other criminal offenders. At least three studies show that convicted rapists are similar to men convicted of other offenses in their attitudes toward women and women's rights (Howells & Wright, 1978; Sattem, Savells, & Murray, 1984; Scully, 1994). In addition, convicted rapists are similar to men convicted of other offenses in their belief in "rape myths" (Hall, Howard, & Boezio, 1986). These studies cast doubt on the idea that sexist attitudes play a causal role in rape. If negative attitudes toward women have a causal effect, then men with these attitudes should show some preference for female targets.

An experimental study of racial prejudice also suggests that negative attitudes toward a particular group are associated with violence generally, not just violence toward that group. Participants who were prejudiced toward black Americans tended to give higher levels of shocks than participants who were not prejudiced, whether the target was white or black (Leonard & Taylor, 1981). The study suggests that mean-spirited people express racial prejudice and mistreat white as well as black people. Perhaps mean-spirited men express negative attitudes toward women and any other group of people regardless of gender.

One could argue that sexism indirectly leads to sexual coercion because it affects male attitudes toward sexuality. According to this perspective, negative attitudes toward women, rather than evolutionary psychology explain male attention to the physical attractiveness of women and their indiscriminate sexuality. Some women, offended by men's attitudes toward sex, accuse men of treating them as "sex objects," an approach that supports the idea that rape is sexually motivated: Male attitudes toward sexuality lead sexually motivated men to coerce and verbally pressure disinterested or ambivalent women.

I would argue that men's sexual behavior reflects their attitudes toward sex, not women. The appearance of their sexual partners is just as important to homosexual men as to heterosexual men, if not more (Blumstein & Schwartz, 1983). In addition, evidence suggests that male attention to female attractiveness is a cultural universal (Buss, 1994). Third, liberal men are more, not less, likely to look at pornographic pictures of women than traditional men (I. L. Reiss, 1986). There is no scientific evidence, but I suspect that men with liberal attitudes about gender roles are just as interested in women's appearance as traditional men and that their wives and girlfriends are just as attractive. Finally, both men and women consider status attributes in choosing partners; they only weigh them differently. Men are more concerned with their partner's physical attractiveness, whereas women are more concerned with their partner's socioeconomic status (e.g., Townsend, 1998). Thus, the difficulties that older professional women have finding partners probably reflect their lack of interest in lower-status men as well as male interest in attractive women. These concerns do not reflect negative attitudes toward the opposite sex.

SEXIST ATTITUDES

Rape Specialization

Are rapists sexist men or just violent men who commit rape along with their other crimes? Sexists should have a history of crimes against women; they should be specialists. On the other hand, if rapists are just as likely to commit other crimes as well as rape—if they are versatile—it would suggest that sexism is not a factor. In addition, if rapists are violent men with no special preference for female targets, then the predictors of rape offending should be similar to the predictors of other types of violence.

The evidence supports versatility. The criminal records of those who have been convicted of rape tend to be similar to the criminal records of those who have been convicted of other crimes (Alder, 1984; Kruttschnitt, 1989). In addition, Ageton (1983) found that adolescent boys who committed sexual assault also engaged in other types of deviant and criminal behavior.

Versatility is also indicated by research that finds that the predictors of rape offending are similar to the predictors of other types of offending. Thus, Hall et al. (1986) found that antisocial attitudes predicted conviction for sexual assault as well as they predicted conviction for pure assault and armed robbery (see also Rapaport & Burkhart, 1984). Ageton (1983) found that boys who committed sexual assault (just like boys who commit other crimes) are more likely to associate with delinquent peers and are less likely to have close family ties. The social-demographic characteristics and family backgrounds of rapists and other types of offenders also tend to be similar (Alder, 1984; Kruttschnitt, 1989).

Men who use sexual coercion tend to have more favorable attitudes toward violence generally (e.g., Burt, 1980; Malamuth, Check, & Briere, 1986). Some researchers interpret this relationship as supporting the idea that the goal of sexual coercion is to harm or dominate the victim (e.g., Burt, 1980; Malamuth et al., 1986). However, attitudes toward coercion involve an attitude toward means, not goals. Favorable attitudes toward violence should lead to different types of violent offending, not specialization in rape.

Although versatility in criminal offending may be the rule, some men do specialize. For those who specialize in sexual coercion, attitudes toward women may be a factor. In addition, the evidence for versatility involves serious sexual assaults and does not necessarily apply to mild forms of coercion. Perhaps there are men who engage in mild forms of sexual coercion who do not engage in other forms of crime and violence. In general, there are offenders who engage in minor crimes but not more serious crimes (Tedeschi & Felson, 1994).

In sum, the evidence suggests that more serious offenders do not specialize in sexual coercion or in violence against women. Instead, they engage in a wide variety of deviant and criminal behaviors, without considering the feelings of victims of either sex. The versatility of rapists suggests that their crime has little or nothing to do with their attitudes toward women. Versatility suggests that the individual difference factors associated with rape are the same ones associated with other forms of deviance and crime. It suggests that rapists, like other criminals, probably lack self-control, value risk-taking, and lack certain moral inhibitions (see Gottfredson & Hirschi, 1990). They are selfish, not sexist.

Hostility Toward Groups

There are other reasons to be skeptical of explanations of interpersonal violence that emphasize hatred for groups. Most homicide and assaults are committed against victims whom the offender believes has engaged in some provocation. That is what is meant when prosecutors attempt to convince the jury that the offender had "motive." Some serial murderers apparently target women, but these crimes are extremely rare. In spite of recent emphasis on "bias crimes," or crimes based on group prejudice, such incidents are also quite rare (Bureau of Justice Statistics, 1993). In addition, if bias toward outgroups was associated with the use of violence, then one might expect a high level of interracial crime based on racial prejudice. Most crimes in the United States, however, including rape, are intraracial (Bureau of Justice Statistics, 1997a).

If interracial rapes reflect prejudice, then one would expect that white men would frequently rape black women. However, the incidence of white men raping black women is extremely rare—only 3% of rapes committed by white men target black women, according to the National Crime Survey (South & Felson, 1990). Its rarity suggests that prejudice inhibits white men from forcing sexual relations on black women—an ironic pattern. Although historical evidence suggests that white slave owners sometimes raped black slaves—how often, no one knows—this may have been due to opportunity and the absence of sanctions.

In contrast to the infrequency of white-on-black rape, about 40% of rapes committed by blacks target white women (South & Felson, 1990). It has been suggested in the literature that interracial rapes by black men reflect hatred of white people (e.g., O'Brien, 1987). This work usually cites a statement by the radical black author and activist Eldridge Cleaver, who wrote that he had raped white women as a young man to obtain vengeance against white men (Cleaver, 1968). The evidence does not support the idea that such motivation is common among African American men. South and Felson found that the level of interracial rape was unrelated to the level of interracial conflict or inequality in metropolitan areas (see also O'Brien, 1987). Rather, the racial patterning of rape was related to the opportunities for personal contact between black and white people. The more interracial contact, the more interracial interaction of all kinds.

In a second analysis we studied rapes committed during robbery to control for opportunity and focus on offender preference. We found that when black men robbed women, they were slightly less likely to commit rape as an afterthought if the victim was white than if she was black. Thus, black men did not have a preference for white women, as one might expect if they were acting on grievances toward white people. Of course, some rapes involving black offenders and white victims may reflect grievances against white people or disinhibition based on group prejudice. In addition, Scully and Marolla (1984) found that some black rapists reported that they chose white women because they otherwise would not have the opportunity to have sexual relations with white women.

Traditionalism

Perhaps traditionalism, not prejudice, leads men to engage in sexual coercion. From a feminist perspective, the belief that men and women should have different roles—that women should be mothers, not breadwinners—is assumed to reflect negative attitudes toward women. However, men and women who believe in a traditional division of labor do not necessarily hold women in low regard. Their beliefs may instead reflect convictions about the importance of mothers raising children. There is some evidence that measures of attitudes toward women reflect traditionalism rather than prejudice. Eagly and Mladinic (1994) found that a standard scale measuring attitudes toward women was positively correlated with attitudes toward equal rights, but not with attitudes toward women as a social group. In addition, scales measuring traditionalism may measure antisocial attitudes and self-interest to some extent. The idea of male dominance is likely to appeal to the self-interest of men because it justifies their getting their way.

The usual assumption is that traditional men are more likely than non-traditional men to use sexual coercion because they believe they have the right to dominate women. However, there are at least two reasons to expect traditional men to be less likely to engage in sexual coercion. First, traditionalism includes a belief in chivalry, and chivalry should discourage sexual coercion just as it deters all violence toward women (see chapter 5). Second, traditional men and women are less likely to engage in consensual sexual activity outside of marriage (Laumann, Gagnon, Michael, & Michaels, 1994). Because most date rapes occur following consensual sexual activity of a less intimate nature, the opportunity for sexual coercion is likely to be lower.

In addition, traditional men are less likely than nontraditional men to desire or expect sexual activity outside of marriage. In support of this perspective, rape rates are twice as high at private colleges and major universities than at religiously affiliated institutions (Koss, Gidycz, & Wisniewski, 1987). However, no one has found at the individual level of analysis that men with traditional attitudes are less likely than nontraditional men to use sexual coercion. I suspect that these studies have measurement problems: The scales they used include a mix of traditionalism, negative attitudes toward women, and antisocial attitudes.

Gender Inequality

Some researchers have examined the role of the status of women using aggregate analyses of the relationship between gender inequality and the frequency of rape. If gender inequality is associated with the subordination of women, one would expect it to predict rapes and other forms of male violence against women. In general, the evidence does not support this hypothesis. For example, L. Ellis and Beattie (1983) found that rape rates in American cities were unrelated to sex disparities in education and occupational status. On the other hand, L. Baron and Straus (1987) found that states with high gender inequality were more likely to have high incidents of rape. Gender inequality was measured by a variety of indicators, such as the ratio of the median income of women to the median income of men and the percentage of women in the state legislature.

Messner and Sampson (1991) provided counterevidence in a study that replicated L. Baron and Straus's methods, but substituted a state's gender-specific homicide rate for the rape rate. If gender inequality is associated with efforts to subordinate women, one would expect it to also predict homicides involving male offenders and female victims and to predict these homicides better than it would predict homicides involving other gender combinations. Instead, Messner found that a state's level of gender inequality predicted homicides between women better than it predicted the homicide rate for other gender combinations. This unpredicted pattern suggests that the correlation between rape rates and gender inequality is probably due to some spurious factor. In addition, Avakame (1998) reported that states with high levels of gender inequality have lower, not higher, rates of intimate violence.

One could also argue, from a feminist perspective, that men feel their status is threatened when women are treated more equally, and commit rape in response. In other words, gender equality could have a positive effect on rape rates (via threat) that counteracts the negative effect discussed above. Whaley (2001) proposes that the short-term effect of gender equality is an increased rape rate, whereas the longer term effect of gender equality is reduced rape rates via an improved social climate toward women. She finds some supporting evidence in an analysis of panel data for U.S. cities over three decades.

There is reason to question whether cites and states are meaningful units of analysis, given the heterogeneity of the population within these aggregates. Do American states and cities really vary much in the extent to which men feel threatened and women are according status? Perhaps meaningful gender disparities are stronger in southern states or rural areas but these are not the areas that have particularly high rape rates.

A more convincing analysis is one that compares rape rates across different cultures. In a cross-national study, Austin and Kim (2000) found that the rape rates were higher in countries with high levels of gender equality than in countries with lower levels of gender equality. This pattern is consistent with the threat hypothesis. The opposite pattern was found in an aggregate analysis of 95 tribal societies (Sanday, 1981). Tribal societies with high levels of male dominance tended to be have a higher rape rate than societies in which women had political or economic power, public influence, or high status. Similarly, I. L. Reiss (1986) reported a positive correlation between a belief in the inferiority of women and the frequency of rape across cultures. These studies indicate that gender roles and the status of women may affect the incidence of sexual coercion in tribal societies. They are consistent with the argument in chapter 5 that if sexism increases violence against women, it is more likely to do so in non-Western societies.

Heterosexual Versus Homosexual Incidents

One method of examining the role of sexism in sexual assault is to compare heterosexual assaults with homosexual assaults. If sexism is involved in rape, then we should observe different patterns when men target men than when men target women. A study of rape using the NCS included 89 male victims, 7.3% of the sample (Felson & Krohn, 1990). Almost all of the offenders were male. Homosexual rapes were similar in most ways to heterosexual rapes. They did not differ in terms of the ages of offenders and victims, the relationship between offenders and victims, or whether weapons or multiple offenders were involved. As indicated in chapter 10, homosexual rapists apparently have the same preference for young victims. However, there was evidence that heterosexual offenders were slightly more likely to injure the victim than homosexual offenders. This finding is consistent with the idea that negative attitudes toward women play a role in heterosexual rapes. However, it also consistent with evidence presented in chapter 4 suggesting that men are more likely to injure women than they are to injure men because of their superior size and strength.

It is interesting that female victims were more likely than male victims to aggressively resist the offender (58% vs. 36%). There could be a selection factor: Offenders may be more likely to rape men who are small, weak, or nonaggressive, whereas men who rape women may pay less attention to these characteristics in choosing a victim. Whatever the explanation, the finding contradicts the assertion that women tend to be compliant when threatened with rape because of their socialization (e.g., Brownmiller, 1975). It also provides an exception to the usual finding that men tend to be much more aggressive than women. When threatened with rape, female victims are more likely to resist aggressively than male victims.

Research has also compared the frequency of sexual coercion for heterosexual and homosexual men and women. That research shows that gay men and lesbians are more likely to be victims of sexual coercion than heterosexuals (Tjaden & Thoennes, 2000; see Waldner-Haugrud & Magruder, 1995, for a review). However, as Waldner-Haugrud and Magruder pointed out, surveys of sexual violence against gay men and lesbians do not typically determine the gender of the perpetrators. The majority of gay men and lesbians have had heterosexual experiences in which they may have experienced coercion. The few studies that examine the gender of the perpetrator as well as the victim have yielded mixed results (Brand & Kidd, 1986; Lie et al., 1991; Waldner-Haugrud & Magruder, 1995).

These studies have serious sampling limitations. In addition, they underestimate gender differences in frequency of offending because they focus on whether an incident has ever occurred rather than frequency, and because they focus on mild forms of coercion and include noncoercive influence tactics. Still, they suggest that sexual coercion probably occurs as often between homosexuals as between heterosexuals. Such encounters are not easily explained in terms of sexism. In addition, the incidence of coercion involving same-sex couples suggests that there are other sources of sexual conflict and coercion than sex differences in sexuality. So do studies that show that men as well as women report that they have experienced instances of unwanted sexual behavior (see chapter 9).

ROLE OF PORNOGRAPHY

Arousal from any source, including pornography, may facilitate and intensify aggressive behavior (Bandura, 1973; Zillmann, 1983). Feminists, on the other hand, have argued that pornography has special effects on violence against women because of the message it communicates (e.g., Dworkin, 1981; MacKinnon, 1984). Exposure to pornography supposedly leads to negative attitudes toward women, which in turn increases the likelihood of rape and other forms of violence against women. It is argued, for example, that pornography leads male viewers to think of women as sex objects or as promiscuous (e.g., Linz & Malamuth, 1993). Furthermore, some erotica portrays scenes of rape and sadomasochism. The female victim may express pleasure during and after being raped, suggesting that women enjoy such treatment. Men who view such films may be induced to believe that forceful sexual acts are desired by women. In addition, unlike characters who commit other forms of criminal violence in films, characters who commit sexual violence in pornographic films rarely suffer negative consequences for doing so (Palys, 1986; D. D. Smith, 1976).

Evidence does not support the hypothesis that exposure to nonviolent pornography leads to violence toward women. Most experimental studies show no difference between participants exposed to pornographic films and control groups in aggression toward women (for a review, see Linz & Malamuth, 1993). Research outside the laboratory has not demonstrated that exposure to pornography and violence toward women are even positively correlated, much less causally related (see Linz & Malamuth, 1993, for a review). In fact, rapists report less exposure to pornography than controls, not more. Studies of the relationship between exposure to pornography and use of sexual coercion among college students have yielded mixed results (Boeringer, 1994; Demare, Lips, & Briere, 1993).

Research using aggregate data has also failed to demonstrate a relationship between exposure to pornography and violence against women. For example, Gentry (1991) found no relationship between rape rates and circulation of sexually oriented magazines across metropolitan areas. Although rape rates are higher in states in which sex-oriented magazines are popular, Ms. magazine was also popular in those same states (L. Baron & Straus, 1987).

Effects of violent pornography, at least under certain conditions, have been reported in laboratory experiments (see Linz & Malamuth, 1993, for a review). Some studies show that an effect is obtained only if the sexual coercion has positive consequences. In the positive consequence condition, participants were told that the woman became a willing participant in the coercive sexual activities, and she is shown smiling and on friendly terms with the man afterwards (e.g., Donnerstein, 1980). However, Fisher and Grenier (1994) found that exposure to a rape scene with positive consequences did not increase participants' aggression toward women. In addition, pornographic films in which the victim of sexual aggression is perceived as experiencing a positive outcome are quite rare (Garcia & Milano, 1990).

It is also important to point out that the "violence" depicted in pornography is not usually coercive. Barron and Kimmel (2000) found that coercion was involved in only 3.8% of the magazine stories depicting violent sex,

5.1% of the videos, and 10.2% of the Internet stories. Most of the scenes apparently involved play violence. In addition, violent pornography does not necessarily involve men targeting women. In magazine stories, women were more likely to be the perpetrator of violence, whereas in videos and Internet stories men were more likely to be the perpetrator. Barron and Kimmel found higher rates of "violence" in pornographic stories, but they included verbal aggression in their measure. The targets, however, were more likely to be women in all three mediums.

Experimenters who show pornographic films communicate information about their values and expectations and thus create demand cues or "sponsor effects." These cues may explain the results of experimental studies involving exposure to pornography. Paik and Comstock's (1994) meta-analysis shows effects of both pornography and violent pornography on antisocial behavior in general. Experimenters who show pornography, especially violent pornography, may imply that they condone or at least are tolerant of taboo behavior (Feshbach & Malamuth, 1978; I. L. Reiss, 1986). Participants may be disinhibited in this permissive atmosphere and engage in more antisocial behavior (see Felson, 1998).

It is possible to avoid sponsor effects by conducting experiments outside the laboratory and concealing from participants that those who showed them the violent films are monitoring their behavior. This condition was met in a field experiment with college students who were exposed to either two films that showed women responding positively to men who had attacked them or two neutral films (Malamuth & Check, 1981). Participants completed a survey that they thought was unrelated to the films several days later. Men who had viewed the violent films with positive consequences showed greater acceptance of violence against women. These films did not involve pornography, nor did they measure actual behavior. In addition, the experimental evidence is mixed concerning whether pornography or violent pornography affects male attitudes toward women, according to Linz's (1989) review of the literature. In fact, as indicated earlier, I. L. Reiss (1986) found that men who were interested in pornography had more (not less) liberal attitudes toward gender roles.

The versatility evidence is also relevant to the literature on pornography and rape. As indicated earlier, most rapists do not specialize in rape or in violent crime (Alder, 1984; Kruttschnitt, 1989). Therefore, theories that emphasize socialization of rape-supportive attitudes, whether learned from the media or elsewhere, have limited utility for understanding why men use sexual coercion.

One factor that is likely to limit the impact of pornography is selective exposure (McGuire, 1986). Media effects are likely to be limited to the extent that viewers choose material that already reflects their values and interests. The argument in regard to media violence is that violence is so pervasive on television that all viewers, including impressionable children, are exposed. In the case of pornography, particularly violent pornography, there is much more selective exposure, because those interested in viewing this material must make a special effort to do so. In addition, the viewers of pornography are usually adults, not children, although pornography on the Internet is probably affecting this pattern.

It is important to note the relationship between pornography and masturbation. Masturbation requires friction and fantasy. The actor can provide his own fantasies or use the fantasies of others through the medium of pornography. Those who use commercially produced fantasies probably select material that they already are interested in and already fantasize about. It is possible that violent pornography broadens the viewer's repertoire of fantasies. However, when viewers substitute commercially produced fantasies for their own fantasies, the content is not necessarily more violent. Palys (1986) found that under 10% of scenes in pornography videos involved some form of aggression. Recall the study of college students showing that approximately 39% of men and women reported that they had fantasized about forced sex (Loren & Weeks, 1986).

In sum, some experimental research suggests that violent pornography that depicts women enjoying the event can lead male participants to engage in violence against women in the laboratory. On the other hand, experimental research does not demonstrate effects of either nonviolent pornography or violent pornography without positive consequences. The experimental effects of violent pornography may reflect the more general experimental effect of exposure to violent films—the sexual element seems irrelevant. In other words, if violent pornography does affect sexual coercion outside the laboratory, it probably is due to the violent content, not the sexual content, of the pornography. However, demand cues and sponsor effects provide an alternative explanation of these results, supported by the finding that exposure affects antisocial behavior generally. The external validity of these studies is questionable given selective exposure and the rarity of these themes in pornography and selective exposure.

CONCLUSION

The possibility that sexism plays some role in sexual coercion cannot be ruled out. Some men may force women to have sex because they hate women or believe in male dominance. Perhaps the male gender role leads them to enjoy overpowering women. Perhaps some of them act as agents of social control, punishing women who violate gender roles. The evidence for these arguments, unlike the evidence for sexual motivation, is limited and not supportive. In general, men who use sexual coercion are versatile: They do not specialize in rape or violence against women. Their attitudes toward women are no different than the attitudes of other criminal offenders. Sexually violent men engage in other antisocial behavior, suggesting that they are more likely to violate rather than enforce social norms. Heterosexual rape is slightly more likely to result in injury than homosexual rape, but this may be due to sex differences in size and strength.

As discussed in chapter 10, men and women often have conflicts over sexual behavior. Many young men are preoccupied with sex, and that interest increases when they become sexually aroused. The conflict can lead men and women to have adversarial beliefs regarding sexual relations. Women, offended by male preoccupation with sex, promiscuity, and pressure, complain about being treated as sex objects. Some men develop callous attitudes, as reflected in their responses to items on the rape myth scale and their responses to questions about whether they would engage in sexual coercion if they were certain they would not get caught (see chapter 9). They believe that "all is fair in love and war," that underhanded tactics are acceptable in the pursuit of sexual relations with women. Such attitudes may disinhibit sexually motivated men to use at least mild forms of sexual coercion. In addition, men have a psychological interest in deceiving themselves about the woman's point of view. Some may have difficulty understanding why women would view sexual activity with them as negative, even if there is some force involved. In addition, they may believe that she will change her mind once the encounter begins. These callous attitudes may stem from selfishness rather than sexism.

12

SEXUAL COERCION AND THE LAW

A feminist approach suggests that rape tends to go unpunished because it is not reported to the police and because when it is, the legal system treats offenders leniently (e.g., Allison & Wrightsman, 1993; Belknap, 2001; Searles & Berger, 1995). Police, prosecutors, judges, and jurors are overly skeptical of testimony from women who claim they have been raped, according to this approach, and they tend to blame the women, not the offenders, for the crime. The police are reluctant to arrest, prosecutors are reluctant to prosecute, and juries and judges are reluctant to convict. The experience of rape victims with the criminal justice system is assumed to be so negative that it is sometimes described as a second victimization (Allison & Wrightsman, 1993).

In this chapter, I discuss the social–legal response to sexual coercion. I examine the feminist argument that the legal system tolerates sexual assault, particularly when it is committed against women who deviate from traditional gender roles. I use the comparative method that I used in earlier chapters, asking whether the legal system responds differently to rape and sexual assault than it responds to other violent crimes. What appears to involve skepticism and victim blaming may simply reflect the adversarial system, the operation of due process, and the principle that the burden of proof should rest on the prosecution. I argue that although there are some differences in the response to sexual and other offenses, these differences are due the importance of victim credibility in these crimes rather than sexism. Before discussing the evidence regarding discrimination, I examine the feminist explanation for why sexual coercion is supposedly tolerated.

SEXUAL COERCION AS SOCIAL CONTROL

As indicated in chapter 11, some feminist scholars have argued that the function of sexual coercion is to control women and keep them in traditional roles (e.g., R. E. Dobash & R. P. Dobash, 1979; Koss et al., 1994). A patriarchal social context supposedly encourages or tolerates sexual coercion against women. For example, in her classic book, Brownmiller (1975) argued that rape is "a conscious process of intimidation by which all men keep all women in a state of fear." She asserted that the male genitals were the vehicle of man's original conquest of women. Men use this "weapon" in rape, and women are disadvantaged because they cannot retaliate in kind. In other words, the shape of male genitals—their ability to insert—is the source of their power over women.

Women look to men to protect them from rape by other men, according to Brownmiller. Thus, women's dependence on men and marriage is based on women's fear of an open season of rape. In exchange for protection, women became the property of men—they were "domesticated" by protective mating. Men passed laws against rape to protect their property.

Brownmiller's (1975) biological emphasis was criticized by Schwendinger and Schwendinger (1983), who preferred to attribute male domination of women and rape to capitalism. In contrast to Brownmiller's depiction of rape as pervasive and universal, they described the relations between the sexes in precapitalist societies as harmonious and rape free. Only under capitalism, they asserted, do men engage in rape. Ethnographic data suggest that both views are incorrect—rape is neither universal nor restricted to capitalist societies (see, e.g., Sanday, 1981).

Brownmiller's statement that all men consciously try to control women using rape is not plausible (for a review of criticism, see Geis, 1977). Ignoring the hyperbole, one can examine the idea that society somehow uses rape to control women. Unless one posits some sort of conspiracy among rapists, legislators, judges, and juries, one must assume that this control motive is unconscious. Still, it is difficult to imagine rapists as agents of social control and society, rather than as deviants, and legal authorities as their accomplices. One could argue that agents of the criminal justice system and other law-abiding citizens develop attitudes sympathetic to rape. However, this is difficult to reconcile with the fact that the punishment for rape is so severe.

Women are more likely than men to restrict their activities because of fear of crime, in spite of their lower risk of violent victimization. Evidence suggests that women's greater fear of crime is due to their fear of rape as well as a lack of confidence in their physical ability to defend themselves (e.g., Riger & Gordon, 1981). Fear of crime leads some women to avoid certain streets at night and to be careful about their surroundings, but it does not lead them to avoid working outside the home or to otherwise conform to traditional gender roles. Women do not marry, at least consciously, for protection, nor is there evidence that high rape rates lead to high marriage rates. Finally, the fact that fear of rape constrains the activities of women does not mean that it was designed for that purpose. The elderly also have greater fear of violent crime (in spite of relatively low victimization rates), but no one argues that violent crime was designed to control them (Kennedy & Sacco, 1998).

Gregor's (1990) description of group rape in a Brazilian tribe—the Mehinaku—shows that rape can be used as a form of social control. The threat of group rape was used in this small group to prevent women from observing certain male ritual objects. Both men and women of the tribe viewed group rape not in sexual terms, but as a terrible punishment that would likely result in the woman's death. Because of their intense fear, the women stayed away from the objects, and a group rape had not occurred for 40 years (and perhaps had never occurred). Apparently, the threat of rape was also used to keep women away from male ritual objects in a number of tropical forest societies in South America and in Highland New Guinea (Sanday, 1981). Rape has been reported to be the prescribed punishment for other offenses committed by women in some societies (e.g., R. F. Murphy, 1959).

For any form of punishment to act as a social control mechanism, there must be clear rules about its application. If sexual coercion is to serve as a sanction, it must be directed at the rule violator, not at all women. Otherwise, it cannot be used as a deterrent to proscribed behaviors. Furthermore, its use must be legitimated, at least among men, and not viewed as a criminal act. This pattern is clear in the societies in which group rape was used and prescribed as a social control mechanism. The men used the threat of rape to deter specific behaviors, not for the vague purpose of controlling women, and their threat targeted the violator. The fact that these patterns are not observed in most societies suggests that rape is rarely used for social control purposes.

A society may punish both men and women for violations of gender roles, and it may do so with similar severity. In addition, the severity of punishment for violations of gender roles may be similar to the severity of punishment for other violations. The relevant comparisons are displayed in Table 12.1. The feminist hypothesis implies that women who violate gender norms—cell c—are treated with particular severity—that is, with rape. It also implies that a society is more punitive toward women who violate gender norms than women who violate general norms (c > d).

One problem with this analysis is the difficulty of distinguishing violations of gender roles from deviant behavior generally. Because men are more

TABLE 12.1
Leniency as a Function of Gender and Type of Norm Violation

Gender	Type of violation	
	Gender norms	Other norms
Male	a	b
Female	c	d

likely to engage in most types of deviant behavior than women, one could consider deviant behavior, in general, a greater violation of expectations for women than men. In addition, few norms apply strictly to women in modern society, although some are influenced by gender. The best candidate is, perhaps, the double standard, or the tendency to judge women more harshly for promiscuity. One could examine, for example, whether a man who rapes a prostitute is treated more leniently than a man who rapes other types of female offenders. This issue has not been examined. However, the legal system is lenient toward prostitutes; when prostitution is prosecuted, it is treated as a low-level misdemeanor. This pattern contradicts the hypothesis that women who violate gender norms are treated more severely than women who engage in other misconduct.

The feminist argument would also imply that women who violate gender norms are treated more harshly than men who violate gender norms (c > a). This seems unlikely, given that the stigma for violating gender roles is much greater for men than women, at least in American society. For example, men in occupations traditionally occupied by women are stigmatized more than women in traditionally male occupations (e.g., Nilson, 1976). In addition, "sissy" is a more pejorative label than "tomboy," male cross-dressing is more stigmatized than female cross-dressing, and male homosexuality is more strongly stigmatized than lesbianism (Posner, 1992).

In sum, the available evidence suggests that we do not respond with special severity when women violate gender roles. Rather, we punish both men and women for deviant behavior, whether the deviance is related to gender roles or not. In fact, we treat female deviance more leniently than male deviance, both inside and outside the criminal justice system, according to the evidence reviewed in chapter 5. We also treat female violations of gender roles more leniently than male violations. The patterns are not consistent with the idea that rape—a severe penalty—is used to punish women who violate gender roles in American society.

UNDERREPORTING

According to the NCVS, sexual assaults (including rape) are less likely to be reported to the police than assault or robbery (Bureau of Justice Statistics, 1997a). In 1994, 31.7% of sexual assaults were reported compared to 40.1% of assaults and 55.4% of robberies. The difference between rape and assault is not that large (8.4%). The reporting gap is larger when the comparisons are restricted to female victims (31.2% vs. 43.1% vs. 63.5%). Surprisingly, sexual assaults involving nonstrangers are slightly more likely to be reported than sexual assaults involving strangers (34.1% vs. 29.5% for female victims).

The earlier version of the survey (the National Crime Survey) indicated that rapes were just as likely to be reported to the police as other violent crimes (Bureau of Justice Statistics, 1993). The difference in results is probably due to the inclusion in the more recent survey of special probes about incidents the respondent may not think of as criminal and special probes about incidents that involve sexual coercion. The more recent survey probably includes more ambiguous and minor incidents of sexual assault than the older survey. If respondents do not believe that an incident was a crime or are uncertain, they are unlikely to report them to the police, and reporting rates will be lower. Thus, the extent to which sexual assaults are underreported depends on one's definition of rape or sexual assault. As indicated in chapter 9, whether these minor incidents are defined as crimes or annoyances may reflect a value judgment.

Victims gave a variety of reasons for not reporting sexual assaults to the police in the NCVS (Bureau of Justice Statistics, 1997a). The two most common reasons were that the crime was a private matter and that the victim feared reprisal if she reported. The reasons given for not reporting sexual assaults appear to be similar to those given by female victims of other crimes.

Tjaden and Thoennes (2000) compared the reporting of sexual and nonsexual violence against intimate partners using data from a large national survey ($N = 16,000$). Intimate partners included current and former dates, spouses, and cohabiting partners. The results (presented in Table 12.2) suggest that sexual assaults are less likely to be reported than other assaults against women but slightly more likely to be reported than assaults against men. However, one must be careful in making comparisons across "crimes," because the questions focused on acts of violence and forced sexual behavior, not incidents that the target identified as assault or rape. In addition, some of the "assaults" may have been minor. The relative frequency of reporting is likely to be affected by the extent to which respondents considered themselves crime victims in what may have been minor or ambiguous incidents.

Victims who did not report the violent incident to the police were asked to give their reasons for not doing so; multiple responses were possible. The most common reasons for not reporting sexual violence were "fear of perpetrator" (21.2%), "minor, one-time incident" (20.3%), and "ashamed, wanted to keep incident private" (16.1%). Only 7.1% of female victims of sexual coercion indicated that it was because "the police wouldn't believe me," compared to 61.3% of female victims of nonsexual violence and 45.1% of male

TABLE 12.2
Legal Outcomes of Sexual and Nonsexual Violence Against Intimate Partners

Legal outcome	Sexual coercion against women (%; N = 441)	Nonsexual violence against women (%; N = 1149)	Nonsexual violence against men (%; N = 541)
Victimization reported to police	17.2	26.7	13.5
Perpetrator prosecuted[a]	7.5	7.3	1.1
Perpetrator convicted[b]	41.9	47.9	c
Perpetrator incarcerated[d]	69.2	64.4	c

Note. Adapted from Tjaden and Thoennes, 2000. [a] Based on those reported to the police. [b] Based on those prosecuted. [c] n < 5. [d] Based on those convicted.

victims of nonsexual violence. Only 13.2% of victims of sexual coercion indicated that the "police couldn't do anything," compared to close to 100% of male and female victims of nonsexual violence. This evidence suggests that lack of confidence in the criminal justice system is not an important factor inhibiting victims of sexual coercion by partners from going to the police. It is a much more important factor inhibiting victims from calling the police for nonsexual violence.

FALSE CHARGES

Anecdotal evidence indicates that the police are more skeptical about rape charges than charges for other crimes (Bryden & Lengnick, 1997). The concern about false charges of rape is long standing. The English jurist Justice Matthew Hale (1680) wrote,

> It is true, rape is a most detestable crime, and therefore ought severely and impartially to be punished with death, but it must be remembered that it is an accusation easily to be made and hard to be proved; and harder to be defended by party accused tho ever so innocent. (p. 364)

Because of skepticism about rape charges, the legal system required corroboration of victim testimony and permitted the introduction of evidence of the accuser's sexual history. Current rape scholars write disparagingly of Hale, claiming that false charges occur no more frequently for rape than for other crimes (e.g., Allison & Wrightsman, 1993; Katz & Mazur, 1979). Their claim appears to be based on a statistic originally presented by Brownmiller (1975) that she based on statements by an appellate judge in New York City. The judge had claimed that a special unit of policewomen estimated that only 2% of rape claims were false. The basis for this estimate is unknown because it is not a published study.

Published research suggests that rape is more likely to involve false charges than other crimes (see Bryden & Lengnick, 1997, for a review). The likelihood that a charge is unfounded is substantially higher for rape than for other crimes (8.4% for rape vs. 1.6% for assault and 3.5% for robbery). However, as Bryden and Lengnick pointed out, the criteria for judging a charge well-founded vary across jurisdiction and over time. In addition, police judgments of victim credibility are not necessarily reliable. A study based on the judgments of 128 police surgeons in Great Britain found that 31.4% of rape charges were judged to be false (Geis, Wright, & Geis, 1977, reported in Bryden & Lengnick, 1997); however, the five female surgeons in the sample gave lower estimates (23.2%). Based on 100 cases of alleged rape in Florida, Schiff (1969) concluded that 7% were definitely not rape and 15% were questionable. Although the variation in these estimates does not inspire confidence, they cast doubt on the 2% estimate typically repeated.

A study of 109 rape cases in a small metropolitan area in the Midwest relied on recantation rather than the judgments of investigators (Kanin, 1994). The study found that 41% of the women who had filed a rape charge later admitted that the charge was false. These admissions were not due to any pressure from the police and typically occurred soon after the charge was made. None of the complainants retracted their recantation after being informed that they would be charged with filing a false complaint. Kanin attributed the particularly high rate of false charges in this jurisdiction to more thorough investigation of rape charges in this low-crime city. In other cities, he claimed, the police do not even record the most obviously false rape reports.

Kanin (1994) also studied false charges among rape complainants in two midwestern universities. A ranking female officer took the complaints and conducted the investigations. The study found that 50% of the 64 complainants recanted their charge.

Why do women sometimes file false charges? In his metropolitan study, Kanin (1994) found that the most frequent motivation was to provide an alibi to avoid punishment (56%). Rape provides a convenient explanation of teenage pregnancies, adulterous relationships, and other misconduct. For example, in one case cited by Kanin, a young woman who was late returning home told her mother she had been raped. The second most important motivation for filing false charges was revenge (27%). For example, in one case, a young woman was angry with her boyfriend for failing to withdraw when he ejaculated during consensual sex. Finally, some false charges stemmed from the victim's desire to gain sympathy (18%). Similar motivations were indicated in the study of false charges at the two universities.

Women may make false charges of rape impulsively, without thinking carefully about the consequences. A false charge is a crime, and people typically commit crime impulsively (e.g., Gottfredson & Hirschi, 1990). In addition, people get "caught up" in their own lies. A woman may make a false claim to family or friends with no intention of going to the police but then feel pressured to do so (Kanin, 1994). For example, if a girl, on impulse, tells her parents that she was raped in order to avoid punishment, her parents may force her to go to the police or may report the incident themselves. Charges of rapes of teenagers are particularly likely to be reported by third parties (Bryden & Lengnick, 1997).

The use of false charges for revenge is consistent with evidence that women are more likely than men to use indirect forms of aggression (Bjorkqvist, Lagerspetz, & Kaukiainen, 1992; see chapter 3). A woman who has a grievance with a man may not view physical violence as an option because of her disadvantage in size and strength. She may use false rape charges to get back at him for some perceived wrong.

It is generally assumed that women would want to avoid charging rape because of the stigma. However, the reputational consequences for rape victims are not clear. Any type of victimization can have positive as well as negative implications for the victim's reputation. Claims of victimization provide an excuse for poor performance on the part of the victim and increase the level of credit for achievements, as the person succeeded in spite of external forces acting against him or her (Heider, 1958). Although rape may stigmatize the victim, it may also gain her sympathy and respect (see chapter 9). The women's movement assigns a heroine's status to rape victims, referring to them and other victims of male violence as "survivors." Kanin, however, attributed only one of the 32 false charges in his university study to a need for attention or sympathy (compared to 18% of the false charges in his city study).

In stranger rape the legal issue is more likely to involve questions of identification than consent. There is strong evidence that wrongful identification is fairly common in rape cases. In approximately 20% of the sexual assault cases referred to the FBI (about 10,000 cases referenced), the primary suspect was excluded by forensic DNA testing (Neufeld & Scheck, 1996). In about 60% of these cases, the DNA matched the DNA of the primary suspect. For the remainder, the results were inconclusive, usually due to an insufficient sample of DNA. Sheck reported that in 25% of the cases the accused was exonerated, but that is not consistent with the numbers he presented. Scheck also reported that an informal survey of private laboratories by the National Institute of Justice revealed a 26% exclusion rate. These referrals typically represent cases where (1) identity is the issue rather than consent; (2) eyewitness testimony linked the suspect to the crime; (3) the suspect had been arrested or indicted based on this evidence; and (4) biological evidence had been collected from a place where the results are virtually dispositive.

The results of these studies support the statement of Matthew Hale in the 1600s. False or mistaken charges of rape are frequent enough to be worrisome. Perhaps a requirement of corroboration of victim testimony is too much of a burden for the prosecution, but we should recognize the problem of false charges. Our anger at rape offenders should not blind us to this problem and lead to a weakening of due process for this crime. Policy issues aside, the evidence suggests that the attention of legal authorities to false rape charges reflects their concern for justice rather than sexism.

BLAMING VICTIMS

Leniency toward rape offenders is mediated by the supposed tendency to attribute blame to the victim rather than the offender. The argument is that because of sexist assumptions, prosecutors, judges, and juries assign more blame to victims than they deserve (e.g., Belknap, 2001; Stanko, 1985). An alternative viewpoint is that discussions of blame in rape reflect the legal battle that takes place in courtrooms for all crime. In many instances, defense attorneys attempt to make the victims look blameworthy while prosecuting attorneys attempt to make offenders look blameworthy. For example, one judge described "putting the deceased on trial" as "the oldest, most common, and most successful tactic in homicide cases" (cited in Bryden & Lengnick, 1997). The degradation of victims is an inevitable consequence of the adversarial process (McBarnet, 1983).

An attribution of blame involves a series of inferences about causality, intention, and negligence. The observer first makes a judgment about whether the actor or some external factor caused the negative outcome (Heider, 1958; Rule & Nesdale, 1976). If a decision is made that the actor caused the outcome, the observer considers whether the outcome was intended or unintended. If the negative outcome is intended, the observer assigns a high level of blame, particularly if the actor's intention was malevolent. However, the actor may also receive some blame for engaging in behavior whose negative consequences were unintended but foreseeable and therefore negligent. Research indicates that if harmful consequences are viewed as foreseeable, then they should have been avoided, and the actor will be blamed for not avoiding them (e.g., Rule & Nesdale, 1976). Blaming individuals for irresponsible or negligent behavior is reasonable because it provides an incentive for them to act with greater care in the future (Hart, 1968). On the other hand, sometimes "20-20 hindsight" is operative: People believe negative outcomes were foreseeable when they were not and blame themselves or others "unfairly."

Blame is sometimes treated as a fixed quantity, such that the more blame assigned to the victim the less assigned to the offender. This zero-sum treatment of blame—the parceling out of a fixed amount of blame to various parties—is apparent in the judgment of contributory negligence in tort cases. In the case of violent crime, it is also possible that if people believe that the victim was careless, they might assign less blame to the offender. Therefore, the prosecutor, and those sympathetic with prosecution, will prefer to deny or minimize blame for the victim, whereas the defense attorney, and those sympathetic to the accused, will do the opposite.

Individuals do not necessarily assign less blame to offenders when victims have made mistakes leading to their victimization. In other words, they sometimes treat blame as a positive-sum, or variable, quantity. For example, some blame will be attributed to a car owner who leaves the keys in the ignition if the car is later stolen. The victim's negligence may be considered irrelevant to judgments about the thief; he is still blameworthy and deserving punishment. On the other hand, sometimes it is argued that the keys tempted the thief, diminishing his responsibility. According to this way of thinking, the blame assigned to the owner of the car lowers the blameworthiness of the thief. Similar thinking might lead to the argument that a victim's provocative clothing tempted the rapist. However, the victim's clothing is not used as a defense in rape trials, at least not those described in the research that follows.

Research has examined the tendency to assign blame to victims in acquaintance rape scenarios. In general, the college student participants assigned a small amount of blame to victims in these scenarios, much less than they attributed to offenders (see Allison & Wrightsman, 1993, for a review). Of course, the distribution of blame assigned depends on the scenario presented. The blame that participants assigned to the victim was typically for irresponsible or negligent behavior. Whether they assigned more blame than they should, or whether blame assigned to the victim reduced the blame assigned to the offender, is not clear.

To my knowledge, no one has examined whether victims of rape are more likely to be blamed than victims of other crimes. Victim blaming may be most prevalent in homicide and assault, where the most common claim of the accused is that they acted in self-defense—that is, in response to the victim's violence (Brereton, 1997; Felson, Baccaglini, & Ribner, 1985). More blame is probably attributed to victims in homicides and assaults than in other crimes because victims play a greater causal role and often engage in intentionally harmful behavior. On the other hand, there is probably a greater tendency to blame victims in rape than in robbery, at least when the crime involves people who know each other. Victim behaviors are more likely to play a causal role and negligence is more likely to be factor in nonstranger rape than in robbery. For example, the victim's intoxication is probably a better predictor of rape than of robbery victimization. In addition, if the acquaintance rape occurs during consensual activity, as many do, the victim's behavior plays a causal role, and some people may assign them blame. Thus, it is not surprising that individuals assign some blame to a woman when a rape occurs when she is drunk and naked with a man in bed, because they consider such behavior irresponsible. They are likely to consider her more blameworthy if they have traditional beliefs about sexual behavior outside marriage and blame her for engaging in consensual sexual behavior. Others will not attribute blame to the victim in these circumstances, because they do not blame women for getting intoxicated or wanting to limit sexual activity. However, they probably attribute less blame to rape victims than homicide and assault victims, because the misbehavior of rape victims is only negligent, whereaas the misbehavior of homicide and assault victims may involve intended wrongs.

One method of examining whether sexism plays a role in victim blaming in sexual assault is to determine whether it is affected by the gender of the offender and victim. R. E. Smith, Pine, and Hawley (1988) compared participants' reactions to a legal case in which two defendants were accused of using a gun to force a stranger to engage in oral sex. The study independently manipulated the gender of the defendants and the accuser. They found that male victims assaulted by female offenders were rated as more likely to have encouraged the assault, more likely to experience pleasure, and less likely to experience trauma than victims in assaults involving other gender combinations. Observers' response to male sexual assaults on men was similar to the response to male sexual assaults of women. The results contradict the idea that observers are particularly likely to blame the victim when men sexually assault women. They suggest that victim blaming in rape is not due to sexism.

Research also shows that male observers are more likely than female observers to blame victims and rate their experience as pleasurable (e.g., Mitchell, Hirschman, & Nagayama Hall, 1999). For example, Smith et al. (1988) found that male participants were particularly likely to think that victims enjoyed the assault if the offender was a woman and the victim a man. Forty-seven percent of male participants rated female assaults on men as pleasurable for the victim, compared to only 9% of female participants. It is striking that almost half the male participants viewed the male victim's experience as pleasurable, in spite of the fact that the female offenders in the scenario were strangers and used a gun. The study demonstrates strong gender difference in attitudes toward forced sexual behavior and suggests that the lack of appreciation of women's aversion to rape that some men reveal is based on male attitudes about sexuality, not their attitudes toward women.

Two other beliefs may also lead to blaming the victim. Women may be attributed blame for enticement or for teasing men sexually. This attribution is not necessarily irrational; a study described in chapter 9 found that many college women reported that they engaged in sexual teasing. Also, the belief that men lack self-control when they are sexually aroused may lead to the assignment of blame to women who give sexual signals or who consent to limited sexual activity but refuse intercourse. Feminist rejection of the sexual motive is probably based, at least in part, on their objection to these excuses for sexual coercion.

The loss of control excuse is not restricted to rape; it is probably much more often used by homicide and assault offenders to explain their behavior

(Felson et al., 1985). For example, these offenders sometimes claim that they lost their temper or that they "just snapped." Criminal defendants and their attorneys are likely to favor theories that assume low levels of self-control, no matter what the crime.

CONSENT AND CREDIBILITY

Because the victim is usually the key witness in rape cases, the case typically depends on her credibility. The legal dispute is frequently concerned with whether she consented: The accused admits to sexual relations but claims it was consensual. Seventy-nine percent of the cases studied by Brereton (1997) in Australia involved disputes over consent. One of three cases studied by LaFree (1989) involved issues of consent. Other types of sexual assault cases included incidents in which the defendant denied that sexual intercourse occurred at all, incidents in which the defendant claimed there is mistaken identification, and (rarely) incidents in which the defendant claims diminished responsibility. LaFree found that cases involving disputes about whether intercourse was consensual or whether it occurred at all were less likely to lead to conviction than cases involving questions of identification and diminished responsibility. Because the issue of consent is much more likely to be in dispute in acquaintance rapes than stranger rapes, it is not surprising that these cases are more difficult to prosecute (Bryden & Lengnick, 1997). Acquaintance rape trials have been described as "swearing contests" or as cases of "he said, she said."

The issue of consent is an issue in sexual assault because defendants use it as a defense. Some sex is consensual, some is forced, and when the accuser and accused give different versions, the courts must sort it out. If defendants in robbery cases claimed that the exchange of money was consensual, then consent would be a factor in robbery trials. There are other crimes where there are disputes over the nature of exchange. One common example is when a defendant accused of failing to repay a loan claims that the money was a gift. Another example is when those accused of theft claim that they took back something that belongs to them. The judge tries to determine who is telling the truth and may use information about the relationship between the parties involved to see if it was one in which a gift would be given. Similarly, a judge or jury might attempt to determine whether the relationship between a defendant and the woman who accused him of rape was one that would be likely to involve consensual sex.

State legislatures introduced a number of reforms in the 1970s that were designed to make conviction for rape easier (Horney & Spohn, 1991). Presumably, these reforms reflected the interests of both feminist legal scholars and conservative male lawmakers who wanted to "get tough on crime." Rape reform laws eliminated the requirement that the victim resist her attacker to demonstrate lack of consent, eliminated the rule requiring corroboration of the testimony of the victim, and placed restrictions on the introduction of evidence of the victim's prior sexual conduct. Research suggests that the effects of these laws on conviction rates have been minimal (e.g., Horney & Spohn, 1991).

It could be argued that the old rules about corroboration, resistance, and sexual history reflected sexist assumptions. Why, for example, was rape the only crime that required corroboration of the victim's testimony? One explanation is that corroboration was required because the victim's testimony was perceived as less reliable in rape than in other crimes. The evidence on false allegations and DNA matching suggests that such perceptions might have had a valid basis.

The requirement that victims resisted the accused to demonstrate lack of consent may be due to difficulties in determining consent in acquaintance rape cases. Because of token resistance and the tendency for passive compliance to communicate consent, the line between consent and coercion is not always clear (see chapter 9). Attention to whether the victim resisted is understandable without invoking sexism.

Finally, the court's tendency to permit testimony about the victim's sexual history was not necessarily due to sexism. The sexual history of the victim in disputes over consent is relevant (or probative), although probably not as much as the criminal history of the defendant. Of course, neither is conclusive. The inclusion of the former but not the latter may reflect the principle that the burden of proof rests on the prosecution. In addition, in the past, when consensual sexual relations outside of marriage were rare, knowing a woman's sexual history could be useful information in determining whether a disputed incident was consensual. A woman who claimed she was forced to have sex was more credible if she was a virgin than if she frequently engaged in consensual sex. The information is much less useful today, because consensual relations outside of marriage are normative. The development of rape shield laws is a response, in part, to changes in the sexual behavior of women. It is also a response to the belief that revealing the victim's sexual history may be prejudicial, although extensive sexual experience outside of marriage is not as stigmatizing as it once was. The sexual history of the victim is permitted in special circumstances currently, and it is sometimes difficult to hide from jurors because it is revealed in the testimony describing the context of the crime (Bryden & Lengnick, 1997).

RESPONSE TO VICTIM MISCONDUCT

If rape is an attempt to encourage women to conform to gender roles and a sexist form of social control, then the legal system should treat offenders who target women who violate gender norms more leniently. Research has examined whether a victim's misconduct, some of which might be interpreted as violations of gender roles, affects legal outcomes. The evidence is mixed. For example, LaFree (1989) examined how outcomes of rape trials were affected by testimony in court that the victim had used drugs or alcohol, engaged in sex outside marriage, or had illegitimate children. Victim misconduct affected outcomes in rape cases only when the defense argued either that the sexual activity was consensual or that intercourse did not occur. The fact that victim misconduct was not a factor in cases of misidentification or diminished responsibility suggested that the jurors did not tolerate sexual assault against a woman who violated gender roles, but rather that they based their judgments about the victim's credibility, to some extent, on their judgments of the victim's character. In addition, Lafree found no differences between male and female jurors in their response to these cases. Nor did the gender-role attitudes of the jurors affect their decisions on rape cases. Some of his evidence suggested that traditional jurors responded more strongly to evidence of victim misconduct, but other evidence has suggested just the opposite (LaFree, 1989).

Horney and Spohn (1996) examined the effect of victim behavior on legal outcomes (e.g., dismissal, conviction) in a large sample of sexual assault cases in Detroit. They found that legal outcomes were unaffected by whether the victim resisted, whether she reported the incident immediately, whether she had engaged in risky behavior immediately before the incident, or whether she had a history of past misconduct. Horney and Spohn also found no evidence that victim behavior was more important in less violent rapes (e.g., date rapes) than in more violent rapes (e.g., those involving strangers). Sexual assaults involving nonstrangers were just as likely to result in conviction as those involving strangers. However, the evidence is mixed on this issue, according to their review of the literature.

The misconduct of crime victims may influence the decisions of judges and jurors for a variety of reasons. First, the conduct of victims is an important consideration in whether they will be viewed as credible witnesses (Baumer, Messner, & Felson, 2000). Victims who have engaged in some form of disreputable behavior are more likely to be viewed as untrustworthy and dishonest, which may decrease the likelihood of indictment and conviction. Second, victim conduct may influence the decisions of judges and jurors by affecting the level of cause and blame attributed to the defendant. As discussed above, to the extent that blame is treated as a fixed quantity, the more blame they can convince the jury to attribute to the victim, the less blame will be attributed to the defendant. Third, victim conduct may affect judgments of the amount of harm or cost to the victim. A crime against an upstanding citizen may be perceived by judges and jurors as a greater harm, and thus a more serious offense, than a crime against someone disreputable (e.g., Black, 1989). Thus, sympathy for the victim and anger toward the defendant are likely to be greater when the victim is someone who is considered reputable.

Victim misconduct, then, is relevant to the issues of credibility, cause, and cost for all types of crime. It is not clear whether victim conduct plays a greater role in rape prosecution than in the prosecution of other violent crimes. To examine that issue requires a comparative approach.

LEGAL RESPONSE TO RAPE VERSUS OTHER CRIMES

A key issue in determining whether sexism plays a role in rape prosecution is to compare the response of the legal system to rape with its response to other crimes. For example, blaming the victim may be a strategy used by defense attorneys in a variety of crimes. Misconduct by the victim may affect legal outcomes for other crimes—rape may not special in this regard. If the victim's conduct affects legal outcomes in general, then it casts doubt on the idea that rape is used to punish and control deviant women. However, even if rape is prosecuted differently, it may be due to the special circumstances of the crime rather than any tendency toward leniency. For example, the credibility of the victim may be a more important issue in prosecuting rape than in prosecuting other crimes. The victim is much more likely to be the only witness in rape cases than in other cases, and therefore her testimony is crucial. To establish that the treatment of rape in the legal system is discriminatory, then, requires two criteria: (1) that rape is handled differently than other crimes—offenders are treated more leniently and victims treated more harshly—and (2) that its special treatment is related to sexism on the part of legal authorities, not special difficulties in prosecuting sexual assault.

At present, sentences for rape in the United States are severe, second only to sentences for homicide (Steffensmeier, 1988). Sentences for rape are more severe than they are in other developed countries, relative to for the severity of sentences for other crimes (Posner, 1992). The U.S. justice system treats sex crimes in general more punitively. A cross-cultural survey of 110 tribal societies from the Human Relations Area Files showed that rape was one of the three most heavily punished crimes, with punishment ranging from payment of compensation to death (Brown, 1952). Why would the punishments be so severe if rape were tolerated or if it were a tool used to control women? Why would Matthew Hale, the English jurist, advocate the death penalty for rape in the 1600s, even though he worried about false charges? If rape were thought of as a property crime, why not punish it with the types of sentences assigned to property crimes? It is interesting that rape is sometimes punished as severely as homicide, when death is considered a much more serious harm than forced sex; indeed, the victim's preference for forced sex over death makes many stranger rapes possible.

The arrest and conviction rates for rape are comparable to the arrest and conviction rates for other crimes. About 52% of rapes known to the police in 1991 resulted in an arrest (Bureau of Justice Statistics, 1993). Only arrest rates for homicide and assault were higher than for rape. Steffensmeier (1988) found that 73% of rape defendants were convicted. This conviction rate was slightly lower than conviction rates for homicide, similar to robbery, and higher than the conviction rates for assault and burglary. Similar results have been reported by Galvin and Polk (1983) and the Bureau of Justice Statistics (1993).

Claims about bias against victims by the legal system typically focus on acquaintance rape. It is useful, therefore, to examine legal outcomes in violence by partners (including "date rapes") using Tjaden and Thoennes's (2000) national survey. They examined whether incidents that were reported to the police were prosecuted, whether those that were prosecuted resulted in conviction, and whether offenders who were convicted received a jail or prison term. The results (presented in Table 12.2) suggest that those accused of sexual coercion were just as likely to be prosecuted as those accused of other violence against women, and they were much more likely to be prosecuted than those accused of violence against men. Among those who were prosecuted, conviction was slightly lower for sexual assaults than nonsexual assaults against women; however, no significance test was performed. On the other hand, offenders convicted of sexual assault were much more likely to be sentenced to jail or prison than offenders convicted of nonsexual assaults. This evidence does not suggest a tolerance of sexual assaults involving acquaintances in the criminal justice system.

In a study of 945 defendants in Indianapolis, Myers and LaFree (1982) compared the legal response to sexual assaults to the response to property crimes and other violent crimes. They examined whether the case was dismissed, whether it proceeded to trial, whether it resulted in a guilty verdict, and whether the offender was sentenced to prison. They found some leniency in treatment related to issues of victim credibility and quality of evidence. Sexual assaults were more likely than other crimes to involve eyewitness identification of the defendant and less likely to involve physical evidence and statements from witnesses or defendants and accomplices. Once evidentiary strength was controlled, defendants accused of sexual assault were not treated more leniently than defendants accused of other crimes.

Brereton (1997) compared rape and serious assault trials in Australia. He found that consent was the most frequent defense in rape cases (79%), whereas self-defense was the most frequent defense in assault cases. All of the assault cases had physical evidence of violence, but the rape cases rarely did. In addition, assault cases were much more likely than rapes to have been witnessed by a third party. The absence of physical evidence and witnesses other than the victim is a factor that makes the prosecution of rape cases more difficult. In spite of these factors, assault offenders were more likely than rape offenders to be acquitted.

Brereton also found that issues related to the character of the complainant were just as likely to be raised in assault trials as they were in rape trials. In cross-examination, complainants were just as likely to be asked questions about their drinking behavior and mental stability and just as likely to be attacked for inconsistencies. Complainants in rape trials were more likely to be asked about their sexual history, but complainants in assault were more likely to be asked about their past criminal record. The single most common instance of questions about sexual history was when the complainant was alleged to be a prostitute and there was a question of whether the incident involved consensual sex with her client. Brereton did find that the cross-examinations were of longer duration in rape cases, but he claimed that this occurred because the rape cases were more complex, more likely to include a charge of aggravating conditions, and more likely to involve disputes about consent between people who knew each other.

Victim misconduct has been shown to affect legal outcomes in a variety of violent crimes, as indicated earlier (see Baumer et al., 2000, for a review). Cases in which there was evidence of disreputable conduct by the victim at the time of the offense (e.g., drinking, using drugs, engaging in criminal behavior) were less likely to be prosecuted and less likely to be convicted if prosecuted (Albonetti, 1986; Baumer et al., 2000; Stanko, 1981; K. M. Williams, 1976). No one has directly compared the effect of victim misconduct on the legal outcomes of rape with those of other violent crimes, however. Given the evidence that female offenders tend to be treated more leniently than male offenders (see chapter 5), it would be surprising if female victims were treated worse than male victims.

CONCLUSION

Rape has been used as a method of deterring certain behaviors of women in a few tribal societies. There is no parallel in U.S. society or any other large society. The fact that rape leads American women to curtail their activities more than men does not imply that rape was designed for this purpose. Rape is too blunt an instrument to serve as a method of social control.

Sexual violence is less likely to be reported to the police than other violence. In particular, female victims of partner violence, including date rape, are much less likely to call the police if sexual violence is involved. The greater reluctance of many women to call the police when they are victims of sexual violence is primarily due to greater concerns for privacy, not to the anticipation of difficulties in obtaining legal redress. In addition, the reluctance to report sexual violence is counteracted to some extent by the fact that women are more likely to call the police than are men.

The evidence suggests that the legal system does not respond more leniently to rape or sexual assault than it responds to other crime—the rates of arrest and conviction are similar. In contrast to the Brazilian tribe that condoned group rape if the woman were to view male ritual objects, the U.S.

justice system punishes rape severely. In some ways the legal system responds to rape in the same way it responds to other violent crimes. In criminal prosecutions generally, the conduct of the alleged victim is often a factor, because it is used to make judgments about credibility, causality, and cost. Deviant targets are more likely than other targets to lack credibility, they may be more likely to be attributed a causal role in the incident, and the cost to them may be perceived as less significant or even deserved. The evidence does not support the idea that rape victims who have engaged in some misconduct themselves have less legal recourse than other crime victims who have engaged in misconduct. Nor is there evidence that women who violate gender roles are treated worse than women who violate other norms. Finally, the assignment of blame to victims of sexual assault is no greater when the victim is a woman and the offender a man than when other gender combinations are involved.

Research shows that rape charges are more likely to be false than charges for other crimes, and DNA evidence suggests that mistaken identification is fairly frequent. Because the victim is typically the key witness in these crimes, and because consent is frequently an issue, victim credibility is likely to be important. Defense attorneys attack victim credibility, no matter what the offense. They are actors in an adversarial legal process designed to determine guilt or innocence, not agents of male domination.

IV

CONCLUSION

13

CONCLUSION

Violence involving women is special, according to the feminist perspective and current conventional wisdom. Academic feminism includes different strands, but most feminists would agree with the following assertions about violence involving women:

1. Sexism plays an important role in male violence against women.
2. Because sexism is pervasive, male violence against women is at epidemic levels, or at least occurs with enough frequency to be considered a special social problem.
3. Violence involving women typically has special motives—sexist men use violence to control women or to demonstrate their power, whereas women use violence to defend themselves.
4. Patriarchal societies support violence against women by blaming the victim and by treating offenders leniently.

I have argued and provided evidence that each of these statements is misleading or false. There is not an epidemic of violence against women: Its frequency reflects the frequency of violence generally. Men are more likely than women to injure their partners, but the pattern reflects gender differences in strength and the tendency to engage in violence, not male domination. The frequency of partner violence reflects the inevitable conflict that exists in intimate relationships, not sexism. Finally, societies are no more likely to blame female victims than male victims or to treat those who attack women more leniently. In fact, societies make a special attempt to protect women and generally treat those who offend against them more severely.

There is evidence for some differences in motives for violence related to gender, however. One study suggests that men's violence against their female partners is more likely to involve a control motive than other types of violence. However, evidence suggests that this pattern does not stem from greater male desire to control their partners: Women try to control their husbands more than men try to control their wives, but they use verbal means. In addition, men are more likely than women to be concerned with displaying an image of power, but primarily in their conflicts with other men. Finally, women are more likely than men to kill in self-defense, but this pattern stems from gender differences in the tendency to use violence and is not restricted to couples.

COMPARATIVE APPROACH

I have used a comparative approach to examine whether men's violence against women or wives is special. The approach is useful in disentangling the effects of gender of perpetrator, gender of target, and whether the perpetrator is an intimate partner of the target. It enables one to convert loosely stated arguments into clear, testable hypotheses.

Table 13.1 shows the relevant comparisons. The cell frequencies (represented by letters) refer to the prevalence of particular motives, attitudes, and behavior. "Intimate partners" refers to spouses, boyfriends, and girlfriends (past and present) as well as dating couples. To simplify the comparisons, I identify a perpetrator and a target, although in many incidents the violence is reciprocal.

The comparisons should apply to both sexual and nonsexual violence. In the case of sexual coercion and partner violence, comparisons must control for the fact that there are many more heterosexual than homosexual people. For example, in computing the frequency of homosexual partner violence (cell a), the denominator might be the number of gay men. The hypotheses implied by the feminist approach and the corresponding evidence are presented and critiqued as follows:

Hypothesis 1

The highest frequency of violence should occur in cells c and d, because there is an epidemic of male violence against women. This hypothesis is not supported:

TABLE 13.1
Comparative Approach to Violence

Perpetrator	Target			
	Male partner	Other man	Female partner	Other woman
Man	a	b	c	d
Woman	e	f	g	h

Violence against women is much less frequent than violence against men. The most frequent type of violence involves men (cell b).

Hypothesis 2

The rate of male violence against women (cells c and d) should vary across cultures and over time independently of other rates of violence. This hypothesis is not supported: Temporal and cross-national variation in homicide victimization rates are similar for men and women. When rates of violence against women are high, rates of violence against men are also high. Cross-national comparisons also reveal that male victimization rates dominate homicide statistics: There is much less variation in rates of homicide against women than in rates in homicide against men. Evidence from international crime victimization surveys does not support the idea that U.S. rape rates are particularly high or that they are high relative to the rate of general violence. American students do report more sexual coercion than Swedish students, but they report more violence generally.

Hypothesis 3

Men who use violence against women should be more likely to have sexist attitudes than men who commit violence against men (c and d > a and b). This hypothesis is not supported: The gender-related attitudes of men who use violence against women are similar to the attitudes of other criminals. Male criminal offenders are more likely than other men to have negative attitudes toward women, but the interpretation is unclear: Offenders express more antisocial attitudes generally.

Hypothesis 4

Men who have committed a violent act against a woman should be more likely to have a history of violence against women than men who have committed a violent act against a man (c and d > a and b). This hypothesis is not supported: Most men who commit violence against women are generalists who target both men and women. Their histories of violence against women are therefore similar to those of men who use violence against men.

Hypothesis 5

Men's violence (and other behavior) directed at female partners should be more likely to involve a control motive than similar behavior involving other gender-relationship combinations (c > all other cells). This hypothesis has mixed support: Male assaults on female partners are more likely to be preceded by threats than assaults involving other gender-relationship combinations, suggesting a more important role for the control motive. However, studies that examine gender differences in the use of nonviolent means of control cast doubt on the idea that men have a greater desire to control their partners than women. Women are just as likely as men (and perhaps more likely) to attempt to control their partner's activities, and this behavior is just as highly related to women's violence as men's violence. In addition, women are more likely than men to complain—a verbal means of control—when they have grievances with their partners. This evidence suggests that when men use violence to control their partners, it is because of their greater coercive power—they are bigger, not bossier.

Hypothesis 6

Men involved in verbal conflicts with their female partners should be particularly likely to use violence, because many men believe that violence is a legitimate method of domination (cell c vs. all other cells). This hypothesis is not supported: Both men and women show greater reluctance to use violence with their partners. Verbal conflicts are less, not more, likely to become physical when the antagonists are partners than when they are strangers. Only minor violence against children is legitimated according to evidence on the relative frequency of violence and verbal aggression.

Hypotheses 7a and 7b

Men should be more likely than women to engage in violence against their heterosexual partners due to sexism and men's desire for control over these partners (cells c vs. e). This difference should exceed gender differences in violence against other targets (cells a, b, and d vs. cells f, g, and h). This hypothesis is not supported: Survey research of minor violence involving heterosexual couples has found that men and women have similar rates. Men are more likely than women to engage in serious violence against their partners, probably because of their greater coercive power. However, the gender difference in partner violence is not as large as the gender difference in stranger violence. The evidence suggests that men are inhibited about using violence against female partners, not specially motivated to use it.

Hypothesis 8

Love triangles should be more likely to motivate men's violence than women's violence, particularly men's violence toward their partners, given the strong male desire to control partners (c > b and a and d> e and f and g and h). This hypothesis is not supported: When men commit homicide it is less likely to stem from love triangles than when women commit homicide. When men kill their partners, it is no more likely to stem from love triangles then when women kill their partners. The evidence suggests that women are just as angry with unfaithful partners; they just are not as violent as men. In addition, male protagonists are much more likely to kill their rivals than their partners. In love triangles involving college students, men are more likely than women to attempt to intimidate or control male rivals than to intimidate or control female partners.

Hypothesis 9

Heterosexual men should be more likely than homosexual men to engage in violence against their partners (c > a). This hypothesis is not supported. In fact, data from the NCVS suggests that gay men are *more* likely to be violent toward their partners than are heterosexual men. In addition, there is some evidence that homosexual men are just as likely as heterosexual men to use sexual coercion. The evidence suggests that violence against women is not a function of male dominance or special attitudes toward women. Rather, men are more violent than women and they sometimes use violence with their partners or those with whom they desire sexual relations, whether the target is a man or woman.

Hypothesis 10

Men's violence against women, particularly their wives, should be less likely to be reported to the police than other violence and less likely to lead to arrest, prosecution, and punishment (c > d > other cells). Authorities and other third parties should be less likely to believe the charges of female victims and more likely to blame them for the crime. This hypothesis is not supported: No statistical interactions between gender and social relationship on reporting and legal treatment were observed. Male violence against female partners is not less likely to be reported, and the reaction of the criminal justice system is not special. There is evidence of gender discrimination in the criminal justice system, but it favors women. In general, violence against women is more likely to be reported than violence against men, and it is more likely to lead to arrest, prosecution, and punishment.

Women are less likely to report sexual assaults to the police than other crimes, particularly sexual assaults committed by acquaintances. However, evidence suggests that the underreporting of sexual assaults by acquaintances is the result of greater privacy concerns, not lack of confidence that the case will be successfully prosecuted. Research has not examined whether female victims are more or less likely than male victims to report sexual assaults to the police. However, women are probably more likely to report sexual assaults than men; research shows that they are more likely to report other crimes, and sexual assault victimization is probably more stigmatizing for male victims.

There is no evidence that the police are more skeptical when women charge their husbands with assault than when men charge their wives; the opposite may occur because of (valid) stereotypes about male violence. Anecdotal evidence suggests that the police are often skeptical of female charges of rape, but we do not know whether the police are more skeptical of female charges of rape than male charges of rape, or of male and female charges of other crimes. If the police are more skeptical about rape charges, there may a good reason for it. Evidence suggests that rape charges are more likely to be false than charges for other crimes. We also know from DNA evidence that there are many cases of misidentification in rape.

Finally, there is evidence that female victims of rape are assigned less, not more, blame than male victims of rape. Observers assign blame to rape victims when they think victims have engaged in irresponsible behavior; however, they assign the bulk of blame to offenders. Finally, prosecution and conviction rates for rape are similar to other violent crimes, and convicted rapists are punished severely relative to most other crimes.

Hypothesis 11

Legal authorities and other observers are more tolerant of violence against women who violate gender roles than violence against men who violate gender roles, and they treat offenders more leniently (c, d, g, and h < a, b, e, and f). This hypothesis is not supported: There is some evidence that we judge men more harshly than women for violations of gender roles. In addition, the criminal justice system does not punish women more for violations of gender roles (e.g., sexual violations) than for other criminal behavior, and it generally punishes women less severely than men for the same crime.

Hypothesis 12

Women's violence against their male partners is more likely to be motivated by self-defense and victim-precipitated than other violence (e vs. other cells). This hypothesis is not supported: Neither victim precipitation nor self-defense is especially prevalent when women kill their male partners. Gender does have additive effects, however: Men are more likely to initiate violence in serious incidents (although not in minor incidents).

In sum, the comparative method is useful for testing theoretical claims that a particular type of violence is special. None of the hypotheses about the distinctiveness of violence against women or wives suggested by a feminist approach are supported. Many are in the opposite direction to the one predicted. The results suggest that the study of partner violence and violence against women be incorporated into the study of violence. Until future evidence suggests otherwise, the parsimony principle suggests that social scientists should prefer more general theories of violence.

DISCRIMINATIVE PREDICTABILITY

Another method used in this book I refer to as "discriminative predictability:" A theoretical explanation can be tested if it implies that variable X affects Y, but not Z. The concept is similar to the concept of discriminative validity, which refers to the ability of a measure to predict the variables it should, and not others, according to theory or common sense. Discriminative predictability is different in that it refers to the validity of a theory rather the validity of measurement.

I used the method of discriminative predictability to address research showing that gender inequality (X) predicts statewide rates of male violence against women (Y), but that it also predicts violence involving other gender combinations (Z). This pattern casts doubt on the feminist explanation for the correlation between statewide measures of inequality and rape rates. I also used the method to examine whether hostility toward women (X) has a causal effect on violence toward women (Y). Research shows that hostility toward women correlates just as strongly with other criminal behavior (Z)—that is, rapists are not different from other criminals in their attitudes. If these hostile attitudes have a causal effect, they should be more highly related to violence against women than other criminal behavior, and they are not.

The method of discriminative predictability should be given more attention in the study of violence and crime. A theory of violence is challenged by evidence that its key causal variables predict nonviolent crime or other behavior as well. For example, Berkowitz's (1989) theory of emotional aggression predicts that negative affect is associated with aggression; the fact that negative affect is associated with any type of risk-taking behavior is a challenge to his theory (Leith & Baumeister, 1996). In addition, research showing that children engage in a variety of misbehaviors after viewing violent films—not just violence—challenges the modeling explanation posited by social learning theory. It suggests the possibility that children are more likely to misbehave when adult sponsors convey permissiveness by showing violent films (Felson, 1996b). The effects of some forms of violent pornography observed in experiments with college men may be due to a similar process.

CONFLICT AND POWER

A basic assertion in this book is that interpersonal violence stems from conflict or divergent interests. I made the controversial argument that all conflict is local—that group conflicts and politics play only a minor role in conflicts between individuals. The fact that men are dominant or have higher status in the public sphere in patriarchal societies does not mean that they dominate their wives. Structural power is different from dyadic power (Guttentag & Secord, 1983). Men may have more economic power in families with a traditional division of labor, but women have other resources at their disposal to counter that power. In addition, exchange principles in marital choice tend to produce couples with similar power to each other.

Conflict is inevitable between people who live together, because their lives are interdependent. Couples have additional conflict because they share resources, have different sexual interests, and are sometimes tempted to stray. Gay and lesbian couples have these same conflicts, so we should not be surprised that they also sometimes engage in violence.

Gender differences contribute to the level of conflict in heterosexual couples and alter the power equation. Three gender differences are particularly large: (1) Men are much bigger and stronger than women; (2) men are much more violent than women; and (3) men have stronger sexual interests and are more indiscriminant in their choice of partners. These differences are important factors in understanding violence involving women. Heterosexual women often live with men who are stronger than they are and are more prone to use injurious violence. When conflicts occur, it is not surprising that some men use violence.

Marital violence occurs because conflicts are frequent and intense, not because the antagonists think it is more legitimate to use violence against their mates. The marriage license is not a hitting license: Society evaluates partner violence at least as negatively as other violence, and probably more so. People are more reluctant to intervene in couple violence than stranger violence, when it is not too serious, because of concerns for privacy, not greater acceptance of the behavior.

Male demand for sex exceeds the supply because of gender differences in sexuality. As a result, some men use coercion and other influence tactics to get their way. In addition, adversarial relations sometimes develop between men and women regarding sexual activity. Men use women for sex, and women use sex to influence men. A dramatic gender difference in willingness to engage in sexual activity with strangers also leads to sexual coercion. Finally, male interest in physically attractive women and their lack of access to these women increases the likelihood of sexual assault.

VICTIM'S ROLE

The theoretical approach used in this book emphasizes the role of social interaction—as opposed to conditions inside the person—in violent behavior. Although the approach recognizes the role of individual differences, the focus is on the role of situational factors in the development of violent interactions. The relationship between the antagonists, the dynamics of the interchange between them, and the presence or absence of third parties are all relevant for explaining the event.

The victim plays at least some causal role in most incidents of dispute-related violence and, to a lesser extent, in predatory violence. Whether an individual kills someone in self-defense or in response to mild criticism, the target's behavior has an effect. I have argued that we should do casual analysis and avoid "blame analysis" in discussions of violence against women. Assigning a causal role to targets does not necessarily imply that they are blameworthy. Whether the victim is blameworthy may be relevant to the legal system, but it is irrelevant to a scientific analysis of violence.

For purpose of crime prevention, it is useful to recognize that crime victims sometimes make mistakes that play a role in their victimization: It is generally more effective to try to change the behavior of potential victims than the behavior of potential offenders. Statements that women (or men) should not have to curtail their activities because of crime are unrealistic. The real world can be a dangerous place, and we must take precautions. No society can be expected to provide full protection from crime.

Many violent disputes between men and women in intimate relationships involve mutual aggression and violence. In minor incidents, women are apparently as likely as men to be the first person to use violence. Violence against partners correlates at least as highly with prior aggression and delinquency for women as it does for men. Thus, women who use violence against their husbands tend to be aggressive in other circumstances as well. We cannot understand disputes if we must constantly worry about the charge of blaming the victim.

In homicides, male victims are more likely than female victims to be the first to use violence, and women are more likely than men to kill in response to violence. Women are also more likely to kill in self-defense, although that is not a typical motive for men or women. The homicide evidence is not consistent with the notion of a battered wife syndrome. As indicated above, men are no more likely to provoke their wives to kill them than they are to provoke other people to kill them. Women who kill their husbands are no less violent than other female homicide offenders. Because men are more violent than women, women are more likely to kill in response to violence, and men are more likely to be killed because of their own violence. Victim precipitation is not special in violence involving couples.

Women's behavior often plays a causal role in sexual coercion involving acquaintances. Their use of token resistance may lead men to use coercion in instances where they misread sincere resistance. Their sexual teasing may anger men or lead to misunderstandings. On the other hand, perhaps the victims who attribute the incident to a misunderstanding misunderstand the incident themselves. Perhaps men who use coercion with acquaintances understand perfectly well when women are disinterested and proceed anyway. The role of misunderstandings in sexual coercion needs further research.

The image of the passive female victim's somehow encouraging further attack is not consistent with the evidence. Women are not particularly reluctant to report assaults by their male partners to the police, nor are they particularly reluctant to file charges. Some wives are inhibited from calling the police because of their fear of reprisal, but fear of future attack is much more likely to lead them to call the police. Women's desire to protect violent male partners is no greater than the desire of victims to protect other violent family members, male or female. In other words, women are not particularly likely to be fooled by their violent but "sweet-talking" husbands. Finally, women threatened with rape are not passive compared to men in the same circumstance. In fact, female victims of rape are more likely to resist than male victims.

MOTIVES

I have argued that people use violence to achieve interpersonal goals. This approach is an alternative to frustration–aggression approaches, which view aggression and violence as a response to frustration or aversive stimuli. The latter viewpoint assumes a biological connection between negative experiences and aggression and a special system of aggressive behavior. Perhaps my presentation of evidence for the instrumental approach was unnecessary: Frustration–aggression approaches are not used to explain violence toward women anyway. However, the rejection of these approaches should be based on empirical evidence, not the reluctance to accept a motive that implies offenders are less blameworthy. If I am wrong, and aversive stimuli instigate (rather than facilitate) emotional aggression, then aversive stimuli must instigate emotional violence against women as well. In other words, feminist researchers are ignoring frustration–aggression approaches for the wrong reason.

My perspective requires an understanding of the phenomenology of actors, who often view their own violence as legitimate and even moralistic. Since the decline of extreme behaviorism, the focus on the actor's perspective is standard practice in the social sciences. To understand why people use violence, it is necessary to examine their perceptions, judgments, expectations, emotions, and values. The perspective of the victim, on the other hand, is not very informative about the offender's motive. For example, outcomes that are critical for rape victims, such as powerlessness or humiliation, may be incidental outcomes for offenders. It is sometimes difficult to focus on the offender's perspective in the study of violence against women because of the tendency to demonize offenders and because we sympathize with female victims and want to avoid assigning them any blame. Both chivalry and ideology interfere with science in this area.

One reason that individuals use violence is their desire to control others. The husband threatens his wife or hits her to influence her to do things his way. The rapist uses coercion to produce sexual compliance. When the target is a partner or acquaintance, he uses violence after other influence methods have failed. The use of violence for purposes of control is not restricted to male violence against women, however. Robbers use violence to control their victims, and men sometimes assault other men for purposes of control. However, the use of violence for control requires superior coercive power. Thus I argued that gender differences in coercive power (and the interdependence of couples) explains why men's violence against their female partners is more likely than other violence to involve a control motive.

Individuals also use violence for retribution when they believe they have been treated wrongly. The justice restoration process goes hand in hand with the control motive. Offended parties (and often third parties) desire punishment for purposes of deterrence and because they believe that justice demands that someone who does wrong deserves to be punished. Grievances play a greater role in violence between people who know each other, for both men and women. Couples fight over sex, children, money, and other issues that arise when people live together and are interdependent. There are gender differences in the content of grievances, however. For example, gender differences in sexual interest lead men to complain about women's sexual withholding and women to complain about male pressure.

Individuals also use violence to assert and protect identities. The schoolyard bully targets other boys in front of classmates to show his power. Individuals retaliate when attacked to avoid appearing weak (as well as to deter and punish). These patterns are more apparent in conflicts between men. Male violence against women, including rape, is unlikely to provide a favorable identity for men, and it may even make them look weak and cowardly. As a result, male violence against women, unlike bullying, is likely to occur in private. The identity argument can explain only some of the reluctance to harm women, however. It cannot explain why women are also reluctant to harm women or why third parties protect women and treat those who harm women more severely. The chivalry norm is useful to explain these patterns.

Men may use violence to demonstrate to themselves that they are powerful and tough, but overpowering men is more likely than overpowering women to accomplish this goal. Men may retaliate when women attack them to avoid appearing weak, but they are more likely to retaliate when their adversary is another man. Violent identity contests are more likely to involve male antagonists.

Some violence between men and women stems from conflict over love triangles. Both male and female protagonists in love triangles have concerns for control, justice, and identity. Both men and women are interested in retribution for the wrongs committed by the partner and rival. Both men and women experience an identity threat, although men who lose face are more likely to respond by using aggression against the rival. Men are also more likely than women to attempt to stop the affair by intimidating their rival.

Certainly sexism plays a role in motivating some violence against women. For example, there are a few serial killers who target only women, apparently out of hatred for the group. Perhaps a belief in male dominance causes some men to use violence to control their wives. However, traditional attitudes also include notions of chivalry, which is likely to offset any effect of male dominance.

There is some evidence that sexism plays a role in violence in some other cultures. At least two studies of tribal societies show a negative correlation between the frequency of rape and the power and status of women (I. L. Reiss, 1986; Sanday, 1981). Also, some studies of Moslem and other non-Western societies have shown a toleration of minor forms of violence against wives, for purposes of "correction." Perhaps sexism played a role in violence against wives historically in Western societies as well. Some judges in previous centuries mentioned the correction principle in their opinions, although they did not seem to accept the principle themselves. The relative strength of the offsetting effects of correction and chivalry historically is unknown.

INHIBITORY FACTORS

Inhibitory factors, as well as incentives, affect decision making. Individuals, to some extent, consider costs, norms, and moral values when they contemplate a violent action. However, many decisions are made impulsively, with little or no consideration for costs and moral values. Impulsive decisions are more likely when the person is in an emotional state, highly stressed, sexually aroused, or under the influence of alcohol or other drugs.

The effect of the state of the perpetrator during the incident appears to be similar for violence against men and women. For example, alcohol and drug use plays an important role in violence against women just as it does in violence against men, suggesting similar causal dynamics. To my knowledge, no one has made explicit comparisons to determine whether alcohol and drug use affects violence against women or intimate partners differently than it does other violence.

The versatility of violent offenders suggests that general inhibitory factors are important for violence against women. Individual differences in self-control, exposure to external controls (e.g., family and school attachments), and general moral values are implicated. If a man who beats his wife also gets in fights in bars and burglarizes homes, then it is unlikely that wife beating reflects his attitude toward women. If sexist men do not treat women worse than men—if they do not discriminate on the basis of gender—then sexism is not a useful concept for explaining their behavior.

In the case of violence against women, I emphasize a special inhibitory factor: Chivalry is the elephant in the violence room that scholars have ignored. The evidence is clear that its inhibitory effect is strong and pervasive, countering the lower costs that promote the use of violence against those who are physically weaker. People are less likely to harm women than men inside and outside the experimental laboratory, and the justice system often treats women more leniently when they violate the law. People are less likely to harm women in front of audiences and mirrors, which are known to inhibit antinormative behavior. Those who harm a woman are judged more harshly and punished more severely. It is clear that hitting women is deviant behavior that male offenders would prefer to conceal from third parties. It is hidden because it is antisocial behavior.

I suspect that even men with liberal attitudes about gender roles are more offended by harm to women than harm to men and feel a stronger obligation than women to protect their partners. They may not want to admit it because of their egalitarian values. Without chivalry, there would be no special concern about violence against women, and this book might not have been written. Chivalry is not dead, but it is hidden because of our egalitarian ethic.

A HYPOTHETICAL EGALITARIAN SOCIETY

Imagine a utopian society where gender roles and patriarchy do not exist. Women would make as much money as men, men would participate equally in child care, and half of the political leaders and corporate executives would be women. Would rates of violence against women be lower in such a society?

Perhaps greater respect for women in traditionally male domains would lead men to be less violent against them. However, the higher status of men in male domains does not protect them from violence—their victimization rates are higher than women's. In addition, evidence suggests that the level of violence is just as high in families in which women are equal breadwinners (Coleman & Straus, 1986; Ronfeldt, Kimmerling, & Arias, 1998).

Women might be expected to be as courageous and tough as men in an egalitarian society, so perhaps the gender difference in violent offending would be reduced. However, although the male threat would be lower, tough women would become a greater threat; the gender difference in the overall level of violence against women might remain the same. Only if men became more like women and women did not become more like men would the overall level of violence be reduced.

Men and women in this egalitarian society would still experience the conflicts of living together. They would still have conflicts over money, children, and sex, given individual differences. Men might still have stronger sex drives and lower sexual selectivity, so they might still have an incentive to use sexual coercion. Women's greater independence and opportunities would probably increase the incidence of love triangles, which, in turn, would increase the rate of couple violence.

The decline of chivalry in an egalitarian society would reduce inhibitions about attacking women—schoolyard bullies would intimidate girls as much as boys. Intoxicated patrons at bars would be just as likely to pick a fight with a woman as a man. Women would still be smaller than men, but chivalry would no longer afford them protection. For these reasons, I suspect that the victimization of women would increase in an egalitarian society.

MINOR VERSUS SERIOUS VIOLENCE

I have argued that it is important to distinguish levels of violence. The distinction between minor and serious violence is particularly important in the study of gender differences in partner violence. Many people have at some point engaged in minor forms of violence against their partners. No one was hurt, neither party considered the event a crime, and no one called the police. Women are just a likely as men to engage in this noninjurious violence, and they are just as likely to be the first one to strike. Although this behavior may offend us, it is not the type of violence that should be of greatest public concern. We should be more concerned about the injurious violence that occurs between couples, the type of violence that is likely to involve a male offender and a female victim. We need shelters for women, not men.

Activists have a tendency to cloud the distinction between minor and serious violence to generate high numbers (e.g., Gilbert, 1991). They count the minor acts and then label the behavior using language that describes its most serious form (e.g., Koss, Gidycz, & Wisniewski, 1987). For example, minor violence against wives is inaccurately labeled "wife beating" or "repeated abuse." Clouding the distinction is useful in generating advocacy numbers, because there are many more instances of minor violence than serious violence. However, it is not legitimate from a scientific perspective because it gives an inaccurate description of the phenomenon that we are trying to explain.

The strategy of confusing minor and serious violence can backfire politically, because gender differences disappear when one counts minor acts of violence. In other words, two ideological goals are at cross-purposes: showing high numbers and showing gender asymmetry. Activists are in a dilemma because their attempts to generate high numbers make it appear that gender differences in partner violence are small or nonexistent. The dilemma has produced a schism between family violence activists and feminist activists.

The involvement of the legal system also depends on the seriousness of the incident. When victims do not consider behavior criminal, they are unlikely to report it to the police. Minor violence that occurs between family members is therefore not reported, whereas the same behavior by a stranger might be. When victims do consider partner violence criminal, they are just as likely to report it to the police. The reaction of third parties also depends on the seriousness of the violence. Third parties are reluctant to intervene or report minor acts of violence involving family members to the police, but they are just as likely to report more serious violence.

Historically, the response of the legal system to violence against wives has depended on the seriousness of the incident. The cases in which the courts were lenient toward violent husbands involved minor acts of violence. The debate in the courts was whether privacy should prevail in these cases. It is inaccurate to say that wife beating was condoned because minor forms of domestic violence were tolerated. Men who committed serious assault could be prosecuted under the assault laws.

The distinction between minor and serious violence is also important in the study of sexual coercion. Many of these incidents involve mild forms of coercion with acquaintances or male pressure that is ambiguous in terms of whether it involves coercion. The victim reports feeling annoyed, not threatened (see chapter 9). She is not hurt physically, she may suffer no psychological harm, and she may not even consider herself a crime victim. These incidents probably dominate in surveys of college students and enable researchers to generate high frequencies. It is not surprising that juries and legal authorities are reluctant to send the young men who commit these acts to prison. In fact, it may be useful to charge men with less serious offenses in order to get convictions.

The distinction between violent rape and minor sexual coercion is also important in the discussion of sexual fantasies. A substantial number of women report fantasies about coercive sex; apparently minor forms of male coercion are exciting to these women. No one should infer from these fantasies that these women want to be raped. But they point to the importance of distinguishing minor from serious forms of sexual coercion.

To make the distinction between a beating and a slap is not to condone slapping. To make the distinction between brutal rapes and sexual advances in the face of protest is not to condone minor forms of sexual coercion. One could just as easily argue that combining the two trivializes the more serious events. The distinctions are necessary for an accurate description of violent incidents and an understanding of how people react to these events.

RACE AND CLASS

I have not said much about the role of race and social class in violence against women. Some scholars would criticize the neglect of these demographic variables, suggesting that it is critical that one study the intersection of "race, class, and gender." The comparative approach and standard statistical language are useful in considering the issue empirically and resolving the problem. We must be concerned with the intersection of race, class, and gender if we observe a three-way statistical interaction between these variables. If the effects of gender on violence depend on both race and socioeconomic status, then we must incorporate interaction terms in our equations and qualifications in our theoretical discussion. If the effects of gender depend on race alone or social class alone, then we need to incorporate two-way interaction terms.

On grounds of parsimony, we should prefer an additive model. If there are theoretical reasons to believe that causal processes are different for different groups, then we should test for statistical interactions; the inclusion or exclusion of class, race, and gender variables should be an empirical question rather than an ideological issue. Because there is usually no theoretical reason to expect statistical interactions, it is not surprising that few have been found. To quote a sociologist I know, "I have been to the corner of class, race, and gender, and I can tell you that the bus doesn't stop there."

There is some evidence of two-way statistical interactions between race and gender in their effects on violence. Recall that there are race differences in the ratio of husband victimization to wife victimization: Black women are more likely than black men to kill their spouses (Wilson & Daly, 1992). Also, recent research suggests that race differences in violence are stronger for adolescent girls than adolescent boys; black girls have higher rates than one would expect given the additive effects of race and gender (Felson, Deane, & Armstrong, 2001).

It is clear that there are class and race differences in violent behavior generally. Higher rates of violence among poor people and among African Americans are typically attributed to discrimination and lack of economic opportunity. It is therefore interesting that this same treatment does not lead women to have higher rates of violence than men—the gender difference is strong and in the opposite direction. The pattern suggests that either women are not subject to much discrimination or that discrimination does not lead to violent crime or that discrimination leads to violent crime only under as yet unspecified conditions. For example, some commentators believe that race and class effects are mediated by neighborhood effects.

IMPLICATIONS FOR RESEARCH STRATEGY

The Violence Against Women Act sets aside money for research funding. There are two related problems with this strategy. First, because the research focuses strictly on violence against women, it ignores the broader patterns described in this book. Second, most of the researchers who work in this area are committed to the idea that violence against women reflects sexism. They are not likely to entertain alternative approaches, particularly those that cast doubt on the rationale for the Violence Against Women Act.

Hopefully, this book will contribute to the understanding of how the study of violence should be organized and where resources should be directed. For example, if we are interested in why women fail to report assaults by their husbands to the police, should we be studying female victims, victims of domestic violence, or victims of violent crime generally? For some outcomes, it will be useful to examine subcategories of violent behavior separately, but for others, we may be missing the larger picture if we do so. We must start by studying violence generally and then determine if some types are special.

IMPLICATIONS FOR COUNSELING

One of the key strategies of activists is to emphasize the seriousness of sexual coercion, including coercion involving acquaintances. This is useful for political reasons, and it might also influence men who consider using sexual coercion to realize the seriousness of their actions. The activists appear to have had some success in affecting perceptions of seriousness. For example, some of my students, typically the more ideologically motivated, believe that rape is worse than death.

Emphasizing the seriousness of these incidents may not be in the victim's interest, however. Convincing women that they have been victimized when they do not think they have may upset them unnecessarily. Convincing them that their victimization is more serious than they realize may increase the trauma. The situation is similar to one in which a person has cancer or some other serious illness. When we visit them at the hospital, we do not want to emphasize the danger or dwell on the seriousness of their predicament. We want to put the best face on their situation and give them hope, while still acknowledging their suffering.

There is an alternative approach. A friend of mine, whose daughter was raped by a stranger, attempted to convince her to view herself as a crime victim, nothing more. He helped her receive counseling, but he did not want to exaggerate the seriousness of the incident, because he believed it would be more difficult for her to recover. Similarly, a rape counselor told me that some of her colleagues at the rape crisis center were disillusioned with the ideological approach they had originally used and had become less directive with their clientele. They now allowed the victims themselves to define their own experience.

Another strategy of the activists is to glorify the female victims of violence. For example, rape victims are now typically referred to as "survivors" rather than victims. This term makes the victim seem more active and heroic and perhaps makes her feel fortunate that she was not killed. However, it may be difficult to convince victims that they are worthy of this glorified image. Female victims of rape and domestic assault, like other crime victims, have often made mistakes that played a causal role in their victimization. To deny this fact is not realistic and may backfire if victims know otherwise. Victims may be reasonably skeptical when counselors tell them that only offenders are blameworthy. They may think their behavior is worse than the behavior of other victims because they did not live up to idealized image of victims promulgated by activists. In addition, the survivor label exaggerates the seriousness of the rape or assault because victims are rarely murdered. The victim may experience more fear and trauma than she might otherwise.

Loseke's (1992) ethnographic study of a shelter for battered women suggests how the impact of ideology can compromise the counseling process. The staff assumed that their clients were victims of severe and continuing abuse. They attributed the victims' drug and alcohol problems, low self-esteem, passivity, and other problems to what they believed was the primary problem: victimization by the male partner. They did not recognize the possibility that the client's behavior might have played a causal role in the violence as well or that their problems were a separate issue. Women who did not fit their ideal type were often denied access to the shelter or evicted. In spite of these practices, not all of the clients wanted to leave their partners, not all were grateful to the staff, some were angry and defiant, and others had extensive problems that could not be attributed to the abuse.

In general, I am suggesting that there may be costs as well as benefits to idealizing female victims and exaggerating the seriousness of their victimization. Setting up impossible standards and "the ideal victim" may lead to more negative self-evaluation and more trauma. An approach that denies that victims can play a causal role in violence, particularly dispute-related violence, is not realistic. Counseling is likely to be less effective when it is guided by ideology rather than evidence and experience.

The understanding of motive is important in the counseling of offenders and victims. If men who assault women also assault men, it makes more sense to teach them anger management than to attempt to change their attitudes toward women. In the case of domestic violence, it may be more useful to counsel couples rather than the male offenders alone. Counselors should not be reluctant to advise victims to avoid behaviors that provoke violence, because victim behavior is often easier to change than offender behavior. Such an approach recognizes the causal role of victims and the interactional dynamics leading to violence.

IMPLICATIONS FOR CRIME PREVENTION

It is very difficult to influence offenders to stop offending. They tend to be impulsive young men who are neither receptive to educational programs nor deterred by marginal increases in punishment severity (e.g., Nagin, 1998). Rape reform laws do not appear to have increased conviction rates (Horney & Spohn, 1991). Arrest for domestic violence is at best an inconsistent deterrent; it sometimes increases the likelihood of a repeated offense. Mandatory arrest laws may be useful, but they are also likely to be exploited by women who have become estranged from their husbands. The law is a weapon that can be used for illegitimate as well as legitimate purposes.

Some scholars argue that the actions of citizens and changes in the physical environment are more effective in reducing crime than increased legal penalties. Much progress has been made under the rubric of situational crime prevention (e.g., Clarke, 1992). The approach is aligned with the routine activity approach, which states that crime is made possible by the contact of motivated offenders and vulnerable targets in the absence of capable guardians (M. Felson, 1998; see chapters 2 and 9). By decreasing the vulnerability of targets and increasing guardianship, we can reduce the opportunity for crime and reduce the crime rate. This approach builds on the everyday crime prevention methods used by individuals (e.g., locking doors, walking in groups). It is consistent with the situational perspective presented in this book.

Situational crime prevention is typically used in the prevention of crime committed by strangers. For example, creating more defensive space and other changes in the physical environment make it more difficult for offenders to commit crimes. Increased supervision of youths, who commit the most crime, is another strategy. There is always the problem of target substitution: An offender deterred from crime in one location commits it elsewhere. However, offenders tend to be impulsive and lazy, so if we can reduce the number of opportunities for crime, the number of offenses is also likely to decrease. These strategies are therefore useful for preventing violence against men and women. To some extent, general crime prevention strategies are the best strategies for the prevention of violence against women.

Women's vulnerability to violence, however, is special in that it is more likely to be committed by people they know. Situational crime prevention is more difficult to apply to domestic violence and acquaintance rape, because these offenses tend to occur in private locations that are difficult for outsiders to alter. Perhaps situational crime prevention could be used in counseling couples at risk of domestic violence how to increase guardianship and decrease victim vulnerability. Another method is to provide women at risk a means of contacting authorities when they are being threatened. Electronic devices can be used to monitor compliance with protective orders and prompt swift police intervention. These include alarm systems in victim's homes or on the victim's person and bracelets worn by offenders that set off alarms if he approaches the victim's home (National Research Council, 1998). Finally, the use of shelters for women to prevent contact with violent husbands is consistent with situational crime prevention strategy.

IMPACT OF IDEOLOGY

Both feminism and chivalry lead those who study violence involving women to attempt to protect the image of women. Scholars avoid ideas that might cast women in a negative light, because such ideas might support stereotypes and encourage sexism. For example, although we can talk about gender differences in violence, it is controversial to mention gender differences in complaining; it sounds like a negative stereotype about women. It is ironic that so many sociologists and other social scientists condemn stereotyping, when they are in the stereotype business. Any discussion of gender differences involves generalizations about men and women. Science suffers when hypotheses about group differences are evaluated according to the image they project for protected groups. The scientific analysis of group differences is often in conflict with the promotion of tolerance and diversity. In the study of human behavior, no group comes out unscathed.

Feminists have had considerable influence on public policy concerning violence against women. For example, there are now special laws regarding domestic violence in most states. The police are much more likely to arrest a husband who assaults his wife rather than seek reconciliation, even if she does not press charges. Sexual harassment suits are now common in the workplace and in universities. The courts prevent the introduction of a victim's sexual history in rape cases and no longer require corroboration of the victim's testimony. Finally, feminists influenced a conservative, and largely male, Congress to pass the Violence Against Women Act (1994).

Feminist activists have had an impact, at least in part, because they have struck a responsive chord among the citizenry. Virtually everyone is sympathetic with crime victims, and high violent crime rates have made many citizens angry and punitive toward criminals. In their approach to violence against women, feminists have become allies of those who want to "get tough on crime," such as political conservatives and the religious right. In addition, feminists and traditionalists share the desire to provide special protections for women. In this context, it is easier to demonize men who have been violent toward women and treat them more punitively.

Like their conservative allies, feminist activists have not shown much concern for civil liberties. For example, sexual harassment codes and restrictions on pornography threaten free speech. Changes making it easier to prosecute rape reduce the likelihood of due process. The charge of sexism may upset the precarious balance between the rights of the victim and the rights of the accused. Sympathy with gender issues and civil liberties push the political left in different directions when women are victims. Civil liberty issues fall by the wayside once the left—their traditional advocates—loses interest.

The development of mandatory arrest policies for domestic violence shows the impact of the alliance of conservatives and the feminist left. The changes came in response to a research study that found that arresting violent husbands deterred them from further violence (Sherman & Berk, 1984). Policy makers usually ignore social science research, but this research was an exception. Almost every state in the union introduced mandatory arrest policies, with feminist support. Because this research supported the punitive inclinations of the more conservative citizenry, it became one of the most influential studies in the history of social science. Later research failed to confirm the earlier findings and showed that arrest sometimes increases subsequent violence, but that research has had no impact on arrest policy (e.g., Berk, Campbell, Klap, & Western, 1992; Sherman & Smith, 1992).

One could argue that, overall, feminist influence has been positive because it drew attention to a social problem. Even if their methods were inadequate and their conclusions erroneous, they influenced the public to devote attention and resources to helping female victims. I do not agree that the end justifies the means in this instance for three reasons: (1) There is no evidence that the feminist approach has had any effect on reducing rates of violence against women, (2) bad research produces bad public policy, and (3) social scientists lose credibility when they generate information on social problems that is later revealed to be false.

I have criticized both frustration–aggression and feminist approaches to violence in this book. Some readers will disagree with some of my criticisms of frustration–aggression or suggest that I have gone too far, but they will not be angry. The reaction to my criticism of the feminist approach to violence will be very different. Many readers will respond with anger and charges of sexism and backlash and ignore the substantive arguments and evidence. My approach has been to take the feminist approach seriously as a scientific theory by stating it in terms of testable hypotheses, considering alternative theories, and discussing relevant evidence. I believe that if feminism is going to have lasting impact in social science, it must compete in a free marketplace of ideas.

REFERENCES

Abbey, A. (1982). Sex differences in attributions for friendly behavior: Do males misperceive females' friendliness? *Journal of Personality and Social Psychology, 42,* 830–838.

Abel, G. G., Barlow, D. H., Blanchard, E. B., & Guild, D. (1977). The components of rapists' sexual arousal. *Archives of General Psychiatry, 34,* 895–903.

Ageton, S. S. (1983). *Sexual assault among adolescents.* Lexington, MA: Lexington Books.

Albonetti, C. A. (1986). Criminality, prosecutorial screening, and uncertainty: Toward a theory of discretionary decision making in felony case processing. *Criminology, 24,* 623–644.

Alder, C. (1984). The convicted rapist: A sexual or a violent offender? *Criminal Justice and Behavior, 11,* 157–177.

Aldis, O. (1975). *Play fighting.* San Diego, CA: Academic Press.

Allison, J. A., & Wrightsman, L. S. (1993). *Rape: The misunderstood crime.* Newbury Park, CA: Sage.

Amir, M. (1971). *Patterns in forcible rape.* Chicago: University of Chicago Press.

Archer, J. (1994). Power and male violence. In J. Archer (Ed.), *Male violence* (pp. 310–331). London: Routledge.

Archer, J. (2000). Sex differences in aggression between heterosexual partners: A meta-analytic review. *Psychological Bulletin, 126,* 651–680.

Ard, B. N. (1977). Sex in lasting marriages: A longitudinal study. *Journal of Sex Research, 13,* 274–285.

Arias, I., & Johnson, P. (1989). Evaluations of physical aggression among intimate dyads. *Journal of Interpersonal Violence, 4,* 298–307.

Arkin, R. M. (1981). Self-presentation styles. In J. T. Tedeschi (Ed.), *Impression management theory and social psychological research* (pp. 311–334). New York: Academic Press.

Austin, R. L., & Kim, Y. K. (2000). A cross-national examination of the relationship between gender equality and official rape rates. *International Journal of Offender Therapy and Comparative Criminology, 44,* 204–221.

Avakame, E. F. (1998). How different is violence in the home? An examination of some correlates of stranger and intimate homicide. *Criminology, 36,* 601–632.

Averill, J. R. (1983). Studies on anger and aggression: Implications for theories of emotion. *American Psychologist, 38,* 1145–1160.

Bachman, R. (1995). Police involvement in domestic violence: The interactive effects of victim injury, offender's history of violence, and race. *Violence and Victims, 10,* 91–107.

Bachman, R., & Saltzman, L. E. (1995). *Violence against women: Estimates from the redesigned survey* (U.S Department of Justice, Bureau of Justice Statistics). Washington, DC: U.S. Government Printing Office.

Bailey, J. M., Kirk, K. M., Zhu, G., Dunne, M. P., & Martin, N. G. (2000). Do individual differences in sociosexuality represent genetic or environmentally contingent strategies? Evidence from the Australian twin registry. *Journal of Personality and Social Psychology, 78,* 537–545.

Bandura, A. (1973). *Aggression: A social learning analysis.* Englewood Cliffs, NJ: Prentice-Hall.

Barber, R. N. (1969). Prostitution and the increasing number of convictions for rape in Queensland. *Australian and New Zealand Journal of Criminology, 2,* 169–174.

Baron, L., & Straus, M. A. (1987). Four theories of rape: A macrosociological analysis. *Social Problems, 34,* 467–489.

Baron, R. A., & Richardson, D. R. (1994). *Human aggression* (2nd ed.). New York: Plenum Press.

Barron, M., & Kimmel, M. (2000). Sexual violence in three pornographic media: Toward a sociological explanation. *Journal of Sex Research, 37,* 161–168.

Barry, H., III, & Schlegel, A. (1984). Measurements of adolescent sexual behavior in the standard sample of societies. *Ethnology, 23,* 315–329.

Baumeister, R. F. (2000). Gender differences in erotic plasticity: The female sex drive as socially flexible and responsive. *Psychological Bulletin, 126,* 347–374.

Baumeister, R. F., Heatherton, T. F., & Tice, D. M. (1994). *Losing control: How and why people fail at self-regulation.* San Diego: Academic Press.

Baumeister, R. F., Smart, L., & Boden, J. M. (1996). Relation of threatened egotism to violence and aggression: The dark side of high self-esteem. *Psychological Review, 103,* 5–33.

Baumeister, R. F., Stillwell, A., & Wotman, S. R. (1990). Victim and perpetrator accounts of interpersonal conflict: Autobiographical narratives about anger. *Journal of Personality and Social Psychology, 59,* 994–1005.

Baumer, E. P., Messner, S. F., & Felson, R. B. (2000). The role of victim character and victim conduct in the disposition of murder cases. *Justice Quarterly, 17,* 281–307.

Baumgartner, M. P. (1988). *The moral order of a suburb*. New York: Oxford University Press.

Baumgartner, M. P. (1993). Violent networks: The origins and management of domestic conflict. In R. B. Felson & J. T. Tedeschi (Eds.), *Aggression and violence: Social interactionist perspective* (pp. 209–231). Washington, DC: American Psychological Association.

Beaulieu, M., & Messner, S. F. (1999). Race, gender, and outcomes in first degree murder cases. *Journal of Poverty, 3*, 47–68.

Belknap, J. (2001). *The invisible woman: Gender, crime, and justice* (2nd ed.). Belmont, CA: Wadsworth.

Bell, A. P., & Weinberg, M. S. (1978). *Homosexualities: A study of diversity among men and women*. New York: Simon and Schuster.

Bem, D. J. (1972). Self-perception theory. In L. Berkowitz (Ed.), *Advances in experimental social psychology* (Vol. 6, pp. 2–62). New York: Academic Press.

Berk, R. A., Campbell, A., Klap, R., & Western, B. (1992). The deterrent effect of arrest in incidents of domestic violence: A Bayesian analysis of four field experiments. *American Sociological Review, 57*, 698–708.

Berkowitz, L. (1989). The frustration–aggression hypothesis: An examination and reformulation. *Psychological Bulletin, 106*, 59–73.

Berkowitz, L. (1993). *Aggression: Its causes, consequences, and control*. Philadelphia: Temple University Press.

Besag, V. (1989). *Bullies and victims in school*. Philadelphia: Open University Press.

Best, J. (1995). *Images of issues: Typifying contemporary social problems* (2nd ed.). New York: A. De Gruyter.

Bettencourt, B. A., & Miller, N. (1996). Gender differences in aggression as a function of provocation: A meta-analysis. *Psychological Bulletin, 119*, 422–447.

Bjorkqvist, K., Lagerspetz, K. M. J., & Kaukiainen, A. (1992). Do girls manipulate and boys fight? Developmental trends in regard to direct and indirect aggression. *Aggressive Behavior, 18*, 117–127.

Black, D. J. (1971). The social organization of arrest. *Stanford Law Review, 23*, 1087–1111.

Black, D. J. (1976). *The behavior of law*. New York: Academic Press.

Black, D. J. (1983). Crime as social control. *American Sociological Review, 48*, 34–45.

Black, D. J. (1989). *Sociological justice*. New York: Oxford University Press.

Blackstone, W. (1836). *Commentaries on the laws of England*. New York: W. E. Dean.

Block, C. R. (1993). The meaning and measurement of victim-precipitated homicide. In C. R. Block & R. L. Block (Eds.), *Questions and answers in lethal and nonlethal violence* (pp. 185–193). Washington, DC: National Institute of Justice.

Block, J. (1983). Differential premises arising from differential socialization of the sexes: Some conjectures. *Child Development, 54*, 1335–1354.

Block, R. (1974). Why notify the police: The victim's decision to notify the police of an assault. *Criminology, 11*, 555–569.

Blood, R. O., & Wolfe, D. M. (1960). *Husbands and wives.* Glencoe, IL: Free Press.

Blumstein, P., & Schwartz, P. (1983). *American couples: Money, work, sex.* New York: Morrow.

Boeringer, S. (1994). Pornography and sexual aggression: Associations of violent and nonviolent depictions with rape and rape proclivity. *Deviant Behavior, 15,* 289–304.

Bograd, M. (1988). Feminist perspectives on wife abuse: An introduction. In M. Bograd & K. A. Yllö (Eds.), *Feminist perspectives on wife abuse* (pp. 11–26). Beverly Hills, CA: Sage Publications.

Bookwala, J., Frieze, I. H., Smith, C., & Ryan, K. (1992). Predictors of dating violence: A multivariate analysis. *Violence and Victims, 7,* 297–311.

Borden, R. J. (1975). Witnessed aggression: Influence of an observer's sex and values on aggressive responding. *Journal of Personality and Social Psychology, 31,* 567–573.

Brand, P. A., & Kidd, A. H. (1986). Frequency of physical aggression in heterosexual and female homosexual dyads. *Psychological Reports, 59,* 1307–1313.

Brereton, D. (1997). How different are rape trials? A comparison of the cross-examination of complainants in rape and assault trials. *British Journal of Criminology, 37,* 242–261.

Briere, J., Malamuth, N. M., & Check, J. V. P. (1985). Sexuality and rape-supportive beliefs. *International Journal of Women's Studies, 8,* 398–403.

Bringle, R. G., & Buunk, B. P. (1991). Extradyadic relationships and sexual jealousy. In K. McKinney & S. Sprecher (Eds.), *Sexuality in close relationships* (pp. 135–153). Hillsdale, NJ: Lawrence Erlbaum.

Brody, L. (1999). *Gender, emotion and the family 1999.* Cambridge, MA: Harvard University Press.

Broude, G. J., & Greene, S. J. (1976). Cross-cultural codes on twenty sexual attitudes and practices. *Ethnology, 15,* 409–429.

Brown, J. S. (1952). A comparative study of deviations from sexual mores. *American Sociological Review, 17,* 135–146.

Browne, A. (1987). *When battered women kill.* New York: Free Press.

Browne, A., & Williams, K. R. (1993). Gender, intimacy, and lethal violence: Trends from 1976 through 1987. *Gender and Society, 7,* 78–98.

Brownmiller, S. (1975). *Against our will: Men, women, and rape.* New York: Simon and Schuster.

Brubaker, J. D. (Producer), & Segal, P. (Director). (2000). *Nutty professor II: The Klumps* [Motion picture]. United States: Universal Pictures.

Bryden, D. P., & Lengnick, S. (1997). Rape in the criminal justice system. *Journal of Criminal Law and Criminology, 87,* 1255–1283.

Bureau of Justice Statistics. (1985). *The crime of rape.* Washington, DC: U.S. Government Printing Office.

Bureau of Justice Statistics. (1993). *Sourcebook of criminal justice statistics—1992*. Washington, DC: U.S. Department of Justice.

Bureau of Justice Statistics. (1995). *Spouse murder defendants in large urban counties*. Washington, DC: U. S. Department of Justice, Bureau of Justice Statistics.

Bureau of Justice Statistics. (1997a). *Criminal victimization in the United States—1994*. Washington, DC: U.S. Government Printing Office.

Bureau of Justice Statistics. (1997b). *Sex difference in violent victimization, 1994*. Washington, DC: U.S. Government Printing Office.

Bureau of Justice Statistics. (2001). *Capital Punishment 2000*. Washington, DC: U.S. Department of Justice.

Burt, M. R. (1980). Cultural myths and support for rape. *Journal of Personality and Social Psychology, 38*, 217–230.

Buss, A. H., & Durkee, A. (1957). An inventory for assessing different kinds of hostility. *Journal of Consulting Psychology, 21*, 343–349.

Buss, D. M. (1989a). Conflict between the sexes: Strategic interference and the evocation of anger and upset. *Journal of Personality and Social Psychology, 56*, 735–747.

Buss, D. M. (1989b). Sex differences in human mate preferences: Evolutionary hypotheses in 37 cultures. *Behavioral and Brain Sciences, 12*, 1–49.

Buss, D. M. (1994). *The evolution of desire: Strategies of human mating*. New York: Basic Books.

Buss, D. M. (1999). *Evolutionary psychology: The new science of the mind*. Boston: Allyn and Bacon.

Buss, D. M. (2000). *The dangerous passion: Why jealousy is as necessary as love and sex*. New York: Free Press.

Buss, D. M., & Cantor, N. (1989). *Personality psychology: Recent trends and emerging directions*. New York: Springer-Verlag.

Buss, D. M., & Malamuth, N. M. (1996). *Sex, power, conflict: Evolutionary and feminist perspectives*. New York: Oxford University Press.

Buzawa, E., Austin, T. L., & Buzawa, C. G. (1995). Responding to crimes of violence against women: Gender differences versus organizational imperatives. *Crime and Delinquency, 41*, 443–466.

Cahalan, D. (1978). Implications of American drinking practices and attitudes for prevention and treatment of alcoholism. In G. A. Marlatt & P. E. Nathan (Eds.), *Behavioral approaches to alcoholism* (pp. 6–26). New Brunswick, NJ: Rutgers Center for Alcohol Studies.

Carver, C. S. (1974). Physical aggression as a function of objective self-awareness and attitudes toward punishment. *Journal of Experimental Social Psychology, 11*, 510–519.

Castan, N. (1976, August). *Divers aspectes de la constrainte maritale, d'apres les documents judiciaires du XVIII siecle [Various aspects of marital compulsion, according to judicial documents of 18th-century France.]*. Paper presented at the annual meeting of the American Sociological Association, New York.

Cazenave, N. A., & Zahn, M. A. (1992). Women, murder and male domination: Police reports of domestic violence in Chicago and Philadelphia. In E. C. Viano (Ed.), *Intimate Violence: Interdisciplinary perspectives* (pp. 83–97). Washington, DC: Hemisphere Publishing. Corp.

Chagnon, N. A. (1977). *Yanomamo: The fierce people*. Holt, Reinhardt & Winston.

Chappell, D., & James, J. (1976, September 8th). *Victim selection and apprehension from the rapist's perspective: A preliminary investigation*. Paper presented at the 2nd International Symposium on Victimology, Boston.

Chesney-Lind, M. (1978). Chivalry reexamined: Women and the criminal justice system. In L. H. Bowker (Ed.), *Women, crime, and the criminal justice system* (pp. 197–223). Lexington, MA: D.C. Heath.

Chesney-Lind, M. (1988). Girls in jail. *Crime and Delinquency, 34*, 150–168.

Choi, A., & Edleson, J. L. (1996). Social disapproval of wife assaults: A national survey of Singapore. *Journal of Comparative Family Studies, 27*, 73–88.

Clark, R. D., & Hatfield, E. (1989). Gender differences in receptivity to sexual offers. *Journal of Psychology and Human Sexuality, 2*, 39–55.

Clarke, R. V. (Ed.). (1992). *Situational crime prevention: Successful case studies*. New York: Harrow and Heston.

Cleaver, E. (1968). *Soul on ice*. New York: Dell-Delta/Ramparts.

Cohen, L. E., & Felson, M. (1979). Social change and crime rate trends: A routine activity approach. *American Sociological Review, 44*, 588–608.

Coleman, D. H., & Straus, M. A. (1986). Marital power, conflict, and violence in a nationally representative sample of American couples. *Violence and Victims, 1*, 141–157.

Cook, P. J. (1976). A strategic-choice analysis of robbery. In W. G. Skogan (Ed.), *Sample surveys of the victims of crime*. Cambridge, MA: Ballinger.

Courtwright, D. T. (1996). *Violent land: Single men and social disorder from the frontier to the inner city*. Cambridge, MA: Harvard University Press.

Craig, M. E., Kalichman, S. C., & Follingstad, D. R. (1989). Verbal coercive sexual behavior among college students. *Archives of Sexual Behavior, 18*, 421–434.

Curtis, L. A. (1974). Victim precipitation and violent crime. *Social Problems, 21*, 594–605.

Daly, K., & Bordt, R. L. (1995). Sex effects and sentencing: An analysis of the statistical literature. *Justice Quarterly, 12*, 141–169.

Daly, M., & Wilson, M. (1988). *Homicide*. New York: Aldine De Gruyter.

Daly, M., Wilson, M., & Weghorst, S. J. (1982). Male sexual jealousy. *Ethology and Sociobiology, 3*, 11–27.

DeKeseredy, W. S., & MacLeod, L. (1997). *Woman abuse: A sociological story*. Toronto, Ontario: Harcourt Brace.

Demare, D., Lips, H. M., & Briere, J. (1993). Sexual violent pornography, antiwomen attitudes, and sexual aggression: A structural equation model. *Journal of Research in Personality, 27*, 285–300.

Deming, M. B., & Eppy, A. (1981). The sociology of rape. *Sociology and Social Research, 64*, 357–380.

Dengerink, H. A. (1976). Personality variables as mediators of attack-instigated aggression. In R. G. Geen & E. C. O'Neal (Eds.), *Perspectives on aggression*. New York: Academic Press.

de Weerth, C., & Kalma, A. P. (1993). Female aggression as a response to sexual jealousy: A sex role reversal. *Aggressive Behavior, 19*, 265–279.

Dobash, R. E., & Dobash, R. P. (1978). Wives: The "appropriate" victims of marital violence. *Victimology, 2*, 426–442.

Dobash, R. E., & Dobash, R. P. (1979). *Violence against wives: A case against the patriarchy*. New York: Free Press.

Dobash, R. E., & Dobash, R. P. (1998). *Rethinking violence against women*. Thousand Oaks, CA: Sage.

Dobash, R. P., & Dobash, R. E. (1981). Community response to violence against wives: Charivari, abstract justice and patriarchy. *Social Problems, 28*, 563–581.

Dobash, R. P., Dobash, R. E., Wilson, M., & Daly, M. (1992). The myth of sexual symmetry in marital violence. *Social Problems, 39*, 71–91.

Dollard, J., Doob, L. W., Miller, N. E., Mowrer, O. H., & Sears, R. R. (1939). *Frustrations and aggression*. New Haven: Yale University Press.

Donnerstein, E. I. (1980). Aggressive erotica and violence against women. *Journal of Personality and Social Psychology, 39*, 269–277.

Donnerstein, E. I., & Hatfield, E. (1982). Aggression and inequity. In J. Greenberg & R. Cohen (Eds.), *Equity and justice in social behavior* (pp. 309–336). New York: Academic Press.

Dutton, D. G. (1988). *The domestic assault of women: Psychological and criminal justice perspectives*. Boston: Allyn and Bacon.

Dworkin, A. (1981). *Pornography: Men possessing women*. New York: G. P. Putnam's Sons.

Eagly, A. H., & Crowley, M. (1986). Gender and helping behavior: A meta-analytic review of the social psychological literature. *Psychological Bulletin, 100*, 283–308.

Eagly, A. H., & Karau, S. J. (1991). Gender and the emergence of leaders: A meta-analysis. *Journal of Personality and Social Psychology, 60*, 685–710.

Eagly, A. H., & Mladinic, A. (1994). Are people prejudiced against women? Some answers from research on attitudes, gender stereotypes, and judgments of competence. *European Review of Social Psychology, 5*, 1–35.

Eagly, A. H., & Steffen, V. J. (1986). Gender and aggressive behavior: A meta-analytic review of the social psychological literature. *Psychological Bulletin, 100*, 309–330.

Eber, L. P. (1981). The battered wife's dilemma: To kill or be killed. *Hastings Law Journal, 32*, 895–931.

Eigenberg, H. M. (2001). *Woman battering in the United States: Till death do us part.* Prospect Heights, IL: Waveland Press.

Elliott, D. S. (1989). Criminal justice procedures in family violence crimes. In L. E. Ohlin & M. H. Tonry (Eds.), *Family violence* (pp. 427–480). Chicago, IL: University of Chicago Press.

Ellis, B. J., & Symons, D. (1990). Sex differences in sexual fantasy: An evolutionary psychological approach. *Journal of Sex Research, 27,* 527–555.

Ellis, L. (1989). *Theories of rape: Inquires into the causes of sexual aggression.* New York: Hemisphere Publishing.

Ellis, L., & Beattie, C. (1983). The feminist explanation of rape: An empirical test. *Journal of Sex Research, 19,* 74–93.

Emerson, R. M. (1972). Exchange theory: Part 1. A psychological basis for social exchange. In J. Berger, M. Zelditch, Jr., & B. Anderson (Eds.), *Sociological theories in progress* (pp. 38–57). Boston: Houghton Mifflin.

Ennis, P. H. (1967). *Criminal victimization in the United States: A report of a national survey.* Washington, DC: President's Commission on Law Enforcement and Administration of Justice.

Epstein, S., & Taylor, S. P. (1967). Instigation to aggression as a function of defeat and perceived aggressive intent of the opponent. *Journal of Personality, 35,* 265–289.

Etzioni, A. (1968). *The active society: A theory of societal and political processes.* New York: Collier-Macmillan.

Eysenck, H. J. (1976). *Sex and personality.* London: Open Books.

Fagan, J., & Browne, A. (1994). Violence between spouses and intimates: Physical aggression between women and men in intimate relationships. In A. J. Reiss, Jr. & J. A. Roth (Eds.), *Understanding and preventing violence* (Vol. 3, pp. 115–292). Washington, DC: National Academy Press.

Fagan, J., Stewart, D., & Hansen, K. (1983). Violent men or violent husbands? Background factors and situational correlates of domestic and extra-domestic violence. In D. Finkelhor, R. J. Gelles, G. T. Hotaling, & M. A. Straus (Eds.), *The dark side of families* (pp. 49–68). Beverly Hill, CA: Sage Publications.

Faragher, T. (1985). The police response to violence against women in the home. In J. Pahl (Ed.), *Private violence and public policy.* London: Routledge & Kegan Paul.

Farrington, D. P. (1989). Early predictors of adolescent aggression and adult violence. *Violence and Victims, 4,* 79–100.

Feder, L. (1998). Police handling of domestic and nondomestic assault calls: Is there a case for discrimination? *Crime and Delinquency, 44,* 335–349.

Feild, H. S. (1978). Attitudes toward rape: A comparative analysis of police, rapists, crisis counselors and citizens. *Journal of Personality and Social Psychology, 36,* 156–179.

Feld, S. L., & Robinson, D. T. (1993, October). *Gender and violence among college students: Norms, identity, and rationality.* Paper presented at the Annual Meeting of the American Society of Criminology, Miami, FL.

Feld, S. L., & Straus, M. A. (1989). Escalation and desistance of wife assault in marriage. *Criminology, 27*, 141–161.

Feldman, S. S., & Cauffman, E. (1999). Sexual betrayal among late adolescents: Perspective of the perpetrator and the aggrieved. *Journal of Youth and Adolescence, 28*, 235–254.

Felson, M. (1998). *Crime and everyday life* (2nd ed.). Thousand Oaks, CA: Pine Forge Press.

Felson, R. B. (1978). Aggression as impression management. *Social Psychology, 41*, 205–213.

Felson, R. B. (1981). An interactionist approach to aggression. In J. T. Tedeschi (Ed.), *Impression management theory and psychological research* (pp. 181–199). New York: Academic Press.

Felson, R. B. (1982). Impression management and the escalation of aggression and violence. *Social Psychology Quarterly, 45*, 245–254.

Felson, R. B. (1983). Aggression and violence between siblings. *Social Psychology Quarterly, 46*, 271–285.

Felson, R. B. (1984). Patterns of aggressive social interaction. In A. Mummendey (Ed.), *Social psychology of aggression: From individual behavior to social interaction* (pp. 107–126). New York: Springer-Verlag.

Felson, R. B. (1991). Blame analysis: Accounting for the behavior of protected groups. *American Sociologist, 22*, 5–23.

Felson, R. B. (1992). "Kick 'em when they're down": Explanations of the relationship between stress and interpersonal aggression and violence. *Sociological Quarterly, 33*, 1–16.

Felson, R. B. (1993). Predatory and dispute-related violence: A social interactionist approach. In R. V. Clarke & M. Felson (Eds.), *Advances in criminological theory* (Vol. 5, pp. 189–235). New Brunswick, NJ: Transaction.

Felson, R. B. (1996a). Big people hit little people: Sex differences in physical power and interpersonal violence. *Criminology, 34*, 433–452.

Felson, R. B. (1996b). Mass media effects on violent behavior. *Annual Review of Sociology, 22*, 103–128.

Felson, R. B. (2000). The normative protection of women. *Sociological Forum, 15*, 91–116.

Felson, R. B., & Ackerman, J. (2001). Arrest for domestic and other assaults. *Criminology, 39*, 501–521.

Felson, R. B., Baccaglini, W., & Gmelch, G. (1986). Bar-room brawls: Aggression and violence in Irish and American bars. In A. Campbell & J. J. Gibbs (Eds.), *Violent transactions* (pp. 153–166). Oxford: Basil Blackwell.

Felson, R. B., Baccaglini, W., & Ribner, S. (1985). Accounting for criminal violence: A comparison of official and offender versions of the crime. *Sociology and Social Research, 70*, 93–95.

Felson, R. B., Deane, G., & Armstrong, D. (2001, March). *Race and adolescent crime and violence: An incident-based analysis.* Paper presented at the Annual Meetings of the Eastern Sociological Society, Philadelphia.

Felson, R. B., & Krohn, M. D. (1990). Motives for rape. *Journal of Research in Crime and Delinquency, 27*, 222–242.

Felson, R. B., & Liska, A. E. (1984). Explanations of the sex-deviance relationship. *Deviant Behavior, 5*, 1–10.

Felson, R. B., Liska, A. E., South, S. J., & McNulty, T. L. (1994). School subcultures of violence and delinquency. *Social Forces, 73*, 155–173.

Felson, R. B., & Messner, S. F. (1996). To kill or not to kill? Lethal outcomes in injurious attacks. *Criminology, 34*, 519–545.

Felson, R. B., & Messner, S. F. (1998). Disentangling the effects of gender and intimacy on victim precipitation in homicide. *Criminology, 36*, 405–423.

Felson, R. B., & Messner, S. F. (2000). The control motive in intimate partner violence. *Social Psychology Quarterly, 63*, 86–94.

Felson, R. B., Messner, S. F., & Hoskin, A. (1999a). The victim–offender relationship and calling the police in assaults. *Criminology, 37*, 931–947.

Felson, R. B., Messner, S. F., & Hoskin, A. (1999b, November). *The whys and why nots of reporting domestic and other assaults to the police*. Paper presented at the American Society of Criminology, Toronto.

Felson, R. B., & Outlaw, M. C. (2002). *Controlling behavior and intimate partner violence*. Unpublished manuscript.

Felson, R. B., & Russo, N. J. (1988). Parental punishment and sibling aggression. *Social Psychology Quarterly, 51*, 11–18.

Felson, R. B., & Steadman, H. J. (1983). Situational factors in disputes leading to criminal violence. *Criminology, 21*, 59–74.

Feshbach, S., & Malamuth, N. (1978). Sex and aggression: Proving the link. *Psychology Today, 11*, 11, 112, 114, 116–117, 122.

Finkelhor, D., & Yllö, K. A. (1985). *License to rape: Sexual abuse of wives*. New York: Rinehart and Wilson.

Fischer, C. S. (1969). The effect of threats in an incomplete information game. *Sociometry, 32*, 301–314.

Fisher, W., & Grenier, G. (1994). Violent pornography, antiwoman thoughts, and antiwoman acts: In search of reliable effects. *Journal of Sex Research, 31*, 23–38.

Follingstad, D. R., Wright, S., Lloyd, S., & Sebastian, J. A. (1991). Sex differences in motivations and effects in dating violence. *Family Relations, 40*, 51–57.

Ford, C. S., & Beach, F. A. (1951). *Patterns of sexual behavior*. New York: Harper and Row.

Fox, J. A. (2001). *Uniform Crime Reports [United States]: Supplementary Homicide Reports, 1976–1999 [Computer file]. ICPSR version*. Ann Arbor, MI: Inter-University Consortium for Political and Social Research.

French, J. R. P., & Raven, B. H. (1959). The bases of social power. In D. Cartwright (Ed.), *Studies in social power* (pp. 150–167). Ann Arbor: University of Michigan Press.

Frieze, I. H., & Browne, A. (1989). Violence in marriage. In L. E. Ohlin & M. H. Tonry (Eds.), *Family violence* (pp. ??–??). Chicago, IL: University of Chicago Press.

Frieze, I. H., & Davis, K. E. (2000). An introduction to stalking and obsessive behaviors in everyday life: Assessments of victims and perpetrators. *Violence and Victims, 15,* 355.

Frost, G. (1995). *Promises broken: Courtship, class and gender in Victorian England.* Charlottesville, VA: University Press of Virginia.

Frude, N. (1994). Marital violence: An interactional perspective. In J. Archer (Ed.), *Male violence* (pp. 153–169). London: Routledge.

Fyfe, J. J., Klinger, D. A., & Flavin, J. (1997). Differential police treatment of male-on-female spousal violence. *Criminology, 35,* 455–473.

Gagnon, J. H. (1977). *Human sexualities.* Glenview, IL: Scott, Foresman & Co.

Gagnon, J. H., & Simon, W. S. (1973). *Sexual conduct: The social sources of human sexuality.* Chicago: Aldine.

Galvin, J., & Polk, K. (1983). Attrition in case processing: Is rape unique? *Journal of Research in Crime and Delinquency, 20,* 126–154.

Gamson, W. A. (1964). Experimental studies of coalition formation. In L. Berkowitz (Ed.), *Advances in experimental social psychology* (Vol. 1, pp. 81–110). New York: Academic Press.

Garcia, L. T., & Milano, L. (1990). A content analysis of erotic videos. *Journal of Psychology and Human Sexuality, 32,* 95–103.

Gebhard, P. H., Gagnon, J. H., Pomeroy, W. B., & Christenson, C. V. (1965). *Sex offenders: An analysis of types.* New York: Harper & Row.

Geis, G. (1977). Forcible rape: An introduction. In D. Chappell, R. Geis, & G. Geis (Eds.), *Forcible rape: The crime, the victim and the offender* (pp. 1–37). New York: Columbia University Press.

Geis, G. (2000). On the absence of self-control as the basis for a general theory of crime. *Theoretical Criminology, 4,* 35–53.

Gelles, R. J. (1983). An exchange/social control theory. In D. Finkelhor, R. J. Gelles, G. T. Hotaling, & M. A. Straus (Eds.), *The dark side of families.* Beverly Hills, CA: Sage Publications.

Gelles, R. J. (1987). *The violent home.* Newbury Park, CA: Sage Publications.

Gentry, C. S. (1991). Pornography and rape: An empirical analysis. *Deviant Behavior, 12,* 277–288.

Gergen, M. (1990). Beyond the evil empire: Horseplay and aggression. *Aggressive Behavior, 16,* 381–398.

Gilbert, N. (1991, Spring). The phantom epidemic of sexual assault. *Public Interest,* 54–65.

Ginsburg, H. J., & Miller, S. M. (1982). Sex differences in children's risk-taking behavior. *Social Psychology Quarterly, 47,* 146–159.

Giordano, P. C., Millhollin, T. J., Cernkovich, S. A., Pugh, M. D., & Rudolph, J. L. (1999). Delinquency, identity, and women's involvement in relationship violence. *Criminology, 37,* 17–37.

Glick, P., & Fiske, S. T. (1999). Gender, power dynamics, and social interaction. In M. M. Ferree, J. Lorber, & B. Hess (Eds.), *Revisioning gender* (pp. 365–398). Thousand Oaks, CA: Sage Publications.

Glueck, S., & Glueck, E. T. (1956). *Physique and delinquency*. New York: Harper.

Goetting, A. (1995). *Homicide in families and other special populations*. New York: Springer.

Goffman, E. (1955). On face-work: An analysis of ritual elements in social interaction. *Psychiatry, 18*, 213–231.

Goffman, E. (1959). *The presentation of self in everyday life*. New York: Doubleday Anchor.

Goldstein, M. J. (1973). Exposure to erotic stimuli and sexual deviance. *Journal of Social Issues, 29*, 197–219.

Goldstein, P. J. (1990). Drugs and violent crime. In N. A. Weiner, M. A. Zahn, & R. J. Sagi (Eds.), *Violence: Patterns, causes, public policy*. San Diego: Harcourt Brace Jovanovich.

Goodchilds, J. D., & Zellman, G. L. (1984). Sexual signaling and sexual aggression in adolescent relationships. In N. M. Malamuth & E. I. Donnerstein (Eds.), *Pornography and sexual aggression* (pp. 233–243). San Diego, CA: Academic Press.

Goode, W. J. (1971). Force and violence in the family. *Journal of Marriage and the Family, 33*, 624–635.

Gordon, L. (1988). *Heroes of their own lives: The politics and history of family violence, Boston 1880–1960*. New York: Viking Press.

Gottfredson, M. R., & Gottfredson, D. M. (1980). *Decision-making in criminal justice*. Cambridge, MA: Ballinger.

Gottfredson, M. R., & Hirschi, T. (1990). *A general theory of crime*. Stanford, CA: Stanford University Press.

Greenberg, M. S., & Ruback, R. B. (1992). *After the crime: Victim decision making*. New York: Plenum Press.

Greenblat, C. S. (1983). A hit is a hit . . . or is it? Approval and tolerance of the use of physical force by spouses. In D. Finkelhor, R. J. Gelles, G. T. Hotaling, & M. A. Straus (Eds.), *The dark side of families* (pp. ??–??) . Beverly Hill, CA: Sage Publications.

Greendlinger, V., & Byrne, D. (1987). Coercive sexual fantasies of college men as predictors of self-reported likelihood to rape and overt sexual aggression. *Journal of Sex Research, 23*, 1–11.

Greer, A. E., & Buss, D. M. (1994). Tactics for promoting sexual encounters. *Journal of Sex Research, 31*, 185–201.

Gregor, T. (1990). Male dominance and sexual coercion. In J. W. Stigler, R. A. Shweder, & G. H. Herdt (Eds.), *Cultural psychology: Essays on comparative human development* (pp. 477–495). Cambridge, NY: Cambridge University Press.

Groth, A. N., & Birnbaum, H. J. (1979). *Men who rape: The psychology of the offender*. New York: Plenum Press.

Groth, A. N., & Burgess, A. W. (1980). Male rape: Offenders and victims. *American Journal of Psychiatry, 137*, 806–810.

Groth, A. N., Burgess, A. W., & Holmstrom, L. L. (1977). Rape: Power, anger, and sexuality. *American Journal of Psychiatry, 134*, 1239–1243.

Gutmann, S. (1990). It sounds like I raped you. *Reason, 22*, 22–27.

Guttentag, M., & Secord, P. F. (1983). *Too many women? The sex ratio question.* Beverly Hills, CA: Sage Publications.

Hagen, R. (1979). *The biosexual factor.* New York: Doubleday.

Haj-Yahia, M. M. (1996). Wife abuse in the Arab society in Israel: Challenge for future change. In J. L. Edleson & Z. C. Eisikovitz (Eds.), *The future of intervention with battered women and their families* (pp. 87–101). Thousand Oaks, CA: Sage Publications.

Haj-Yahia, M. M. (1998). A patriarchal perspective of beliefs about wife beating among Palestinian men from the West Bank and the Gaza Strip. *Journal of Family Issues, 19*, 595–621.

Hale, M. (1680). *History of the pleas of the crown* (Vol. 1). (Emlyn ed., 1847).

Hall, E. R., Howard, J. A., & Boezio, S. L. (1986). Tolerance of rape: A sexist or antisocial attitude. *Psychology of Women Quarterly, 10*, 101–118.

Harris, M. (1997). *Culture, people, nature: An introduction to general anthropology.* New York: Harper & Row.

Harris, M. B. (1991). Effects of sex of aggressor, sex of target, and relationship on evaluations of physical aggression. *Journal of Interpersonal Violence, 6*, 174–186.

Harris, M. B. (1992). Sex and ethnic differences in past aggressive behaviors. *Journal of Family Violence, 7*, 85–102.

Hart, H. L. A. (1968). *Punishment and responsibility: Essays in the philosophy of law.* New York: Oxford University Press.

Hartford, T. C. (1978). Contextual drinking patterns among men and women. In F. A. Seixas (Ed.), *Currents in alcoholism* (Vol. 4, pp. 287–296). San Francisco: Grune & Stratton.

Hartford, T. C., & Gerstel, E. K. (1981). Age-related patterns of daily alcohol consumption in Metropolitan Boston. *Journal of Studies on Alcohol, 42*, 1062–1066.

Harway, M., & O'Neil, J. M. (1999). *What causes men's violence against women?* Thousand Oaks, CA: Sage Publications.

Heider, F. (1958). *The psychology of interpersonal relations.* New York: Wiley.

Hickey, E. W. (1991). *Serial murderers and their victims.* Belmont, CA: Wadsworth.

Hickman, S. E., & Muehlenhard, C. L. (1999). By the semi-mystical appearance of a condom: How young women and men communicate consent in heterosexual situations. *Journal of Sex Research, 36*, 258–272.

Hickson, F. C. I., Davies, P. M., Hunt, A. J., Weatherburn, P., McManus, T. J., & Coxon, A. P. M. (1994). Gay men as victims of nonconsensual sex. *Archives of Sexual Behavior, 23*, 281–294.

Hilton, N. Z., Harris, G. T., & Rice, M. E. (2000). The functions of aggression by male teenagers. *Journal of Personality and Social Psychology, 79*, 988–994.

Hirschon, R. (Ed.). (1984). *Women and property.* New York: St. Martins.

Holmstrom, L., & Burgess, A. W. (1978). *The victim of rape: Institutional reactions.* New York: Wiley.

Holmstrom, L. L., & Burgess, A. W. (1979). Rapists talk. *Deviant Behavior, 1,* 101–125.

Holtzworth-Munroe, A., & Stuart, G. L. (1994). Typologies of male batterers: Three subtypes and the differences among them. *Psychological Bulletin, 116,* 476–497.

Hooton, E. A. (1939). *Crime and the man.* New York: Greenwood Press.

Horney, J., & Spohn, C. C. (1991). Rape law reform and instrumental change in six urban jurisdictions. *Law and Society Review, 25,* 117–153.

Horney, J., & Spohn, C. C. (1996). The influence of blame and believability factors on the processing of simple versus aggravated rape cases. *Criminology, 34,* 135–162.

Hornstein, H. A. (1965). The effects of different magnitudes of threat upon interpersonal bargaining. *Journal of Experimental Social Psychology, 1,* 282–293.

Hotaling, G. T., & Sugarman, D. B. (1986). An analysis of risk markers in husband to wife violence: The current state of knowledge. *Violence and Victims, 1,* 101–124.

Howells, K., & Wright, E. (1978). The sexual attitudes of aggressive sexual offenders. *British Journal of Criminology, 18,* 170–173.

Huesmann, L. R. (1988). An information processing model for the development of aggression. *Aggressive Behavior, 14,* 13, 24.

Hull, J. G. (1981). A self-awareness model of the causes and effects of alcohol consumption. *Journal of Abnormal Psychology, 90,* 586–600.

Jackson, S. (1978). The social context of rape: Sexual scripts and motivation. *Women's Studies International Quarterly, 1,* 27–38.

Jay, T. B. (1980). Sex roles and dirty word usage: A review of the literature and a reply to Haas. *Psychological Bulletin, 88,* 614–621.

Johnson, G. D., Palileo, G. J., & Gray, N. B. (1992). Date rape on a southern campus: Reports from 1991. *Sociology and Social Research, 76,* 37–41.

Johnson, M. P. (1995). Patriarchal terrorism and common couple violence: Two forms of violence against women. *Journal of Marriage and the Family, 57,* 283–294.

Johnson, M. P. (1999, November). *Two types of violence against women in the family: Identifying patriarchal terrorism and common couple violence.* Paper presented at the National Council on Family Relations, Irvine, CA.

Jurik, N., & Winn, R. (1990). Gender and homicide: A comparison of men and women who kill. *Violence and Victims, 5,* 227–242.

Juster, F. T., & Stafford, F. P. (1991). The allocation of time: Empirical findings, behavioral models and problems measurement. *Journal of Economic Literature, 29,* 471–522.

Kahn, M. W. (1980). Wife beating and cultural context: Prevalence in an Abonginal and Islander Community in northern Australia. *American Journal of Community Psychology, 8,* 727–731.

Kaleta, R. J., & Buss, A. H. (1973, May). *Aggression intensity and femininity of the victim*. Paper presented at the meeting of the Eastern Psychological Association.

Kanekar, S. V., Nanji, J., Kolsawalla, M. B., & Mukerji, G. S. (1981). Perception of an aggressor and victim of aggression as a function of sex and retaliation. *Journal of Social Psychology, 114*, 139–140.

Kanin, E. J. (1965). Male sex aggression and three psychiatric hypotheses. *Journal of Sex Research, 1*, 227–229.

Kanin, E. J. (1967). An examination of sexual aggression as a response to sexual frustration. *Journal of Marriage and the Family, 3*, 429–433.

Kanin, E. J. (1969). Selected dyadic aspects of male sex aggression. *Journal of Sex Research, 5*, 12–28.

Kanin, E. J. (1985). Date rapists: Differential sexual socialization and relative deprivation. *Archives of Sexual Behavior, 14*, 219–231.

Kanin, E. J. (1994). False rape allegations. *Archives of Sexual Behavior, 23*, 81–92.

Kanin, E. J., & Parcell, S. R. (1977). Sexual aggression: A second look at the offended female. *Archives of Sexual Behavior, 6*, 67–76.

Kaplan, R., & Felson, R. B. (1999, November). *The (in)frequency of family violence*. Paper presented at the American Society of Criminology, Toronto.

Karmen, A. (1996). *Crime victims: An introduction to victimology* (3rd ed.). Belmont, CA: Wadsworth.

Kasof, J. (1993). Sex bias in the naming of stimulus persons. *Psychological Bulletin, 113*, 140–163.

Katz, J. (1988). *Seductions of crime: Moral and sensual attractions of doing evil*. New York: Basic Books.

Katz, S., & Mazur, M. A. (1979). *Understanding the rape victim: A synthesis of research findings*. New York: Wiley.

Keen, M. (1984). *Chivalry*. New Haven, CT: Yale University Press.

Kelly, H. A. (1994). Rule of thumb and the folklaw of the husband's stick. *Journal of Legal Education, 44*, 341–365.

Kennedy, L. W., & Sacco, V. F. (1998). *Crime victims in context*. Los Angeles, CA: Roxbury.

Kertzer, D. I. (1993). *Sacrificed for honor: Italian infant abandonment and the politics of reproductive control*. Boston: Beacon Press.

Kipnis, D., & Schmidt, S. M. (1983). An influence perspective on bargaining in organizations. In M. Bazerman & R. Lewicki (Eds.), *Negotiating in organizations* (pp. 303–319). Beverly Hills, CA: Sage Publications.

Kleck, G., & McElrath, K. (1991). The effects of weaponry on human violence. *Social Forces, 69*, 669–692.

Koss, M. P. (1992). The underdetection of rape: Methodological choices influence incidence estimates. *Journal of Social Issues, 48*, 61–75.

Koss, M. P., & Dinero, T. E. (1987). *Predictors of sexual aggression among a national sample of male college students*. Paper presented at the New York Academy of

Sciences Conference, "Human Sexual Aggression: Current Perspectives," New York.

Koss, M. P., Dinero, T. E., Seibel, C. A., & Cox, S. L. (1988). Stranger and acquaintance rape: Are there differences in the victim's experience? *Psychology of Women Quarterly, 12,* 1–24.

Koss, M. P., Gidycz, C. A., & Wisniewski, N. (1987). The scope of rape: Incidence and prevalence of sexual aggression and victimization in a national sample of students in higher education. *Journal of Consulting and Clinical Psychology, 55,* 162–170.

Koss, M. P., Goodman, L. A., Browne, A., Fitzgerald, L. F., Keita, G. P., & Russo, N. F. (1994). *No safe haven: Male violence against women at home, at work, and in the community* (1st ed.). Washington, DC: American Psychological Association.

Koss, M. P., Leonard, K. B., Beezley, D. A., & Oros, C. J. (1985). Non-stranger sexual aggression: A discriminate analysis classification. *Sex Roles, 12,* 981–992.

Kowalski, R. M. (1996). Complaints and complaining: Function, antecedents and consequences. *Psychological Bulletin, 119,* 179–196.

Kruttschnitt, C. (1989). A sociological, offender-based, study of rape. *Sociological Quarterly, 30,* 305–329.

Kruttschnitt, C. (1994). Gender and interpersonal violence in intimate relationships. In A. J. Reiss, Jr., & J. A. Roth (Eds.), *Understanding and preventing violence* (pp. 293–376). Washington, DC: National Academy Press.

Kumagai, F., & Straus, M. A. (1983). Conflict resolution tactics in Japan, India, and the USA. *Journal of Comparative Family Studies, 14,* 377–392.

Kurz, D. (1989). Social science perspectives on wife abuse: Current debates and future directions. *Gender and Society, 3,* 489–505.

LaFree, G. D. (1989). *Rape and criminal justice: The social construction of sexual assault.* Belmont, CA: Wadsworth.

Lalumiere, M. L., Chalmers, L. J., Quinsey, V. L., & Seto, M. C. (1996). A test of the mate deprivation hypothesis of sexual coercion. *Ethology and Sociobiology, 17,* 299–318.

Landes, R. (1971). *The Ojibwa woman.* New York: Norton.

Langan, P. A., & Dawson, J. M. (1995). *Spouse murder defendants in large urban counties* (NCJ-153256). Washington, DC: Bureau of Justice Statistics.

Langhinrichsen-Rohling, J., Palereea, R. E., Cohen, J., & Rohling, M. L. (2000). Breaking up is hard to do: Unwanted pursuit behaviors following dissolution of a romantic relationship. *Violence and Victims, 15,* 73–90.

Laumann, E. O., Gagnon, J. H., Michael, R. T., & Michaels, S. (1994). *The social organization of sexuality: Sexual practices in the United States.* Chicago: University of Chicago Press.

Lawler, E. J. (1986). Bilateral deterrence and conflict spiral: A theoretical analysis. In E. J. Lawler (Ed.), *Advances in group processes* (Vol. 3, pp. 107–130). Grenwich, CT: JAI Press.

Leitenberg, H., & Henning, K. (1995). Sexual fantasy. *Psychological Bulletin, 117*, 469–496.

Leith, K. P., & Baumeister, R. F. (1996). Why do bad moods increase self-defeating behavior? Emotion, risk taking, and self-regulation. *Journal of Personality and Social Psychology, 71*, 1250–1267.

Leland, J. (1982). Gender, drinking and alcohol abuse. In I. Al-Issa (Ed.), *Gender and psychopathology* (pp. 201–220). San Francisco: Academic Press.

Le Maire, L. (1956). Danish experiences regarding the castration of sexual offenders. *Journal of Criminal Law, Criminology, and Police Science, 47*, 294–310.

Leonard, K. E., & Taylor, S. P. (1981). Effects of racial prejudice and race on target on aggression. *Aggressive Behavior, 7*, 205–214.

Levine, R. A. (1959). Gusii sex offenses: A study in social control. *American Anthropologist, 61*, 189–226.

Levinson, D. (1989). *Family violence in cross-cultural perspective*. Newbury Park, CA: Sage Publications.

Lie, G.-Y., Schilit, R., Bush, J., Montagne, M., & Reyes, L. (1991). Lesbians in currently aggressive relationships: How frequently do they report aggressive past relationships? *Violence and Victims, 6*, 121–135.

Lieberman, B. (1988). Extrapremarital intercourse: Attitudes toward a neglected sexual behavior. *Journal of Sex Research, 24*, 291–298.

Lilly, J. R., & Marshall, P. (2000). Rape—Wartime. In C. D. Bryant (Ed.), *Encyclopedia of criminology and deviant behavior* (Vol. 3, pp. 310–322). Philadelphia: Taylor and Francis.

Linz, D. (1989). Exposure to sexually explicit materials and attitudes toward rape: A comparison of study results. *Journal of Sex Research, 26*, 50–84.

Linz, D., & Malamuth, N. M. (1993). *Pornography*. Newbury Park, CA: Sage Publications.

Lips, H. M. (1991). *Women, men, and power*. Mountain View, CA: Mayfield.

Lipton, D. N., McDonel, E. C., & McFall, R. M. (1987). Heterosocial perception in rapists. *Journal of Consulting and Clinical Psychology, 55*, 17–21.

Lisak, D., & Roth, S. (1988). Motivational factors in nonincarcerated sexually aggressive men. *Journal of Personality and Social Psychology, 55*, 795–802.

Liska, A. E., Felson, R. B., Chamlin, M. B., & Baccaglini, W. (1984). Estimating attitude–behavior relations within a theoretical specification. *Social Psychology Quarterly, 47*, 15–23.

Lizotte, A. J. (1986). Determinants of completing rape and assault. *Journal of Quantitative Criminology, 2*, 203–217.

Lockwood, D. (1980). *Prison sexual violence*. New York: Elsevier.

Loewenstein, G., Nagin, D. S., & Paternoster, R. (1997). The effect of sexual arousal on expectations of sexual forcefulness. *Journal of Research in Crime and Delinquency, 34*, 443–473.

Logan, T. K., Leukefeld, C., & Walker, B. (2000). Stalking as a variant of intimate violence: Implications from a young adult sample. *Violence and Victims, 15*, 91–111.

Lonsway, K. A., & Fitsgerald, L. F. (1995). Attitudinal antecedents of rape myth acceptance: A theoretical and empirical reexamination. *Journal of Personality and Social Psychology, 68,* 704–711.

Loren, R. E. A., & Weeks, G. (1986). Sexual fantasies of undergraduates and their perceptions of the sexual fantasies of the opposite sex. *Journal of Sex Education and Therapy, 12,* 31–36.

Loseke, D. R. (1992). *The battered women and shelters: The social construction of wife abuse.* Albany, NY: SUNY Press.

Lottes, I. L., & Weinberg, M. S. (1996). Sexual coercion among university students: A comparison of the United States and Sweden. *Journal of Sex Research, 34,* 67–76.

Luckenbill, D. F. (1977). Criminal homicide as a situated transaction. *Social Problems, 25,* 176–186.

Luckenbill, D. F. (1980). Patterns of force in robbery. *Deviant Behavior: An Interdisciplinary Journal, 1,* 361–378.

MacDonald, J. (1971). *Rape: Offenders and their victims.* Springfield, IL: Charles C Thomas.

MacKinnon, C. (1984). Not a moral issue. *Yale Law and Policy Review, 2,* 321–345.

Mahoney, P., Williams, L. M., & West, C. M. (2001). Violence against women by intimate relationship partners. In C. M. Renzetti, J. L. Edleson, & R. K. Bergen (Eds.), *The sourcebook on violence against women* (pp. 143–178). Thousand Oaks, CA: Sage Publications.

Malamuth, N. M. (1981). Rape proclivity among males. *Journal of Social Issues, 37,* 138–157.

Malamuth, N. M. (1986). Predictors of naturalistic sexual aggression. *Journal of Personality and Social Psychology, 50,* 953–962.

Malamuth, N. M., & Check, J. V. P. (1981). The effects of mass media exposure on acceptance of violence against women: A field experiment. *Journal of Research in Personality, 15,* 436–446.

Malamuth, N. M., Check, J. V. P., & Briere, J. (1986). Sexual arousal in response to aggression: Ideological, aggressive and sexual correlates. *Journal of Personality and Social Psychology, 50,* 330–340.

Malin, H., Wilson, R., Williams, G., & Aitken, S. (1986). 1983 alcohol/health practices. *Alcohol Health and Research World, 10,* 48–50.

Mann, C. R. (1988). Getting even? Women who kill in domestic encounters. *Justice Quarterly, 5,* 33–51.

Marcus-Newhall, A., Pedersen, W. C., Carlson, M., & Miller, N. (2000). Displaced aggression is alive and well: A meta-analytic review. *Journal of Personality and Social Psychology, 78,* 670–689.

Marion, M. (1983). Child compliance: A review of the literature with implications for family life education. *Family Relations, 32,* 545–555.

Marshall, W. L., & Barbaree, H. E. (1984). A behavioral view of rape. *International Journal of Law and Psychiatry, 7,* 51–77.

Marsot, A. L. S. (1984). The changing Arab–Muslim family. In M. Kelly (Ed.), *Islam: The religious and political life of a world community* (pp. 243–257). New York: Praeger Special Studies.

Martin, D. (1976). *Battered wives*. San Francisco: Glide Publications.

Marvell, T. B., & Moody, C. E. (1999). Female and male homicide victimization rates: Comparing trends and regressors. *Criminology, 37*, 879–900.

Matsueda, R. L. (1988). The current state of differential association theory. *Crime and Delinquency, 34*, 277–306.

Mayhew, P., & van Dijk, J. J. M. (1997). *Criminal victimisation in eleven industrialised countries*. London: Information and Publications Group, Home Office.

Mazur, A., & Booth, A. (1998). Testosterone and dominance in men. *Behavioral and Brain Sciences, 21*, 353–397.

McBarnet, D. (1983). Victim in the witness box: Confronting victimology's stereotype. *Contemporary Crises, 7*, 293–303.

McDermott, M. J. (1979). *Rape victimization in 26 American cities*. Washington, DC: U.S. Department of Justice.

McDonald, G. W. (1980). Family power: The assessment of a decade of theory and research, 1970–1979. *Journal of Marriage and the Family, 10*, 841–854.

McGuire, W. J. (1986). The myth of massive media impact: Savagings and salvagings. *Public Communication and Behavior, 1*, 175–257.

McManus, P. A., & DiPrete, T. A. (2001). Losers and winners: The financial consequences of separation and divorce for men. *American Sociological Review, 66*, 246–268.

Medea, A., & Thompson, K. (1974). *Against rape*. New York: Farrar Straus and Giroux.

Melburg, V., & Tedeschi, J. T. (1989). Displaced aggression: Frustration or impression management. *European Journal of Social Psychology, 19*, 139–145.

Merlo, A. V., & Pollock, J. M. (1995). *Women, law, and social control*. Boston: Allyn and Bacon.

Messner, S. F., & Rosenfeld, R. (1994). *Crime and the American dream*. Belmont, CA: Wadsworth.

Messner, S. F., & Sampson, R. J. (1991). The sex ratio, family disruption, and rates of violent crime: The paradox of demographic structure. *Social Forces, 69*, 693–713.

Mikula, G., & Heimgartner, A. (1992). *Experiences of injustice in intimate relationships*. Unpublished manuscript: University of Graz, Austria.

Milburn, T. W., & Watman, K. (1980). *On the nature of threats: A social psychological analysis*. New York: Praeger.

Mitchell, D., Hirschman, R., & Nagayama Hall, G. C. (1999). Attributions of victim responsibility, pleasure, and trauma in male rape. *Journal of Sex Research, 36*, 369–373.

Moffitt, T. E., Krueger, R. F., Caspi, A., & Fagan, J. (2000). Partner abuse and general crime: How are they the same? How are they different? *Criminology, 38*, 199–232.

Moffitt, T. E., Robins, R. W., & Caspi, A. (2001). A couples analysis of partner abuse with implications for abuse-prevention policy. *Criminology and Public Policy, 1*, 5–36.

Mooney, J. (2000). *Gender, violence, and the social order*. New York: St. Martin's Press.

Morley, R. (1994). Wife beating and modernization: The case of Papua New Guinea. *Journal of Comparative Family Studies, 25*, 25–52.

Muehlenhard, C. L. (1988). Misinterpreted dating behaviors and the risk of date rape. *Journal of Social and Clinical Psychology, 6*, 20–37.

Muehlenhard, C. L., & Cook, S. W. (1988). Men's self-reports of unwanted sexual activity. *Journal of Sex Research, 24*, 58–72.

Muehlenhard, C. L., & Hollabaugh, L. C. (1988). Do women sometimes say no when they mean yes? The prevalence and correlates of women's token resistance to sex. *Journal of Personality and Social Psychology, 54*, 872–879.

Muehlenhard, C. L., & Linton, M. A. (1987). Date rape and sexual aggression in dating situations: Incidence and risk factors. *Journal of Counseling Psychology, 34*, 186–196.

Mugford, J., & Mugford, S. (1989). Social justice, public perceptions, and spouse assault in Australia. *Social Justice, 16*, 103–123.

Mummendey, A., Linneweber, V., & Loschper, G. (1984). Actor or victim of aggression? Divergent perspectives—divergent evaluations. *European Journal of Social Psychology, 14*, 291–311.

Murnen, S. K., Perot, A., & Byrne, D. (1989). Coping with unwanted sexual activity: Normative responses, situational determinants, and individual differences. *Journal of Sex Research, 26*, 85–106.

Murphy, R. F. (1959). Social structure and sex antagonism. *Southwestern Journal of Anthropology, 15*, 89–123.

Murphy, W. D., Coleman, E. M., & Haynes, M. R. (1986). Factors related to coercive sexual behavior in a nonclinical sample of males. *Violence and Victims, 1*, 255–278.

Myers, M. A., & LaFree, G. D. (1982). Sexual assault and its prosecution: A comparison with other crimes. *Journal of Criminal Law and Criminology, 73*, 1282–1305.

Nacci, P. L., & Tedeschi, J. T. (1977). Displaced aggression: Drive reduction of equity restoration. *Human Relations, 30*, 1157–1167.

Nagayama Hall, G. C., Shondrick, D. D., & Hirshman, R. (1993). The role of sexual arousal in sexually aggressive behavior: A meta-analysis. *Journal of Consulting and Clinical Psychology, 61*, 1091–1095.

Nagin, D. S. (1998). Criminal deterrence research at the outset of the twenty-first century. In M. H. Tonry (Ed.), *Crime and justice: A review of research* (Vol. 23, 1–42). Chicago: University of Chicago Press.

National Research Council. (1998). *Violence in families: Assessing prevention and treatment programs*. Washington, DC: National Academy Press.

Neufeld, P., & Scheck, B. C. (1996). Commentary by Peter Neufeld, Esq. and Barry C. Scheck. In E. Connors, T. Lundregan, N. Miller, & T. McEwen (Eds.), *Convicted* by juries, exonerated by science: Case studies in the use of DNA evidence to establish innocence after trial (pp. 29–32). Washington, DC: National Institute of Justice.

Nilson, L. B. (1976). The occupational and sex related components of social standing. *Sociology and Social Research, 60*, 328-336.

O'Brien, R. M. (1987). The interracial nature of violent crimes: A reexamination. *American Journal of Sociology, 92*, 817–835.

Oliver, M. B., & Hyde, J. S. (1993). Gender differences in sexuality: A meta-analysis. *Psychological Bulletin, 114*, 29–51.

Olweus, D. (1978). *Aggression in the schools: Bullies and whipping boys*. Washington, DC: Hemisphere Press.

Olweus, D. (1979). Stability of aggressive reaction patterns in males: A review. *Psychological Bulletin, 86*, 852–875.

Olweus, D. (1984). Aggressors and their victims: Bullying at school. In N. Frude & H. Gault (Eds.), *Disruptive behaviors in schools* (pp. 57–76). New York: Wiley.

O'Sullivan, L. F., & Allgeier, E. R. (1998). Feigning sexual desire: Consenting to unwanted sexual activity in heterosexual dating relationships. *Journal of Sex Research, 35*, 234–243.

Pagelow, M. D. (1984). *Family violence*. New York: Praeger.

Paik, J., & Comstock, G. A. (1994). The effects of television violence on antisocial behavior: A meta-analysis. *Communications Research, 21*, 516–545.

Palmer, C. T. (1988). Twelve reasons why rape is not sexually motivated: A skeptical examination. *Journal of Sex Research, 25*, 512–530.

Palmer, C. T. (1991). Human rape: Adaptation or by-product? *Journal of Sex Research, 28*, 365–386.

Palys, T. S. (1986). Testing the common wisdom: The social content of video pornography. *Canadian Psychology, 27*, 22–35.

Pan, H. S., Heidig, P. H., & O'Leary, K. D. (1994). Male–female and aggressor–victim differences in the factor structure of the modified conflict tactics scale. *Journal of Interpersonal Violence, 9*, 366–382.

Parke, R. D., & Collmer, C. W. (1975). Child abuse: An interdisciplinary analysis. In E. M. Hetherington (Ed.), *Review of child development research* (Vol. 5, pp. 509–590). Chicago: University of Chicago Press.

Patterson, G. R., Littman, R. A., & Bricker, W. (1967). Assertive behavior in children: A step toward a theory of aggression. *Monographs of the Society for Research in Child Development, 32*.

Paul, L., Foss, M. A., & Galloway, J. (1993). Sexual jealousy in young women and men: Aggressive responsiveness to partner and rival. *Aggressive Behavior, 19*, 401–420.

Pence, E., & Paymar, M. (1993). *Education groups for men who batter: The Duluth model*. New York: Springer.

Peterson, E. S. L. (1999). Murder as self-help: Women and intimate partner homicide. *Homicide Studies, 3*, 30–46.

Peterson, R. R. (1996). A re-evaluation of the economic consequences of divorce. *American Sociological Review, 61*, 528–536.

Peterson del Mar, D. (1996). *What trouble I have seen: A history of violence against wives.* Cambridge, MA: Harvard University Press.

Pleck, E. H. (1979). Wife beating in nineteenth-century America. *Victimology, 4,* 60–74.

Pleck, E. H. (1987). *Domestic tyranny.* Oxford: Oxford University Press.

Pleck, E. H. (1989). Criminal approaches to family violence. In L. E. Ohlin & M. H. Tonry (Eds.), *Family violence: Crime and justice: An annual review of research* (pp. 19–57). Chicago: University of Chicago Press.

Pleck, J. H. (1985). *Working wives/working husbands.* Beverly Hills, CA: Sage Publications.

Ploughman, P., & Stensrud, J. (1986). The ecology of rape victimization: A case study of Buffalo, New York. *Genetic, Social, and General Psychology Monographs, 112,* 303–342.

Polk, K. (1997). A reexamination of the concept of victim-precipitated homicide. *Homicide Studies, 1,* 141–168.

Posner, R. A. (1992). *Sex and reason.* Cambridge, MA.: Harvard University Press.

Pratto, F. (1996). Sexual politics: The gender gap in the bedroom, the cupboard, and the cabinet. In D. M. Buss & N. M. Malamuth (Eds.), *Sex, power, conflict: Evolutionary and feminist perspectives* (pp. 179–230). New York: Oxford University Press.

Preston, K., & Preston, S. K. (1987). What's the worst thing . . . ? Gender directed insults. *Sex Roles, 17,* 209–219.

Pruitt, D. G., & Rubin, J. Z. (1986). *Social conflict: Escalation, stalemate, and settlement.* New York: Random House.

Ptacek, J. (1988). Why do men batter their wives? In K. A. Yllö & M. Bograd (Eds.), *Feminist perspectives on wife abuse* (pp. 133–157). Newbury Park, CA: Sage Publications.

Queen's Bench Foundation. (1976). Rape prevention and resistance (pp. 59–76, 79–87, 92–94). San Francisco: Queen's Bench Foundation.

Quigley, B. M., & Leonard, K. E. (1996). Desistance of husband aggression in the early years of marriage. *Violence and Victims, 11,* 355–370.

Quinsey, V. L., Chaplin, T. C., & Varney, G. A. (1981). A comparison of rapists' and non-sex offender's sexual preference for mutually consenting sex, rape, and physical abuse of women. *Behavioral Assessment, 3,* 127–135.

Rada, R. T., Laws, D. R., & Kellner, R. (1976). Plasma testosterone levels in the rapist. *Psychosomatic Medicine, 38,* 257–268.

Rapaport, K., & Burkhart, B. R. (1984). Personality and attitudinal characteristics of sexually coercive college males. *Journal of Abnormal Psychology, 93,* 216–221.

Reiss, A. J., Jr. (1971). *The police and the public.* New Haven, CT: Yale University Press.

Reiss, A. J., Jr., & Roth, J. A. (Eds.). (1993). *Understanding and preventing violence* (Vol. 1). Washington, DC: National Academy Press.

Reiss, I. L. (1986). *Journey into sexuality: An exploratory voyage*. Englewood Cliffs, NJ: Prentice Hall.

Rennison, C. M. (2001). *Intimate partner violence and age of victim, 1993–1999*. Washington, DC: Bureau of Justice Statistics.

Renzetti, C. M., Edleson, J. L., & Bergen, R. K. (2001). *The sourcebook on violence against women*. Thousand Oaks, CA: Sage Publications.

Richardson, D. R., & Green, L. R. (1999). Social sanctions and threat explanations of gender effects on direct and indirect aggression. *Aggressive Behavior, 25,* 425–434.

Riger, S., & Gordon, M. (1981). The fear of rape: A study in social control. *Journal of Social Issues, 37,* 71–92.

Ronfeldt, H. M., Kimerling, R., & Arias, I. (1998). Satisfaction with relationship power and the perpetration of dating violence. *Journal of Marriage and the Family, 60,* 70–78.

Roscoe, B., Cavanaugh, L. E., & Kennedy, D. R. (1988). Dating infidelity: Behaviors, reasons, and consequences. *Adolescence, 13,* 35–43.

Rosenbaum, A. (1986). Of men, macho, and marital violence. *Journal of Family Violence, 1,* 121–129.

Ross, L., Greene, D., & House, P. (1977). The false consensus effect: An egocentric bias in social perception. *Journal of Experimental Social Psychology, 13,* 279–301.

Rossi, P. H., Waite, E., Bose, C., & Berk, R. E. (1974). The seriousness of crime: Normative structure and individual differences. *American Sociological Review, 39,* 224–237.

Roy, M. (1977a). *Battered women: A psychological study of domestic violence*. New York: Van Nostrand Reinhold.

Roy, M. (1977b). Some thoughts regarding the criminal justice system and wife-beating. In M. Roy (Ed.), *Battered women: A psychosociological study of domestic violence* (pp. 138–139). New York: Van Nostrand Reinhold.

Ruback, R. B., & Ivie, D. L. (1988). Prior relationship, resistance, and injury in rapes: An analysis of crisis central records. *Violence and Victims, 3,* 99–111.

Rule, B. G., & Nesdale, A. R. (1976). Moral judgments of aggressive behavior. In R. G. Geen & E. C. O'Neal (Eds.), *Perspectives on aggression* (pp. 37–60). New York: Academic Press.

Russell, D. E. H. (1975). *The politics of rape: The victim's perspective*. New York: Stein and Day.

Sanday, P. R. (1981). The socio-cultural context of rape: A cross-cultural study. *Journal of Social Issues, 37,* 5–27.

Sarrel, P. M., & Masters, W. H. (1982). Sexual molestation of men by women. *Archives of Sexual Behavior, 11,* 117–131.

Sattem, L., Savells, J., & Murray, E. (1984). Sex-role stereotypes and commitment of rape. *Sex Roles, 11,* 849–860.

Saunders, D. G. (1986). When battered women use violence: Husband-abuse or self-defense? *Violence and Victims, 1*, 47–60.

Saunders, D. G. (1992). A typology of men who batter women: Three types derived from cluster analysis. *American Orthopsychiatry, 62*, 264–275.

Schafer, S. (1977). Sociosexual behavior in male and female homosexuals: A study of sex differences. *Archives of Sexual Behavior, 6*, 355–364.

Scheier, M. F., Fenigstein, A., & Buss, A. H. (1974). Self-awareness and physical aggression. *Journal of Experimental Social Psychology, 10*, 264–273.

Schiff, A. F. (1969). Statistical features of rape. *Journal of Forensic Science, 14*, 102–108.

Schlegel, A. (1972). *Male dominance and female autonomy: Domestic authority in matrilineal societies.* New Haven, CT: HRAF Press.

Schmidt, J. D., & Hochstedler, S. (1989). Prosecutorial discretion in filing charges in domestic violence cases. *Criminology, 27*, 487–510.

Schreder, C. (Producer), & Greenwald, R. (Director). (1984). *The burning bed* [Motion picture]. United States: 20th Century Fox.

Schwartz, M. D., & DeKeseredy, W. S. (1993). The return of the "battered husband syndrome" through the typification of women as violent. *Crime, Law, and Social Change, 20*, 249–265.

Schwartz, M. D., & Pitts, V. L. (1995). Exploring a feminist routine activities approach to explaining sexual assault. *Justice Quarterly, 12*, 9–31.

Schwendinger, J. R., & Schwendinger, H. (1983). *Rape and inequality.* Beverly Hills, CA: Sage Publications.

Scott, M. B., & Lyman, S. M. (1968). Accounts. *American Sociological Review, 33*, 46–62.

Scully, D. (1990). *Understanding sexual violence: A study of convicted rapists.* Cambridge, MA: Unwin Hyman.

Scully, D., & Marolla, J. (1984). Convicted rapists' vocabulary of motive: Excuses and justifications. *Social Problems, 31*, 530–544.

Scully, D., & Marolla, J. (1985). Riding the bull at Gilley's: Convicted rapists describe the rewards of rape. *Social Problems, 32*, 251–263.

Searles, P., & Berger, R. J. (1995). *Rape and society: Readings on the problem of sexual assault.* Boulder, CO: Westview Press.

Selznick, D. O. (Producer), & Fleming, V. (Director). (1939). *Gone with the wind* [Motion picture]. United States: MGM.

Sermat, V. (1967). The possibility of influencing the other's behavior and cooperation: Chicken vs. prisoner's dilemma. *Canadian Journal of Psychology, 21*, 204–219.

Sherman, L. W. (1992). *Policing domestic violence.* New York: Free Press.

Sherman, L. W., & Berk, R. A. (1984). The specific deterrent effects of arrest for domestic assault. *American Sociological Review, 49*, 261–272.

Sherman, L. W., & Smith, D. A. (1992). Crime, punishment and stake in conformity: Legal and informal control of domestic violence. *American Sociological Review, 57,* 680–690.

Shields, W. M., & Shields, L. M. (1983). Forcible rape: An evolutionary perspective. *Ethology and Sociobiology, 4,* 115–136.

Shortell, J. R., & Miller, H. B. (1970). Aggression in children as a function of sex of subject and of opponent. *Developmental Psychology, 3,* 143–144.

Shotland, R. L., & Craig, J. M. (1988). Can men and women differentiate between friendly and sexually interested behavior? *Social Psychology Quarterly, 51,* 66–73.

Shotland, R. L., & Straw, M. K. (1976). Bystander response to an assault: When a man attacks a woman. *Journal of Personality and Social Psychology, 34,* 990–999.

Simpson, J. A., & Gangestad, S. W. (1991). Individual differences in sociosexuality: Evidence of convergent and discriminant validity. *Journal of Personality and Social Psychology, 60,* 870–883.

Singer, B., & Toates, F. M. (1987). Sexual motivation. *Journal of Sex Research, 23,* 481–501.

Skocpol, T. (1992). *Protecting soldiers and mothers: The political origins of social policy in the United States.* Cambridge, MA: Belknap Press of Harvard University Press.

Smith, D. A. (1987). Police response to interpersonal violence: Defining the parameters of legal control. *Social Forces, 65,* 767–782.

Smith, D. D. (1976). The social content of pornography. *Journal of Communication, 29,* 16–24.

Smith, M. D. (1990). Patriarchical ideology and wife beating: A test of a feminist hypothesis. *Violence and Victims, 5,* 257–274.

Smith, R. E., Pine, C. J., & Hawley, M. E. (1988). Social cognitions about adult male victims of female sexual assault. *Journal of Sex Research, 24,* 101–112.

Smith, W. P., & Leginski, W. A. (1970). Magnitude and precision of punitive power in bargaining strategy. *Journal of Experimental Social Psychology, 6,* 57–76.

Sommers, C. H. (1995). *Who stole feminism? How women have betrayed women.* New York: Touchstone/Simon & Schuster.

Sommers, C. H. (2000). The war against boys. *Atlantic Monthly, 287,* 59–74.

Sorenson, S. B., Stein, J. A., Siegel, J. M., Golding, J. M., & Burnam, M. A. (1987). The prevalence of adult sexual assault: The Los Angeles epidemiologic catchment area project. *American Journal of Epidemiology, 126,* 1154–1164.

South, S. J., & Felson, R. B. (1990). The racial patterning of rape. *Social Forces, 69,* 71–93.

Stafford, M. C., & Gibbs, J. P. (1993). A theory about disputes and the efficacy of control. In R. B. Felson & J. T. Tedeschi (Eds.), *Aggression and violence: Social interactionist perspectives* (pp. 69–98). Washington, DC: American Psychological Association.

Stanko, E. A. (1981). The impact of victim assessment on prosecutor's screening decisions: The case of the New York district attorney's office. *Law and Society Review, 16,* 225–239.

Stanko, E. A. (1985). *Intimate intrusions: Women's experiences of male violence.* London: Routledge and Kegan Paul.

Steffensmeier, D. J. (1988). The uniqueness of rape? Disposition and sentencing outcomes of rape in comparison to other major felonies. *Sociology and Social Research, 72,* 192–198.

Steffensmeier, D. J., Kramer, J., & Streifel, C. (1993). Gender and imprisonment decisions. *Criminology, 31,* 411–446.

Steinmetz, S. K., & Straus, M. A. (1974). *Violence in the family.* New York: Harper and Row.

Stets, J. E., & Burke, P. J. (1996). Gender, control, and interaction. *Social Psychology Quarterly, 59,* 193–220.

Stets, J. E., & Straus, M. A. (1990). Gender differences in reporting marital violence and its medical and psychological consequences. In M. A. Straus & R. J. Gelles (Eds.), *Physical violence in American families: Risk factors and adaptation to violence in 8,145 families* (pp. 151–165). New Brunswick, NJ: Transaction Press.

Straus, M. A. (1980). Stress and child abuse. In C. H. Kempe & R. F. Helfer (Eds.), *The battered child* (3rd ed., pp. 86–103). Chicago: University of Chicago Press.

Straus, M. A. (1993). Physical assaults by wives: A major social problem. In R. J. Gelles & D. R. Loseke (Eds.), *Current controversies on family violence* (pp. 67–87). Newbury Park, CA: Sage Publications.

Straus, M. A. (1999). The controversy over domestic violence by women: A methodological, theoretical, and sociology of science analysis. In X. B. Arriaga & S. Oskamp (Eds.), *Violence in intimate relationships* (pp. 17–44). Thousand Oaks, CA: Sage Publications.

Straus, M. A., & Gelles, R. J. (1986). Societal change and change in family violence from 1975 to 1985 as revealed by two national surveys. *Journal of Marriage and the Family, 48,* 465–479.

Straus, M. A., Gelles, R. J., & Steinmetz, S. K. (1980). *Behind closed doors: Violence in the American family.* Garden City, NY: Anchor Press/Doubleday.

Straus, M. A., Kantor, G. K., & Moore, D. W. (1994). *Change in cultural norms approving marital violence from 1968 to 1994.* Paper presented at the annual meeting of the American Sociological Association, New York.

Struckman-Johnson, C., Struckman-Johnson, D., Rucker, L., Bumby, K., & Donaldson, S. (1996). Sexual coercion reported by men and women in prison. *Journal of Sex Research, 33,* 67–76.

Sturup, G. K. (1960). Sex offenses: The Scandinavian experience. *Law and Contemporary Problems, 25,* 361–375.

Sugarman, D. B., & Hotaling, G. T. (1989). Courtship violence. In M. A. Pirog-Good & J. E. Stets (Eds.), *Violence in dating relationships* (pp. 3–32). New York: Praeger.

Sundberg, S. L., Barbaree, H. E., & Marshall, W. L. (1991). Victim blame and the disinhibition of sexual arousal to rape vignettes. *Violence and Victims, 6*, 103–120.

Sykes, G. M., & Matza, D. (1957). Techniques of neutralization: A theory of delinquency. *American Sociological Review, 41*, 664–670.

Symons, D. (1979). *The evolution of human sexuality*. New York: Oxford University Press.

Tang, C. S.-K., Critelli, J. W., & Porter, J. F. (1993). Motives in sexual aggression: The Chinese context. *Journal of Interpersonal Violence, 8*, 435–445.

Taylor, S. P., & Epstein, S. (1967). Aggression as a function of the interaction of the sex of the aggressor and the sex of the victim. *Journal of Personality, 35*, 474–485.

Tedeschi, J. T. (1970). Threats and promises. In P. Swingle (Ed.), *The structure of conflict* (pp. 155–192). New York: Academic Press.

Tedeschi, J. T., & Felson, R. B. (1994). *Violence, aggression, and coercive actions*. Washington, DC: American Psychological Association.

Tedeschi, J. T., & Norman, N. M. (1985). A social psychological interpretation of displaced aggression. In E. J. Lawler (Ed.), *Advances in group processes: Theory and research* (Vol. 2, pp. 29–56). Greenwich, CT: JAI Press.

Thar, A. E. (1981). The admissibility of expert testimony on battered wife syndrome: An evidentiary analysis. *Northwestern University Law Review, 77*, 348–373.

Thibaut, J. W., & Kelley, H. H. (1959). *The social psychology of groups*. New York: Wiley.

Thornhill, R., & Palmer, C. T. (2000). *A natural history of rape: Biological bases of sexual coercion*. Boston: MIT Press.

Thornhill, R., & Thornhill, N. W. (1983). Human rape: An evolutionary analysis. *Ethology and Sociobiology, 4*, 137–173.

Tjaden, P., & Thoennes, N. (2000). *Extent, nature, and consequences of intimate partner violence: Finding from the National Violence against Women Survey*. Washington, DC: National Institute of Justice.

Toch, H. H. (1993). Good violence and bad violence: Self-presentations of aggressors through accounts and war stories. In R. B. Felson & J. T. Tedeschi (Eds.), *Aggression and violence: Social interactionist perspectives* (pp. 193–208). Washington, DC: American Psychological Association.

Tonizzo, S., Howells, K., Day, A., Reidpath, D., & Froyland, I. (2000). Attributions of negative partner behavior by men who physically abuse their partners. *Journal of Family Violence, 15*, 155–166.

Townsend, J. M. (1998). *What women want—what men want: Why the sexes still see love and commitment so differently*. Oxford: Oxford University Press.

Turrel, S. C. (2000). A descriptive analysis of same-sex relationship violence for a diverse sample. *Journal of Family Violence, 15*, 281–293.

van Dijk, J. J. M., Mayhew, P., & Killias, M. (1990). *Experiences of crime across the world: Key findings of the 1989 International Crime Survey*. Deventer, The Netherlands: Kluwer.

Vera Institute of Justice. (1977). *Felony arrests: Their prosecution and disposition in New York City's courts*. New York: Vera Institute of Justice.

Visher, C. A. (1983). Gender, police arrest decisions, and notions of chivalry. *Criminology, 21*, 5–28.

Wade, W. C. (1992). *The Titanic: End of a dream*. New York: Penguin.

Waldner-Haugrud, L. K., & Magruder, B. (1995). Male and female sexual victimization in dating relationships: Gender differences in coercion techniques and outcomes. *Violence and Victims, 10*, 203–215.

Walker, L. E. (1979). *The battered woman* (1st ed.). New York: Harper & Row.

Walker, L. E. (1984). *The battered woman syndrome*. New York: Springer.

Websdale, N. (1999). *Understanding domestic violence*. Boston: Northeastern University Press.

Weis, K., & Borges, S. S. (1973). Victimology and rape: The case of the legitimate victim. *Issues in Criminology, 8*, 71–115.

Whaley, R. B. (2001). The paradoxical relationship between gender inequality and rape: Toward a refined theory. *Gender and Society, 15*, 531–555.

Whiting, B. B., & Edwards, C. P. (1988). *Children of different worlds: The formation of social behavior*. Cambridge, MA: Harvard University Press.

Wicklund, R. A. (1975). Objective self-awareness. In L. Berkowitz (Ed.), *Advances in experimental social psychology* (Vol. 8, pp. 233–275). New York: Academic Press.

Wilbanks, W. (1984). *Murder in Miami: An analysis of homicide patterns and trends in Dade County (Miami) Florida, 1917–1983*. Lanham, MD: University Press of America.

Williams, J. E., & Best, D. L. (1977). Sex stereotypes and trait favorability on the adjective check list. *Educational and Psychological Measurement, 37*, 101–110.

Williams, K. M. (1976). The effects of victim characteristics on the disposition of violent crimes. In W. F. McDonald (Ed.), *Criminal justice and the victim* (pp. 177–213). Beverly Hills, CA: Sage Publications.

Wills, T. A. (1981). Downward comparison principles in social psychology. *Psychological Bulletin, 90*, 245–271.

Wilson, M., & Daly, M. (1992). Who kills whom in spouse killings? On the exceptional sex ratio of spousal homicides in the United States. *Criminology, 30*, 189–215.

Wolfgang, M. E. (1958). *Patterns in criminal homicide*. Montclair, NJ: Patterson Smith.

Wolfgang, M. E., & Ferracuti, F. (1967). *The subculture of violence: Towards an integrated theory in criminology*. London: Tavistock Publications.

World Health Organization (WHO). (various years). *World health statistics annual*. Geneva: WHO.

Wright, J. D., Rossi, P. H., & Daly, K. (1983). *Under the gun: Weapons, crime, and violence in America*. New York: Aldine de Gruyter.

Wright, R. T., & Decker, S. H. (1997). *Armed robbers in action: Stickups and street culture*. Boston: Northeastern University Press.

Yegidis, B. L. (1986). Date rape and other forced sexual encounters among college students. *Journal of Sex Education and Therapy, 12*, 51–54.

Yllö, K. A. (1988). Political and methodological debates in wife abuse research. In K. A. Yllö & M. Bograd (Eds.), *Feminist perspectives on wife abuse* (pp. 28–50). Newbury Park, CA: Sage Publications.

Yllö, K. A., & Straus, M. A. (1984). Patriarchy and violence against wives: The impact of structural and normative factors. *Journal of International and Comparative Social Welfare, 1*, 16–29.

Young, D. M., Beier, E. G., Beier, P., & Barton, C. (1975). Is chivalry dead? *Journal of Communication, 25*, 57–64.

Zillmann, D. (1983). Arousal and aggression. In R. G. Geen & E. I. Donnerstein (Eds.), *Aggression: Theoretical and empirical reviews* (Vol. 1, pp. 75–101). New York: Academic Press.

Zimring, F. E. (1989). Toward a jurisprudence of family violence. In L. E. Ohlin & M. H. Tonry (Eds.), *Family violence* (Vol. 11, pp. 547–569). Chicago: University of Chicago Press.

AUTHOR INDEX

Numbers in italics refer to listings in the reference section.

Abbey, A., 132
Abel, G. G., 156
Ackerman, J., 60, 76, 91, 150
Ageton, S. S., 160, 170, 172
Aiken, S., 25
Albonetti, C. A., 199
Alder, C., 152, 172, 179
Aldis, O., 58
Allgeier, E. R., 126
Allison, J. A., 163, 183, 188, 192
Amir, M., 132, 140, 152, 158, 167
Archer, J., 6, 41, 42, 44, 45, 67, 95
Ard, B. N., 147
Arias, I., 41, 60, 75, 102, 215
Arkin, R. M., 19
Austin, R. L., 176
Austin, T. L., 91
Avakame, E. F., 175
Averill, J. R., 13, 21

Baccaglini, W., 20, 103, 171, 192
Bachman, R., 91
Bailey, J. M., 145
Bandura, A., 177
Barbaree, H. E., 157
Barber, R. N., 153
Barlow, D. H., 156
Baron, L., 175, 178
Baron, R. A., 71
Barron, M., 178
Barry, H., III, 74, 140
Baumeister, R. F., 15, 16, 17, 18, 23, 126, 146, 154, 165, 209
Baumer, E. P., 196, 199
Baumgartner, M. P., 38, 76, 80
Beach, F. A., 148, 154
Beattie, C., 175
Beaulieu, M., 75
Beezley, D. A., 170
Beier, E. G., 58, 71
Beier, P., 58, 71
Belknap, J., 3, 4, 31, 45, 154, 183, 191
Bell, A. P., 159
Bem, D. J., 171
Berger, R. J., 183
Berk, R. A., 223

Berk, R. E., 74
Berkowitz, L., 13, 14, 15, 26, 209
Besag, V., 24
Best, D. L., 62
Best, J., 31, 43, 139
Bettencourt, B. A., 25, 28, 33, 58
Birnbaum, H. J., 151, 162, 163
Bjorkquist, K., 22, 34, 190
Black, D. J., 20, 79, 91, 131, 161, 196
Blackstone, W., 77
Blanchard, E. B., 156
Block, C. R., 44
Block, J., 24
Block, R., 85, 86
Blood, R. O., 52
Blumstein, P., 114, 171
Boden, J. M., 165
Boeringer, S., 178
Boezio, S. L., 171
Bograd, M., 3, 31, 67
Bookwala, J., 71
Booth, A., 16
Borden, R. J., 25
Bordt, R. L., 72
Borges, S. S., 3, 131
Bose, C., 74
Brand, P. A., 177
Brereton, D., 192, 194, 198
Bricker, W., 54
Briere, J., 170, 172, 178
Bringle, R. G., 111, 114
Brody, L., 22
Broude, G. J., 148
Brown, J. S., 197
Browne, A., 28, 37, 41, 46, 71, 78, 79, 84, 95, 135
Brownmiller, S., 3, 4, 20, 67, 69, 143, 167, 168, 177, 184, 188
Brubaker, J. D., 72
Bryden, D. P., 188, 189, 190, 191, 194, 195
Bumby, K., 134
Bureau of Justice Statistics, 33, 34, 35, 37, 41, 42, 70, 72, 75, 133, 134, 158, 159, 164, 173, 187, 197, 198
Burgess, A. W., 24, 27, 145, 157, 158, 165
Burke, P. J., 22, 103

Burkhart, B. R., 170, 172
Burnam, M. A., 136
Burt, M. R., 170, 172, 173
Buss, A. H., 71, 73, 170
Buss, D. M., 16, 20, 23, 107, 123, 145, 147, 149, 152, 159, 172
Buunk, B. P., 111, 114
Buzawa, C. G., 91
Buzawa, E., 90, 91
Byrne, D., 127, 139

Cahalan, D., 25
Campbell, A., 223
Carlson, M., 26
Carver, C. S. 73
Caspi, A., 41, 105
Castan, N., 77
Cauffman, E., 108, 113, 114
Cavanaugh, L. E., 113
Cazenave, N. A., 67
Chagnon, N. A., 76, 80
Chalmers, L. J., 152
Chamlin, M. B., 103, 171
Chaplin, T. C., 156
Chappell, D., 160, 161, 166
Check, J. V. P., 139, 170, 172, 179
Chesney-Lind, M., 69, 74
Choi, A., 80
Christenson, C. V., 154
Clark, R. D., 145
Clarke, R. V., 221
Cleaver, E., 174
Cohen, L. E., 140, 159
Coleman, D. H., 102, 215
Coleman, E. M., 132
Collmer, C. W., 20
Comstock, G. A., 179
Cook, P. J., 55, 126
Cook, S. W., 126
Courtwright, D. T. 104
Cox, S. L., 123, 158
Craig, J. M., 132
Craig, M. E., 170
Critelli, J. W., 154
Crowley, M., 72
Curtis, L. A., 48

Daly, K., 59, 72
Daly, M., 23, 43, 107, 108, 109, 110, 111, 112, 218
Davis, K. E., 112
Dawson, J. M., 48

Day, A., 21
Decker, S. H., 150
DeKeseredy, W. S., 3, 46
Demare, D., 178
Deming, M. B., 163
Dengerink, H. A., 71
de Weerth, C., 113
Dinero, T. E., 123, 158, 170
DiPrete, T. A., 52
Dobash, R. E., 3, 4, 20, 28, 38, 51, 63, 67, 76, 77, 91, 95, 167, 184
Dobash, R. P., 3, 4, 20, 28, 38, 41, 45, 46, 51, 63, 67, 76, 77, 91, 95, 167, 184
Dollard, J., 14, 28
Donaldson, S., 134
Donnerstein, E. I., 27, 178
Doob, L. W., 14
Durkee, A., 170
Dutton, D. G., 95
Dworkin, A., 178

Eagly, A. H., 52, 53, 58, 62, 72, 174
Eber, L. P., 46
Edleson, J. L., 80
Edwards, C. P., 100
Eigenberg, H. M., 3, 28, 45, 76
Elliott, D. S., 91
Ellis, B. J., 145
Ellis, L., 147, 170, 175
Emerson, R. M., 52, 60
Ennis, P. H., 159
Eppy, A., 163
Epstein, S., 16, 71
Etzioni, A., 52
Eysenck, H. J., 145, 149

Fagan, J., 41, 70, 71, 78, 95, 105, 135
Faragher, T., 91
Farrington, D. P., 48
Feder, L., 91
Feild, H. S., 166
Feld, S. L., 43, 85
Feldman, S. S., 108, 113, 114
Felson, M., 6, 20, 71, 140, 159, 221
Felson, R. B., *ix, x*, 4, 7, 11, 13, 15, 18, 20, 22, 24, 26, 38, 40n1, 44, 45, 46, 47, 48, 53, 54, 55, 57, 59, 71, 73, 76, 85, 86, 89, 91, 97, 98, 99, 100, 101, 103, 111, 113, 114, 115, 133, 151, 155, 157, 159, 161, 171, 173, 174, 176, 179, 192, 194, 196, 209, 218
Fenigstein, A., 73

Ferracuti, F., 44, 48
Feshbach, S., 179
Finkelhor, D., 161
Fischer, C. S., 54
Fisher, W., 178
Fiske, S. T., 53, 69
Fitsgerald, L. F., 170
Flavin, J., 91
Fleming, V., 125
Follingstad, D. R., 95, 170
Ford, C. S., 148, 154
Foss, M. A., 113
French, J. R. P., 124
Frieze, I. H., 71, 84, 112
Frost, G., 68, 69
Froyland, I., 21
Frude, N., 73
Fyfe, J. J., 91

Gagnon, J. H., 126, 128, 132, 145, 146, 150, 154, 175
Galloway, J., 113
Galvin, J., 198
Gamson, W. A., 55
Gangestad, S. W., 145
Garcia, L. T., 178
Gebhard, P. H., 154
Geis, G., 184, 189
Gelles, R. J., 33, 41, 59, 79, 83, 102
Gentry, C. S., 178
Gerstel, E. K., 25
Gibbs, J. P., 38
Gidycz, C. A., 133, 158, 175, 216
Gilbert, N., 123, 137, 138, 216
Ginsburg, H. J., 24
Giordano, P. C., 45
Glick, P., 53, 69
Glueck, E. T., 132
Glueck, S., 132
Gmelch, G., 20
Goetting, A., 46
Goffman, E., 21, 129
Golding, J. M., 136
Goldstein, M. S., 21, 154
Goodchilds, J. D., 130, 170
Goode, W. J., 54
Gordon, L., 77
Gordon, M., 6, 185
Gottfredson, D. M., 84
Gottfredson, M. R., 16, 17, 84, 132, 161, 173, 189
Gray, N. B., 125

Green, L. R., 22, 34
Greenberg, M. S., 84
Greenblat, C. S., 75
Greendlinger, V., 139
Greene, D., 21, 132
Greene, S. J., 148
Greenwald, R., 47
Greer, A. E., 123
Gregor, T., 121, 130, 145, 185
Grenier, G., 178
Groth, A. N., 24, 27, 145, 151, 157, 162, 163, 165
Guild, D., 156
Guttentag, M., 52, 53, 210
Gutmann, S., 139

Hagen, R., 151
Haj-Yahia, M. M., 80
Hale, M., 188
Hall, E. R., 171, 172
Hansen, K., 70
Harris, M., 24, 64, 75, 164
Hart, H. L. A., 191
Hartford, T. C., 25
Harway, M., 3, 6
Hatfield, E., 27, 145
Hawley, M. E., 193
Haynes, M. R., 132
Heatherton, T. F., 15, 16, 17
Heider, F., 156, 190, 191
Heidig, P. H., 41
Heimgartner, A., 23
Henning, K., 126
Hickey, E. W., 26
Hickman, S. E., 128
Hickson, F. C. I., 134
Hilton, N. Z., 73
Hirschi, T., 16, 17, 132, 161, 173, 188
Hirschman, R., 193
Hirschon, R., 64
Hirshman, R., 157
Hochstedler, S., 91
Hollabaugh, L. C., 125, 127, 129
Holmstrom, L. L., 24, 27, 157, 158, 165
Holtzworth-Munroe, A., 105
Hooton, E. A., 57
Horney, J., 194, 195, 196, 221
Hornstein, H. A., 54
Hoskin, A., 86, 89
Hotaling, G. T., 71, 96, 97, 103
House, P., 21, 132
Howard, J. A., 171

Howells, K., 21, 171
Huesmann, L. R., 17
Hull, J. G., 18
Hyde, J. S., 145

Ivie, D. L., 123

James, J., 160, 161, 166
Jay, T. B., 25
Johnson, G. D., 125, 129, 137
Johnson, M. P., 95, 96, 97
Johnson, P., 41, 75
Jurik, N., 48
Juster, F. T., 53

Kaleta, R. J., 71
Kalichman, S. C., 170
Kalma, A. P., 113
Kanekar, S. V., 75
Kanin, E. J., 123, 130, 131, 136, 140, 152,
        153, 154, 155, 156, 167, 170, 189,
        190
Kantor, G. K., 75
Kaplan, R., 38
Karau, S. J., 53
Karmen, A., 44
Kasof, J., 62
Katz, J., 18, 115, 188
Katz, S., 188
Kaukiainen, A., 22, 34, 190
Keen, M., 68
Kelley, H. H., 52, 56, 60, 69
Kellner, R., 170
Kelly, H. A., 77, 78
Kennedy, D. R., 113, 185
Kennedy, L. W., 185
Kertzer, D. I., 70
Kidd, A. H., 177
Killias, M., 35, 136
Kim, Y. K., 176
Kimerling, R., 60, 102, 215
Kimmel, M., 178
Kipnis, D., 54
Klap, R., 223
Kleck, G., 59
Klinger, D. A., 91
Kolsawalla, M. B., 75
Koss, M. P., 3, 4, 28, 31, 51, 67, 95, 123,
        131, 133, 135, 136, 137, 138, 143,
        158, 161, 167, 170, 175, 184, 216
Kowalski, R. M., 22, 34, 35, 104
Kramer, J., 72

Krohn, M. D., x, 151, 155, 159, 161, 176
Krueger, R. F., 105
Kruttschnitt, C., 37, 58, 172, 179
Kumagai, F., 43
Kurz, D., 3

LaFree, G. D., 194, 196, 198
Lagerspetz, K. M. J., 22, 34, 190
Lalumiere, M. L., 152, 154
Landes, R., 76, 80
Langan, P. A., 48
Langhinrichsen-Rohling, J., 112
Laumann, E. O., 42, 126, 175
Lawler, E. J., 54, 55
Laws, D. R., 170
Leginski, W. A., 54
Leitenberg, H., 126
Leith, K. P., 15, 18, 209
Leland, J., 25
Le Maire, L., 154
Lengnick, S., 188, 189, 190, 191, 194, 195
Leonard, K. E., 43, 170, 171
Levine, R. A., 129, 130, 140, 153
Levinson, D., 23, 76, 80
Lie, G.-Y., 177
Lieberman, B., 112
Lilly, J. R., 168, 169
Linneweber, V., 23
Linton, M. A., 133, 170
Linz, D., 178, 179
Lips, H. M., 52, 67, 107, 178
Lipton, D. N., 132
Lisak, D., 170
Liska, A. E., 24, 103, 171
Littman, R. A., 54
Lizotte, A. J., 133
Lloyd, S., 95
Lockwood, D., 134, 160
Loewenstein, G., 155
Logan, T. K., 112
Lonsway, K. A., 170
Loren, R. E. A., 126, 180
Loschper, G., 23
Loseke, D. R., 96, 97, 220
Lottes, I. L., 136, 140
Luckenbill, D. F., 26, 44, 55, 100, 115, 157,
        158
Lyman, S. M., 129

MacDonald, J., 158
MacKinnon, C., 178
MacLeod, L., 3

Magruder, B., 124, 129, 177
Mahoney, P., 3
Malamuth, N. M., 139, 165, 169, 170, 172,
    173, 178, 179
Malin, H., 25
Mann, C. R., 46, 49
Marcus-Newhall, A., 26
Marion, M., 19
Marolla, J., 122, 133, 160, 162, 166, 170, 174
Marshall, P., 168, 169
Marshall, W. L., 157
Marsot, A. L. S., 80
Martin, L., 127, 139
Marvell, T. B., 36, 105
Masters, W. H., 128, 145
Matsueda, R. L., 154
Matza, D., 103, 166, 170
Mayhew, P., 35, 136
Mazur, A., 16
Mazur, M. A., 188
McBarnet, D., 191
McDermott, M. J., 133, 140
McDonald, G. W., 52
McDonel, E. C., 132
McElrath, K., 59
McFall, R. M., 132
McGuire, W. J., 179
McManus, P. A., 52
Medea, A., 143
Melburg, V., 27
Merlo, A. V., 3
Messner, S. F., 47, 55, 59, 70, 75, 86, 89,
    99, 100, 111, 157, 175, 196
Michael, R. T., 126, 175
Michaels, S., 126, 175
Mikula, G., 23
Milano, L., 178
Milburn, T. W., 100
Miller, H. B., 71
Miller, N., 25, 26, 28, 33, 58
Miller, N. E., 14
Miller, S. M., 24
Mitchell, D., 193
Mladinic, A., 52, 62, 174
Moffitt, T. E., 41, 46, 105
Moody, C. E., 36, 105
Mooney, J., 75
Moore, D. W., 75
Morley, R., 80
Mowrer, O. H., 14
Muehlenhard, C. L., 125, 126, 127, 128,
    129, 131, 132, 133, 170

Mugford, J., 80
Mugford, S., 80
Mukerji, G. S., 75
Mummendey, A., 23
Murnen, S. K., 127
Murphy, R. F., 185
Murphy, W. D., 132
Murray, E., 171
Myers, M. A., 198

Nacci, P. L., 27, 113
Nagayama Hall, G. C., 156, 193
Nagin, D. S., 155, 221
Nanji, J., 75
National Research Council, 222
Nesdale, A. R., 191
Nilson, L. B., 186
Norman, N. M., 27

O'Brien, R. M., 174
O'Leary, K. D., 41
Oliver, M. B., 145
Olweus, D., 24, 54, 56, 164
O'Neill, J. M., 3, 6
Oros, C. J., 170
O'Sullivan, L. F., 126
Outlaw, M. C., 53, 97

Pagelow, M. D., 33, 38, 46, 60, 84
Paik J., 179
Palileo, G. J., 125
Palmer, C. T., 148, 149, 151, 165
Palys, T. S., 178, 180
Pan, H. S., 41
Parcell, S. R., 131, 140
Parke, R. D., 20
Paternoster, R., 155
Patterson, G. R., 54
Paul, L., 113
Paymar, M., 3, 4
Pederson, W. C., 26
Pence, E., 3, 4
Perot, A., 127
Peterson del Mar, D., 77
Peterson, E. S. L., 21
Peterson, R. R., 60

Pine, C. J., 193
Pitts, V. L., 140
Pleck, E. H., 77, 78
Pleck, J. H., 53
Ploughman, P., 159

Polk, K., 44, 198
Pollock, J. M., 3
Pomeroy, W. B., 154
Porter, J. F., 154
Posner, R. A., 186, 197
Pratto, F., 100
Preston, K., 25
Preston, S. K., 25
Pruitt, D. G., 53, 100
Ptacek, J., 3

Queens's Bench Foundation, 160
Quigley, B. M., 43
Quinsey, V. L., 152, 156

Rada, R. T., 170
Rapaport, K., 170, 172
Raven, B. H., 124
Reidpath, D., 21
Reiss, A. J., Jr., 37, 79, 83, 84
Reiss, I. L., 132, 145, 172, 176, 179, 214
Ribner, S., 192
Richardson, D. R., 22, 34, 71
Riger, S., 6, 185
Robins, R. W., 41
Robinson, D. T., 85
Rogers, C. R., 17, 29
Ronfeldt, H. M., 60, 102, 215
Roscoe, B., 113
Rosenbaum, A., 71
Rosenfeld, R., 70
Ross, L., 21, 132
Rossi, P. H., 59, 74
Roth, J. A., 37, 79, 84
Roth, S., 170
Roy, M., 91
Ruback, R. B., 84, 123
Rubin, J. Z., 53, 100
Rucker, L., 134
Rule, B. G., 191
Russell, D. E. H., 143
Russo, N. J., 55
Ryan, K., 71

Sacco, V. F., 185
Saltzman, L. E., 91
Sampson, R. J., 175
Sanday, P. R., 176, 184, 185, 214
Sarrel, P. M., 128, 145
Sattem, L., 171
Saunders, D. G., 46, 105
Savells, J., 171

Schafer, S., 146
Scheier, M. F., 73
Schlegel, A., 74, 80, 140
Schmidt, J. D., 91
Schmidt, S. M., 54
Schreder, C., 47
Schwartz, M. D., 46, 140
Schwartz, P., 114, 171
Schwendinger, H., 184
Schwendinger, J. R., 184
Scott, M. B., 129
Scully, D., 122, 133, 160, 162, 166, 170, 171, 174
Searles, P., 183
Sears, R. R., 14
Sebastian, J. A., 95
Secord, P. F., 52, 53, 210
Segal, P., 72
Seibel, C. A., 123, 158
Selznick, D. O., 125
Sermat, V., 16
Seto, M. C., 152
Sherman, L. W., 56, 223
Shields, L. M., 147, 151
Shields, W. M., 147, 151
Shondrck, D. D., 157
Shortell, J. R., 71
Shotland, R. L., 88, 132
Siegel, J. M., 136
Simon, W. S., 132, 145, 146
Simpson, J. A., 145
Singer, B., 152
Skocpol, T., 70
Smart, L., 165
Smith, C., 71
Smith, D. A., 91, 223
Smith, D. D., 178
Smith, M. D., 80, 95
Smith, R. E., 193
Smith, W. P., 54
Sommers, C. H., 63, 77
Sorenson, S. B., 136
South, S. J., 173, 174
Spohn, C. C., 194, 195, 196, 221
Stafford, F. P., 53
Stafford, M. C., 38
Stanko, E. A., 3, 191, 199
State v. Rhodes (1868), 79
Steadman, H. J., 44
Steffen, V. J., 58
Steffensmeier, D. J., 72, 197, 198
Stein, J. A., 136

Steinmetz, S. K., 33, 38, 59, 83, 103
Stensrud, J., 159
Stets, J. E., 22, 41, 103
Stewart, D., 70
Stillwell, A., 23
Straus, M. A., 33, 38, 40, 41, 42, 43, 55, 59, 75, 83, 85, 95, 102, 175, 178, 215
Straw, M. K., 88
Streifel, C., 72
Struckman-Johnson, C., 134
Struckman-Johnson, D., 134
Stuart, G. L., 105
Sturup, G. K., 154
Sugarman, D. B., 71, 96, 97, 103
Sundberg, S. L., 157
Sykes, G. M., 103, 166, 170
Symons, D., 145, 146, 148, 149, 151, 152

Tang, C. S.- K., 154
Taylor, S. P., 16, 71, 171
Tedeschi, J. T., 7, 11, 13, 15, 27, 44, 54, 71, 73, 97, 100, 101, 113, 114, 133, 173
Thar, A. E., 46
Thibaut, J. W., 52, 56, 60, 69
Thoennes, N., 42, 44, 93, 135, 177, 187, 188, 198
Thompson, K., 143
Thornhill, N. W., 148, 149, 151, 159
Thornhill, R., 148, 149, 151, 159
Tice, D. M., 15, 16, 17
Tjaden, P., 42, 44, 93, 135, 177, 187, 188, 198
Toates, F. M., 152
Toch, H. H., 97
Tonizzo, S., 21
Townsend, J. M., 172
Turrel, S. C., 42

van Dijk, J. J. M., 35, 136
Varney, G. A., 156
Vera Institute of Justice (1977), 91
Visher, C. A., 69

Wade, W. C., 68
Waite, E., 74

Waldner-Haugrud, L. K., 124, 129, 177
Walker, L. E., 28, 31, 46, 60
Watman, K., 100
Websdale, N., 46, 107
Weeks, G., 126, 180
Weghorst, S. J., 107
Weinberg, M. S., 136, 140, 159
Weis, K., 3, 131
West, C. M., 3
Western, B., 223
Whaley, R. B., 176
Whiting, B. B., 100
Wicklund, R. A., 73
Wilbanks, W., 48, 111
Williams, G., 25
Willians, J. E., 62
Williams, K. M., 199
Williams, K. R., 37, 79, 84
Williams, L. M., 3
Wills, T. A., 27
Wilson, M., 23, 43, 107, 108, 109, 110, 218
Wilson, R., 25
Winn, R., 48
Wisniewski, N., 133, 158, 175, 216
Wolfe, D. M., 52
Wolfgang, M. E., 44, 48, 79, 97, 109
World Health Organization, 36
Wotman, S. R., 23
Wright, E., 171
Wright, J. D., 59
Wright, R. T., 159
Wright, S., 95
Wrightsman, L. S., 163, 183, 188, 192

Yegidis, B. L., 166
Yllö, K. A., 46, 95, 161
Young, D. M., 58, 71

Zahn, M. A., 67
Zellman, G. L., 130, 170
Zillmann, D., 177
Zimring, F. E., 82

SUBJECT INDEX

Achievement motive, sexual relations, 166
Acquaintance rape. *See also* Date rape
    legal outcomes, 198
    miscommunication factor, 131
    prosecution of, difficulty, 194
    and sexual arousal, 155
    victim blaming, 192
Adolescents, status perceptions, 63
Age factors
    rape victims, 159–161
    and sex offender nontactical violence,
        161
Aggression. *See* Instrumental aggression
Alarm systems, 222
Alcohol use
    and coercive sex ambiguity, 127–128
    and male identity, 25
    rape factor, 133
    violence role, 214–215
"All conflict is local" argument, 210
Altruism, gender differences, 72
Ambiguity, in sexual coercion, 124–128,
    212
Ambivalence, in unwanted sexual activity,
    127
Anger
    versus aggression, 13
    and control motive, 103–104
    gender differences, 23, 103–104
    love triangle reaction, women, 114
Antisocial behavior, rapists, 172–173
Arab societies, 80–81
Arousal, aggression link, 17–18
Arranged marriages, women as property, 64
Arrest policies
    chivalry effect, 76
    determinants, 90–94
    feminism effect, 223
    gender differences, 207–208
    leniency hypothesis, 91–94, 207
    and partner violence deterrence, evi-
        dence, 223
    rape versus other crimes, 197–198
Assault victims. *See* Criminal assault
"Asshole" slur, 25
Attitudes toward women

versus attitudes toward men, 62
    rapists, 172–173
    sexual coercion effects, 169–173
    in traditional men, 174–175
Attractiveness factor
    and male attitudes toward sex, 171–172
    rape victims, 159–160
Attribution of blame
    aggression link, 16, 21
    causal inference process, 191
    in love triangles, 114
Audience effects
    aggression motivation, 24–25
    and chivalry norm, 73
Aversive stimuli, and "reactive" aggression,
    15

Battered wife syndrome
    ideology impact, 220
    male control motive link, 96–98
    patriarchal terrorism role, 96–98
    qualitative data weaknesses, 96
    research limitations, 43–44
    as spousal homicide defense, 46–47
    evidence limitations, 48–49
Bias, self-report surveys, 41–42
"Bitch" slur, 25
Black-on-white rape, 173–174
Blame
    aggression link, 15–16, 21
    in love triangles, 113–114
Blaming the victim. *See also* Victim precipi-
    tation
    battered women, 96–97
    versus causal analysis approach, 211–
        212
    and rape, 191–197, 208
    sexism in, 193
Bodily force, and sexual coercion, 122
Bossiness, in women, 97–98, 103
Brideprice, 153
Bullying
    and coercive power, 54
    coercive sex link, 164
    motivation for, 24

Capitalist societies, rape in, 184
Castration, coercive sex effect, 154
Casual sex, gender differences, 145–146
Causal analysis, and victim precipitation, 45, 211–212
Child protection, chivalry norm link, 69–70
Chivalry norm, 67–82, 215
    in arrest decisions, 92
    "benevolent sexism" in, 69
    and domestic violence intervention, 76–78
    double standard exception, 73–74
    and female criminality punishment, 72
    versus male dominance norm, 67
    origins, 68–70
    and reactions to domestic violence, 80–81
    and reluctance to harm women, 70–76
    as violence inhibitory factor, 214
Civil liberties, and rape reform laws, 223
Coalition formation, motivation, 55
Coercive power. *See* Power motive
Coercive sex, 121–141. *See also* Rape
    alcohol use factor, 127–128, 133
    ambiguity in, 124–128, 212
    and rape statistics, 137–139
    versus consensual encounters, 123–124
    control motive evidence, 167–172
    cross-cultural studies, 136–137
    decision-making impairment, 132–133
    definition, 122–123
    frequency statistics, 133–136
    self-report discrepancies, 135–139
    skepticism about, 136–139
    legal system response, 183–200
    male expectations factor, 130–131
    minor versus serious, 213–218
    offender preference question, 156–157
    opportunity factor, 139–140
    overt behavior ambiguity in, 124–126, 212
    power motive evidence, 163–167
    sexism, 163–181
    in sexual fantasies, 126
    sexual motivation evidence, 149–162
    and sexual scripts, 128–130, 212
    versus unwanted sexual activity, 126–127
College students, rape statistic discrepancies, 135–136

Communication problems, coercive sex, 131–132, 212
Comparative approach, 204–209
Competition, aggression distinction, 13
Complaining
    and control motive, 103–104
    gender differences, 22–23, 103–104
Complaint signing, victims, 92–94
Compliance motive, aggression, 19–20
Compulsive aggression, motivation, 16–18
Conflict Tactics Scale, 41–42
Consensual sex, 121–141
    versus coercive sex, 123–124
    overt behavior ambiguity, 124–126
    sex offender preference question, 156–157
    sexual scripts in, 128–130
Consent disputes, rape, 194–195
Conservatives, feminists' alliance with, 222–223
Continual partner violence, 43–44
Control motive, 95–106. *See also* Dominance motive; Power motive
    and aggression, 18–20
    feminist perspective, 4, 95–96, 101–106, 206
    gender differences, 101–104, 206
    comparative studies, 206
    in legal system, 184–186
    in love triangles, 110–112
    in patriarchal terrorism, 96–98
    and sexism, 101–105, 206
    statistical study, 100–102
    threat communication link, 101–101
Conviction rates, rape versus other crimes, 197–198
Cooperative face work, 129, 131
"Correction" principle, 214
Counseling, 219–221
Criminal assaults. *See also* Serious violence
    gender differences, victims, 34–35
    police intervention factors, 83–94
    reports to police, 86–88
Criminal justice system. *See* Legal system
Criminal punishment
    chivalry norm effect, 75–78
    gender differences, 72, 75–76, 207–208
    sexual coercion, 197–199
Criminal records, rapists, 172–173
Cross-cultural studies
    attitudes toward women, 62
    chivalry norm differences, 76

domestic violence reactions, 80–81
double standard, 74
gender inequality and rape rates, 176
homicide statistics, 205
partner violence gender differences, 42–43
rape frequency, 136–139
sexism effects, 214
"Cuckolded," 115
Cultural factors. *See* Cross-cultural studies

Date rape
coercion methods in, 124
consensual sex link, 123–124
legal outcomes, 198
and male expectations, 130–131
and sexual arousal, 155–156
stranger rape motivation differences, 155
Death penalty, gender differences, 72
Decision-making
aggressive behavior role, 16–18
coercive power factor, 56
and control motive, 102–103
gender differences, partners, 52–53, 102
impairments in coercive sex, 132–133
Delinquency, adolescent females, 46
Dependency
partner violence factor, 60–61
power motive link, 52, 60–61
Deprivation hypothesis, sexual coercion, 151–153
Deviance, in women, 167–168
"Discriminative predictability," 209–210
Displaced aggression
motivation for, 26–27
sex offenders, 162, 165
Dispute-related violence, 18–19
DNA matching, 190, 195
Domestic violence. *See also* Partner violence
chivalry norm effects, 74–78
cultural factors, 80–81
frequency statistics, 36–38, 43–44, 96
police response factors, 90–94
and privacy, 78–80
reporting of, 83–90
Dominance motive. *See also* Control motive;
Power motive
versus chivalry norm, 67
as domestic violence justification, 76–77, 79–80

gender differences, 52–53, 101–104
motivation for, 99
and partner violence statistics, 42
sex offenders, 165
and spousal decision-making, evidence, 52–53
Double standard
chivalry norm exception, 73–74, 186
token resistance link, 125
Drug use, violence role, 214–215
Due process changes, 223

Economic dependency, and partner violence, 60
Egalitarian society effects, 215–216
Electronic alarm devices, 222
"Emotional" aggression, 15–17
Emotional dependency factor, 60
Epidemic of violence against women
"behind closed doors" factor, 83
lack of evidence for, 34–36, 204–205
rape, 136–139
statistics, 34–36
Erectile dysfunction, rapists, 151
Escalation of violence
audience factor, 24
domestic conflicts versus strangers, 40
Evidentiary concerns, arrest factor, 92–93
Evolutionary psychology
and double standard, 74
and love triangle reactions, 107–110, 116
sexuality gender differences explanation, 147–149
Exchange processes, in sex, 131
Extramarital affairs, frequency in rapists, 154

False consensus effect, 132
False rape charges, 188–191
motivation for, 189–190
published research, 189
Family violence. *See* Domestic violence
Fathers, violence frequency, 33
Fear of reprisal, reporting factor, 90
Feminist perspective
conservative allies, 222–223
control motive, 4, 95–96, 101–106, 167–172
impact of, 222–223
pornography, 177–178
sexism and violence, 3–6
sexual coercion motivation, 163–181

women's status, 61–62
Firearm use, 59
Fraternity group members, 154
Frustration-aggression hypothesis
    and attribution of blame, 16
    displaced aggression explanation, 26–27
    versus instrumental aggression, 14–16, 212
Fundamental attribution error, 21

Game playing, in sexual activity, 125
Gay men
    versus lesbians, sexuality, 146
    partner violence statistics, 42, 207
    versus heterosexual couples, 207
    sexual coercion frequency, 177
Gender differences
    aggression motivation, 22–25
    control motive, 101–104, 206
    indirect aggression, 22–23
    legal system treatment, 207–208
    love triangle homicides, 108–110, 116
    partner violence, 40–43, 45–48
    physical power, 57–59
    in power and status, 51–65
    in rape offending, 144–145
    resistance to rape, 177, 212
    sexual conflict source, 147
    in sexuality, 144–149
    victimization frequencies, 34–36
    violence frequency, 32–34
    in violence history, offenders, 205
Gender equality, and rape rates, 176
Gender inequality
    cross-cultural studies, 176
    discriminative predictability, 209
    and rape frequency, 175–176, 209
Gender norm violations, 185–186, 195–196
Gender role identity, and aggression, 24–25
Gender roles
    and chivalry, 71
    and male control motive, 167–168
    and male power motive, 164
Genetics. *See* Evolutionary psychology
Gossip, gender differences, 22–23, 33–34 ,
Gratuitous violence, sex offenders, 157–162
Grievances
    aggression motivation, 20–23
    sex offender motive, 160–162
Group rape
    as social control mechanism, 185

statistics, 164
Gun use, 59
Gusii of southwestern Kenya, 129–130, 140, 153

Habitual aggression, 17
Harm, aggression component, 13–14
Hatred against women, 5
Helping behavior, gender differences, 72
"Hitting license" concept, 38, 40, 210
Homicide. *See also* Partner homicide
    gender differences, statistics, 34–36
    and victim precipitation, 44–49, 211–212
Homosexuality
    partner violence statistics, 42, 207
    versus heterosexual couples, 207
    rape patterns, versus heterosexuals, 176–177
    sexuality gender differences, 146
Hostility toward women
    discriminative predictability, 209
    and sexual coercion, 169–171, 209
Humor, chivalry norm effects, 72–73

Impotence, rapists, 151
Impulsive behavior, and aggression, 16–18
Indirect aggression
    and false rape charges, 190
    gender differences, 22–23, 33–34
Infidelity. 112–114. *See also* Love triangles
Inhibiting factors
    chivalry role, 215
    in reporting assault, 89–90
    in violence, 214–215
    Instrumental aggression, 11–28, 212–214
    versus frustration-aggression hypothesis, 14–16
    motivation in, 18–28, 212–214
Insults, gender factors, 25
Intent to harm standard
    aggression component, 13–14
    in coercive sex, 125
International Crime Survey, 35
Internet pornography, 179
Interpersonal aggression, definition, 12
Interracial rape, 173–174
Intimidation
    in love triangles, 111
    and preemptive aggression, 55
Intoxication

and coercive sex ambiguity, 127–128
and rape, 133
Irrational violence, 16–18

Jealousy
as homicide motive, 108–110
in love triangles, 107–110
Justice motive. *See* Retributive justice

Koran teachings, 80–81

Leadership, gender differences, 53
Legal system, 183–200
and false charges of rape, 188–191
family privacy considerations, 78–80
feminism impact on, 223
feminist attitudes toward, 183
gender norm violations response, 184–186
partner violence response, 90–94, 223
rape response, 183–200
versus other crimes, 197–199
sexism in, 183–200, 207–208
comparative data, 207–208
sexual coercion response, 183–200
Legalized prostitution, and rape incidence, 152–153
Leniency hypothesis
arrest decisions, 91–94, 208
gender differences comparative data, 208
rape versus other crimes, 197–199
and victim blaming, rape, 191–194
Lesbians
versus gay men, sexuality, 146
partner victimization statistics, 42
Liberal men
chivalry values, 215
sex attitudes, 172
Lies, in love triangles, 114
Loss of face. *See* "Saving face"
Love triangles, 107–117, 207
control motive in, 110–112, 207
evolutionary psychology, 107, 116
gender differences in reaction to, 108–110, 116, 207
and homicide, 108–112, 207
choice of victim, 111–112
humiliation factor, 115
identity concerns, 115
retributive justice in, 112–114
violence motivation, 107–117

Male rape victims
age factor, 159
survey data, 134–135, 138
Mandatory arrests
feminism impact, 223
limitations of, 221
spousal violence effect, 55–56, 223
Marital rape, 130
Marital status, and sexual deprivation hypothesis, 152
Marital violence. *See* Partner violence
Masculinity, aggression motivation, 24–25
Masturbation
and pornography, 180
and sex offender preferences, 150
Mehinaku Indians of Brazil, 130, 185
Minor violence, 216–218
men and women offenders, 217
serious violence difference, 216–218
in sexual coercion, 217–218
Mirror experiments, chivalry norm, 73
Misogyny, 5
Misunderstandings, in coercive sex, 131–132, 212
Moral condemnation, violence against women, 74–75
Moslem societies, 214
Mothers
protection of, chivalry norm, 69–70
violence against, frequency, 33
Motivation for aggression, 18–28, 212–214
Myths about rape. *See* Rape myth beliefs

Nagging, control motive, 103–104
National Crime Victimization Survey
censoring factor, 87, 138
description of, 32–33
reporting violence to police, 86–87
sexual assault, 133–134, 138
underreporting, 186–187
violence gender differences, 32–37, 41
National Violence Against Women Survey
arrest statistics, 93
control behavior data, 97
violence gender differences, 42
Negative emotionality, women, 46
Nontactical violence, sex offenders, 157–162

Opportunity factors
and crime prevention, 221
and sex offender preferences, 167–168

sexual coercion, 139–140
Orgasm frequency needs, 153–154

Parental violence
    gender differences, 33
    verbal aggression ratio, 39–40
Partner homicide
    battered wife syndrome defense, 46–49
    evidence limitations, 47–49
    control motive, 99
    criminal punishment gender differ-
        ences, 75–76
    gender differences, 43
    love triangle motive, 108–112
    victim precipitation concept, 44–49,
        211–212
Partner violence
    "all conflict is local" factor in, 210–211
    arrest policy as deterrent, evidence, 223
    chivalry norm effects, 74–78
    control motive, sexism perspective, 206
    cultural factors, 80–81
    frequency statistics, 40–42, 206
    grievance sources, 23
    minor versus serious, 216–218
    physical size/strength factor, 54–56
    police response factors, 90–94
    power and status factors, 51–65, 210–
        211
    and privacy, 78–80, 83–94
    repetition of, misleading statistics, 43–
        44
    reporting of, 83–90
    verbal conflict ratio, 38–40
    victim precipitation concept, 44–47
    victimization statistics, 36–38, 43–44
Passive female image, 212
Patriarchal societies
    and control motive, 96–98
    relative influence in partner conflicts,
        210
    sexual coercion toleration in, 184
Patriarchal terrorism, 96–98
Peer group pressure, and coercive sex, 154
Penile tumescence studies, 156
Physical attractiveness
    and male attitudes toward sex, 171–172
    sexual coercion factor, 159–160, 171–
        172
Physical power
aggression role, 56–59
offsetting factors, 58–59

"Planned" rapes, 132
Play fighting, in consensual sex, 125–126
Police intervention
    arrest determinants, 93–94
    gender factors, 90–94
    leniency hypothesis, 90–94
    privacy factor, 83–94
    reporting factor, 83–90
Polyandry, 148
Polygamy, 148
Pornography
    and discriminative predictability, 209–
        210
    feminists' position, 177–178
    masturbation relationship, 180
    and rape rates, 178
    violence toward women effects, evi-
        dence, 177–180
    violent form of, 178–180
Power motive. See also Control motive;
        Dominance motive
    characteristics, 51–54
    in coercive sex, 124, 163–167
    complex relationship to violence, 54–
        56
    in consensual sex, 124, 150–151
    control motive difference, 167
    gender differences, in marriage, 51–65
    physical size/strength factor, 56–59
    rapists' report, 165–167
    versus sexual motive, coercive sex,
        143–162
Predatory violence
    definition, 18
    motivation, 18–19
Preemptive aggression, 55, 59
Prejudice, men versus women, 62
Pretend violence, 130
Prisons
    rape statistics, 134
    rape victim attractiveness, 160
    sexual deprivation, 153
Privacy
    and chivalry norm, 73
    and domestic violence, 78–80
    and police intervention, 83–94
Proarrest laws, leniency policy offset, 91–92
Promiscuity
    double standard for, 73–74
    gender differences, 146
Property metaphor, 63–64
Prosecution of violence, 197–198, 207

Prostitution
    gender differences, 146
    legal system response, 186
    and sex offender preferences, 150
    sexual deprivation role in use of, 152–153
Public behavior, chivalry norm, 73
Public policy, feminism impact, 222–223
Punishment. *See also* Criminal punishment
    aggression motive, 20–23
    and sexual activity, gender differences, 147

Racial factors, 173–174
    gender interactions, 218–219
    and rape, 173–174, 218–219
Rape. *See also* Coercive sex; Date rape
    ambiguity factor, 137–138
    control motive evidence, 167–172
    cross-cultural studies, 136–139
    counseling, 219–220
    decision-making impairment, 132–133
    evolutionary explanations, 149
    false charges, 188–191, 208
    frequency statistics, 133–139
    self-report discrepancies, 135–137
    skepticism about, 137–139
    gender differences, 34–35, 144–145
    legal system response, 183–200, 207–208
    in males, 134–135
    miscommunication factor, 131–132
    opportunity factor, 139–140
    pornography effects, 177–180
    power motive, 163–167
    proclivity, 139
    resistance to, gender differences, 177
    sexism evidence, 163–181
    sexual motivation, evidence, 149–162
    underreporting evidence, 186–188, 208
    victim blaming, 191–194, 208
    victim credibility, 194–197
Rape counseling, 219–220
Rape epidemic
    cross-cultural comparisons, 136–137
    skepticism, 137–139
Rape myth beliefs, 170–171
Rape proclivity, 139
Rape reform laws, 194–195
"Rape survivor" label
    connotations, 136, 190

counseling implications, 220
Rapists
    self-reports of, 165–167
    sexual motivation, evidence, 149–162
    social information processing deficits, 132
    specialization evidence, 172–173
    tactical versus gratuitous violence, 157–162
"Reactive" aggression, 15
Recreational sex, 145–146
"Relational distance" concept, 79
Repeated partner violence, 43–44
Reporting violence
    gender factors, 84–91
    comparison data, 207–208
    inhibiting factors, 89–90
    motivations, 89–90
    seriousness of incident factor, 86–88
    sexual assault, 186–188, 207–208
    third-party factors, 87–88
    by victims, 86–89
Reproductive strategies, gender differences, 148
Research strategies, 219
Resistance to rape, gender differences, 177, 212
Retribution motive
    aggression, 18–23
    and infidelities, 112–114
    sex offenders, 160–162, 164
Robberies
    black-on-white rape during, 174
    tactical violence in, 157–158
    victim age factor, 159–160
Romantic interests, gender differences, 145–146
Rough-and-tumble play, 58
"Rule of thumb" idea, 77

"Saving face," 23–25. *See also* Self-image protection
    aggression motive, 23–26
    in love triangles, 115
    sexual script function, 129
"Scoring" motive, 166
"Scripted behavior"
    and aggression, 17
    in sexual activity, 128–130
Self-blame, aggression link, 15
Self-control factors
    aggression role, 17–18

and rape defense, 193–194
Self-defense motive
    battered wife syndrome defense, 46–49
    evidence limitations, 47–49
    and victim precipitation concept, 44–49, 208
Self-help violence, 20–21
Self-image protection
    aggression motive, 18–19, 23–26, 55
    in love triangles, 115
    sexual scripts function, 129
Self-report surveys. *See* Survey data
Self-righteous motivation, 21
Sentences for rape, 197–198
Serial killers, 26, 214
Serious violence
    legal system involvement, 217
    versus minor violence, 216–217
    reports to police, 86–88
    in sexual coercion, 217–218
Sex differences. *See* Gender differences
Sex drive, gender differences, 145–146
"Sex objects" attitudes, 171
Sex offenders. *See also* Rapists
    sexual motivation, evidence, 149–160
    tactical versus gratuitous violence, 157–162
Sexism
    coercive sex link, evidence, 163–181
    and control motive, 101–104
    cultural differences, 214
    feminists' perspective, 3–6, 205
    as inhibitor of violence, 5
    and spousal violence specialization, 105
    and victim blaming, rape, 191–194
    and violence against women, 205, 214
Sexual arousal
    and coercive sex, 133
    and date rape, 155–156
"Sexual aspirations" factor, 153–155
Sexual assault. *See also* Rape
    gender differences statistics, 34–35
    underreporting, 186–188
Sexual coercion. *See* Coercive sex
Sexual deprivation
    sexual coercive relationship, 151–153
    sexual desire link, 152
Sexual dysfunction, rapists, 151
Sexual fantasies
    coercive sex theme in, 126, 157
    gender differences, 145
    and pornography, 180

Sexual harassment codes, 222–223
Sexual history testimony, 195, 199
Sexual motivation
    versus power motive, 143–162
    in sex offenders, 149–162
Sexual scripts, 128–130
Sexual selectivity, gender differences, 148–149
Sexual teasing, 193, 212
Sexuality, gender differences, 144–149
Shock delivery experiments, 71, 73
Sibling aggression, 55
Signing of complaint, victims, 92–94
Single fathers, violence frequency, 33
Single mothers, violence frequency, 33
Situational crime prevention, 221–222
Size/strength factor, aggression, 56–59
Social class, 218–219
Social control
    aggression motive, 19–20
    sexual coercion role in, 184–186
    women as agents of, 104
Social norms, and coercive power use, 56
Social relationship factor, and reporting, 84–91
Specialization argument, spousal violence, 105
Spousal violence. *See* Partner violence
Stalking behavior, gender differences, 112
Statistics, 31–50
Status motive
    in consensual sex, 150–151
    feminist approach, 61
    gender differences, 62–63
Stereotypes, of men versus women, 62
Stigma, rape charge consequence, 190
Stranger rape
    date rape motivation difference, 155
    intervention factors, 133
    risk factors, 140
    statistics, 134–135
    underreporting data, 187
    wrongful identification, 190
Stranger violence, reporting to police, 85–88
Stress, aggression relationship, 22
Survey data
    minor violence focus of, 86–87
    partner violence gender differences, 41–42, 73
    versus qualitative reports, battered women, 96

reporting bias, 41–42, 73
sexual coercion, 133–136
report discrepancies explanation, 135–136
"Survivor" label
connotations, 136, 190
counseling implications, 220
Sweden, sexual coercion rates, 136–137

Tactical violence, sex offenders, 157–159
Teenage rape, false charges, 190
Temperament, aggression influence, 16
Temporary insanity plea, 46
Testosterone, aggression influence, 16
Third-party reporting, 87–88
Threat communication
control motivation in, 100–101
and sexual coercion, 122–123
"Token resistance"
in consensual sex, 125–126
frequency of, 125
function of, 125–126, 129, 212
in sexual script, 129
Traditional men
and chivalry norm, 71–72, 175
sex attitudes, 172
sexual coercion use, 174–175
violence against women, 71–72, 105
Tribal societies
domestic violence acceptance, 80
gender inequality and rape rates, 176
rape punishment, 197
sexism effects, 214
sexual scripts, 129–130

Underreporting. See also Reporting violence
reasons for, 187–188, 208
sexual assaults, 186–188
Uniform Crime Reports, 33–34
Unwanted sexual activity, 126–127

Value judgments, aggression definition, 14
Verbal conflict
violence link, gender factors, 206

violence ratio, partners and families, 38–40
Victim blaming. See Blaming the victim
"Victim" label
connotations, 136, 190
counseling implications, 219–220
Victim misconduct, 195–197, 199
Victim precipitation. See also Blaming the victim
causal analysis, 211–212
conceptual aspects, 44–45
counseling implications, 220
gender factors, 45–46, 208, 211
in homicide, 46–49, 208, 211–212
Victims of violence
blame analysis versus causal analysis, 211
counseling, 219–221
as evidentiary source, 92–93
gender difference statistics, 34–36
role of, 211–212. See also Victim precipitation
violence history of, 97
Video pornography, 179
Violence Against Women Act, 219, 222
Violence levels
and legal system involvement, 217
in sexual coercion, 217–218
and rate of violence statistics, 216–217
Violent pornography, 178–180, 210
Violent sex, offender preference question, 156–157

War, and rape, 168–169
"Weakness is strength" principle, 55–56
Weapons use, 59
Welfare system, protection of mothers, 70
White-on-black rape, 173–174
Wife abuse. See Partner violence
Witnesses to assault, 85–87
Women as property, 63–64

Younger women, as rape victims, 159–160

ABOUT THE AUTHOR

Richard B. Felson, PhD, is professor of crime, law, and justice and of sociology at Pennsylvania State University. He obtained his PhD in sociology at Indiana University in 1977, specializing in social psychology. In the past decade, Dr. Felson moved into the field of criminology, concentrating his research on the study of interpersonal violence. He has written extensively in this area, on such topics as situational factors in homicide and motives for rape and domestic violence. His articles have appeared in a variety of journals, including *Journal of Personality and Social Psychology*, *Social Forces*, *Social Psychology Quarterly*, and *Criminology* (where he serves on the editorial board). He is a coauthor or coeditor of three other books published by the American Psychological Association: *Violence, Aggression and Coercive Actions* (1994, with James T. Tedeschi); *Aggression and Violence: Social Interactionist Perspectives* (1993, edited with James T. Tedeschi); and *Psychological Perspectives on Self and Identity* (2000, edited with Abraham Tesser and Jerry M. Suls).